The Key to Theosophy, Being a Clear Exposition, in the Form of Question and Answer, of the Ethics, Science, and Philosophy for the Study of Which the Theosophical Society Has Been Founded, With a Copious Glossary of General Theosophical Terms

THE
KEY TO THEOSOPHY

BEING A CLEAR EXPOSITION, IN THE FORM
OF QUESTION AND ANSWER, OF THE

ETHICS, SCIENCE, AND PHILOSOPHY, FOR THE STUDY OF
WHICH THE THEOSOPHICAL SOCIETY
HAS BEEN FOUNDED

WITH A

COPIOUS GLOSSARY OF GENERAL
THEOSOPHICAL TERMS

BY

H. P. BLAVATSKY

Second and Revised American Edition

NEW YORK
THEOSOPHICAL PUBLISHING COMPANY
144 MADISON AVENUE
1896

DEDICATED

BY

" H. P. B."

TO ALL HER PUPILS,
THAT
THEY MAY LEARN AND TEACH
IN THEIR TURN.

PREFACE.

THE purpose of this book is exactly expressed in its title, THE KEY TO THEOSOPHY, and needs but few words of explanation. It is not a complete or exhaustive text-book of Theosophy, but only a key to unlock the door that leads to the deeper study. It traces the broad outlines of the Wisdom-Religion, and explains its fundamental principles; meeting, at the same time, the various objections raised by the average Western inquirer, and endeavoring to present unfamiliar concepts in a form as simple and in language as clear as possible. That it should succeed in making Theosophy intelligible without mental effort on the part of the reader would be too much to expect; but it is hoped that the obscurity still left is of the thought, not of the language; is due to depth, not to confusion. To the mentally lazy or obtuse Theosophy must remain a riddle; for in the world mental as in the world spiritual each man must progress by his own efforts. The writer cannot do the reader's thinking for him, nor would the latter be any the better off if such vicarious thought were possible. The need for such an exposition as the present has long been felt among those interested in the Theosophical Society and its work, and it is hoped that it will supply information, as free as possible from technicalities, to many whose attention has been awakened, but who, as yet, are merely puzzled and not convinced.

Some care has been taken in disentangling some part of

what is true from what is false in Spiritualistic teachings as
to the post-mortem life, and in showing the true nature of
Spiritualistic phenomena. Previous explanations of a similar kind have drawn much wrath upon the writer's devoted
head, the Spiritualists, like too many others, preferring to
believe what is pleasant rather than what is true, and becoming very angry with any one who destroys an agree-
able delusion.   For the past year Theosophy has been the
target for every poisoned arrow of Spiritualism, as though
the possessors of a half-truth felt more antagonism to the
possessors of the whole truth than those who had no share
to boast of.

Very hearty thanks are due from the author to many
Theosophists who have sent suggestions and questions, or
have otherwise contributed help during the writing of this
book.   The work will be the more useful for their aid, and
that will be their best reward.

H. P. B.

LONDON, 1889.

PREFACE TO THE SECOND EDITION.

In order to further facilitate the study of Theosophy, which the KEY has already made an easy task, I have added a copious Glossary of all the technical terms found in it. Most of the definitions and explanations are transcriptions or abbreviations from the larger *Theosophical Glossary*. It is hoped that both Glossaries will supply a long-felt want, and that the larger one will cover the whole range of occult terminology as completely as possible.

H. P. B.

London, 1890.

PREFACE TO THE SECOND AND REVISED AMERICAN EDITION.

The main features of the revision attempted are: (1) a systematic use of italics and capitals; (2) a consistent transliteration of Sanskrit words; (3) the correction of some mistakes intimated by H. P. B. while still living; (4) the removal of some obscurities of style; (5) the omission of some passages of a controversial nature which are no longer of general interest.

It is thought that a change of form in the mechanical construction of the book will be welcomed by most students, numerous complaints having been made concerning the size and generally unwieldy form of all the preceding editions.

New York, 1895.

CONTENTS.

SECTION V.

THE FUNDAMENTAL TEACHINGS OF THEOSOPHY.

SECTION VI.

THEOSOPHICAL TEACHINGS AS TO NATURE AND MAN.

SECTION VII.

ON THE VARIOUS POST-MORTEM STATES.

SECTION VIII.

ON REINCARNATION OR REBIRTH.

SECTION IX.

ON KÂMALOKA AND DEVACHAN.

SECTION XIV.

The "Theosophical Mahâtmâs."

CONCLUSION.

THE KEY TO THEOSOPHY.

I.

THEOSOPHY AND THE THEOSOPHICAL SOCIETY.

THE MEANING OF THE NAME.

INQUIRER.—*Theosophy and its doctrines are often referred to as a new-fangled religion. Is it a religion?*

THEOSOPHIST.—It is not. Theosophy is Divine Knowledge or Science.

INQ.—*What is the real meaning of the term?*

THEO.—Divine Wisdom, Theosophia (θεοσοφία), or Wisdom of the Gods, as Theogonia (θεογονία), Genealogy of the Gods. The word θεός means a God in Greek, one of the divine beings; certainly not "God" in the sense attached in our day to the term. Therefore it is not "Wisdom of God," as translated by some, but Divine Wisdom such as that possessed by the Gods. The term is many thousand years old.

INQ.—*What is the origin of the name?*

THEO.—It comes to us from the Alexandrian philosophers, called lovers of truth, Philaletheians, from *phil* (φιλ), "loving," and *aletheia* (ἀλήθεια), "truth." The name The-

1

osophy dates from the third century of our era, and began
with Ammonius Saccas and his disciples, who started the
Eclectic Theosophical system, and were also called Analogeticists. As explained by Professor Alexander Wilder, M.D.,
F.T.S., in his *New Platonism and Alchemy*,* they were so
called—

Because of their practice of interpreting all sacred legends and narratives, myths and mysteries, by a rule or principle of analogy and
correspondence, so that events which were related as having occurred
in the external world were regarded as expressing operations and experiences of the human soul.

They were also denominated Neoplatonists. · Though
Theosophy, or the Eclectic Theosophical system, is generally attributed to the third century, yet, if Diogenes Laertius
is to be credited, its origin is much earlier, as he attributed
the system to an Egyptian priest, Pot Amun, who lived in
the early days of the Ptolemaic dynasty. The same author
tells us that the name is Coptic, and signifies one consecrated
to Amun, the God of Wisdom. Theosophy is the equivalent of the Sanskrit Brahma-Vidyâ, Divine Knowledge.

Inq.—*What was the object of this system ?*

Theo.—First of all to inculcate certain great moral truths
upon its disciples and all those who were "lovers of the
truth." Hence also the motto adopted by the Theosophical Society : "There is no religion higher than truth."

Eclectic Theosophy was divided under three heads:
(1) Belief in one absolute, incomprehensible, and supreme
Deity, or infinite essence, which is the root of all Nature,
and of all that is, visible and invisible. (2) Belief in man's
eternal immortal nature, which, being a radiation of the
Universal Soul, is of an identical essence with it. (3) The-

---

* *A Sketch of the Doctrines and Principal Teachers of the Eclectic or Alexandrian School ; also an Outline of the Interior Doctrines of the Alchemists of the
Middle Ages.* Albany, N. Y., 1869.

urgy, or "divine work," or producing a work of Gods; from *theoi*, "Gods," and *ergein*, "to work." The term is very old, but, as it belongs to the vocabulary of the Mysteries, was not in popular use. It was a mystic belief—practically proven by initiated Adepts and priests—that, by making one's self as pure as the incorporeal beings—i.e., by return-ing to one's pristine purity of Nature—man could move the Gods to impart to him Divine Mysteries, and even cause them to become occasionally visible, either subjectively or objectively. It was the transcendental aspect of what is now called "Spiritualism"; but having been abused and misconceived by the populace, it had come to be regarded by some as necromancy, and was generally forbidden. A travestied practice of the Theurgy of Iamblichus lingers still in the ceremonial magic of some modern Kabalists. Modern Theosophy avoids and rejects both these kinds of magic and necromancy as being very dangerous. Real *divine* Theurgy requires an almost superhuman purity and holiness of life; otherwise it degenerates into mediumship or black magic. The immediate disciples of Ammonius Saccas, who was called Theodidaktos, "God-taught"—such as Plotinus and his follower Porphyry—rejected Theurgy at first, but were finally reconciled to it through Iamblichus, who wrote a work to that effect entitled *De Mysteriis*, under the name of his own master, a famous Egyptian priest called Abammon. Ammonius Saccas was the son of Christian parents; but being from his childhood repelled by dogmatic spiritualistic Christianity, he became a Neo-platonist, and, like Jakob Böhme and other great seers and mystics, is said to have had Divine Wisdom revealed to him in dreams and visions. Hence his name of Theodidaktos. He resolved to reconcile every system of religion, and, by demonstrating their identical origin, establish one universal creed based on ethics. His life was so blameless and pure, his learning so profound and vast, that several church fathers were his secret disciples. Clemens Alexandrinus speaks very highly of him. Plotinus, the "St. John" of Ammonius, was also a man universally respected and esteemed, and of the most profound learning and integrity. When thirty-nine years of age he accompanied the Roman Emperor Gordian and his army to the East, to be instructed by the sages of Bactria and India. He had a school of philosophy in Rome. Porphyry, his disciple, a Hellenized Jew, whose real name was Malek, collected all the writings of his master. Porphyry was also himself a great author, and gave an allegorical interpretation of some parts of Homer's writings. The system of meditation the Philaletheians resorted to was ecstasy, a system akin to Indian Yoga-practice. What is known of the Eclectic school is due to Origen, Longinus, and Plotinus, the immediate disciples of Ammonius.*

The chief aim of the founders of the Eclectic Theosophical school was one of the three objects of its modern successor, the Theosophical Society, namely, to reconcile all religions, sects, and nations under a common system of ethics based on eternal verities.

INQ.—*What have you to show that this is not an impossible dream, and that all the world's religions are based on the one and the same truth?*

THEO.—Their comparative study and analysis. The "Wisdom-Religion" was one in antiquity; and the sameness of primitive religious philosophy is proven to us by the identical doctrines taught to the Initiates during the Mysteries, an institution once universally diffused. As Dr. Wilder says:

All the old worships indicate the existence of a single Theosophy anterior to them. The key that is to open one must open all; otherwise it cannot be the right key.

---

* For further information see Dr. Wilder's pamphlet.

THE POLICY OF THE THEOSOPHICAL SOCIETY.

INQ.—*In the days of Ammonius there were several great ancient religions, and the sects in Egypt and Palestine alone were numerous. How could he reconcile them?*

THEO.—By doing that which we again try to do now. The Neoplatonists were a large body, and belonged to various religious philosophies; so do our Theosophists.

It was under Philadelphus that Judaism established itself in Alexandria, and forthwith the Hellenic teachers became the dangerous rivals of the College of Rabbis of Babylon. As the author of *New Platonism* very pertinently remarks:

> The Buddhistic, Vedântic, and Magian systems were expounded along with the philosophies of Greece. It was not wonderful that thoughtful men supposed that the strife of words ought to cease, and considered it possible to extract one harmonious system from the various teachings. . . . Pantænus, Athenagoras, and Clement were thoroughly instructed in the Platonic philosophy, and comprehended its essential unity with the Oriental systems.

In those days the Jew Aristobulus affirmed that the ethics of Aristotle represented the esoteric teachings of the law of Moses; Philo Judæus endeavored to reconcile the Pentateuch with the Pythagorean and Platonic philosophy; and Josephus proved that the Essenes of Carmel were simply the copyists and followers of the Egyptian Therapeutæ, or Healers. So it is in our day. We can show the line of descent of every Christian religion, as of every —even the smallest—sect. The latter are the minor twigs or shoots grown on the larger branches; but shoots and branches spring from the same trunk—the Wisdom-Religion. To prove this was the aim of Ammonius, who endeavored to induce Gentiles and Christians, Jews and idolaters, to lay aside their contentions and strifes, remembering only that they were all in possession of the same

truth under various vestments, and were all the children of
a common mother. This is the aim of Theosophy likewise.

Says Mosheim of Ammonius:

Conceiving that not only the philosophers of Greece, but also all
those of the different barbarous nations, were perfectly in unison with
each other with regard to every essential point, [he] made it his busi-
ness so to expound the tenets of all these various sects as to make it
appear they had all originated from one and the same source, and
tended all to one and the same end.

If the writer on Ammonius in the *Edinburgh Encyclopedia* knows what he is talking about, then he describes
the modern Theosophists, their beliefs and their work, for
he says, speaking of the Theodidaktos:

He adopted the doctrines which were received in Egypt [the esoteric
were those of India] concerning the universe and the Deity, considered as constituting one great whole; concerning the eternity of the
world. . . . He also established a system of moral discipline which allowed the people in general to live according to the laws of their country
and the dictates of Nature, but required the wise to exalt their mind by
contemplation.

INQ.—*What are your authorities for saying all this of the
ancient Theosophists of Alexandria?*

THEO.—An almost countless number of well-known
writers. Mosheim—one of them—says that Ammonius
taught that—

The religion of the multitude went hand in hand with philosophy,
and with her had shared the fate of being by degrees corrupted and ob-
scured with mere human conceits, superstition, and lies; and it ought,
therefore, to be brought back to its original purity by purging it of this
dross and expounding it upon philosophical principles; and the whole
which Christ had in view was to reinstate and restore to its primitive
integrity the Wisdom of the ancients; to reduce within bounds the universally prevailing dominion of superstition; and in part to correct, and
in part to exterminate, the various errors that had found their way into
the different popular religions.

This, again, is precisely what the modern Theosophists say; only while the great Philaletheian was supported and helped in the policy he pursued by two church fathers, Clement and Athenagoras, by the learned rabbis of the synagogue, by the philosophers of the Academy and the Grove, and while he taught a common doctrine for all, we, his followers on the same line, receive no recognition, but, on the contrary, are abused and persecuted. People fifteen hundred years ago are thus shown to have been more tolerant than they are in this " enlightened " century.

INQ.—*Was Ammonius encouraged and supported by the church because, notwithstanding his heresies, he taught Christianity and was a Christian?*

THEO.—Not at all. He was born a Christian, but never accepted church Christianity. As said of him by Dr. Wilder:

He had but to propound his instructions " according to the ancient pillars of Hermes, which Plato and Pythagoras knew before, and from them constituted their philosophy." Finding the same in the prologue of the Gospel according to John, he very properly supposed that the purpose of Jesus was to restore the great doctrine of Wisdom in its primitive integrity. The narratives of the Bible and the stories of the Gods he considered to be allegories illustrative of the truth, or else fables to be rejected.

Moreover, as says the *Edinburgh Encyclopedia:*

He acknowledged that Jesus Christ was an excellent *man* and the friend of God, but alleged that it was not his design entirely to abolish the worship of demons [Gods], and that his only intention was to purify the ancient religion.

THE WISDOM-RELIGION ESOTERIC IN ALL AGES.

INQ.—*Since Ammonius never committed anything to writing, how can one feel sure that such were his teachings?*

THEO.—Neither did Buddha, Pythagoras, Confucius, Orpheus, Socrates, nor even Jesus, leave behind them any

writings. Yet most of these are historical personages, and
their teachings have all survived. The disciples of Ammonius, among whom were Origen and Herennius, wrote
treatises and explained his ethics. Certainly the latter are
as historical, if not more so, than the apostolic writings.
Moreover, his pupils—Origen, Plotinus, and Longinus,
counselor of the famous Queen Zenobia—have all left records of the Philaletheian system—so far, at all events, as
their public profession of faith was known; for the school
was divided into exoteric and *esoteric* teachings.

INQ.—*How have the latter tenets reached our day, since
you hold that what is properly called the Wisdom-Religion
was esoteric?*

THEO.—The Wisdom-Religion was ever one and the
same, and being the last word of possible human knowledge, was therefore carefully preserved. It preceded by
long ages the Alexandrian Theosophists, reached the mod
ern, and will survive every other religion and philosophy.

INQ.—*Where and by whom was it so preserved?*

THEO.—Among Initiates of every country; among profound seekers after truth—their disciples; and in those parts
of the world where such topics have always been most
valued and pursued—in India, central Asia, and Persia.

INQ.—*Can you give me some proofs of its esotericism?*

THEO.—The best proof you can have of the fact is that
every ancient religious, or rather philosophical, cult consisted of an esoteric or secret teaching, and an exoteric or
outward public worship. Furthermore, it is a well-known
fact that the Mysteries of the ancients comprised with every
nation the Greater (secret) and Lesser (public) Mysteries—
as, for instance, in the celebrated solemnities called the
Eleusinia, in Greece. From the Hierophants of Samothrace,
Egypt, and the initiated Brâhmans of the India of old, down
to the later Hebrew rabbis, all, for fear of profanation, kept

their real *bona-fide* beliefs secret. The Jewish rabbis called their secular religious series the Mercavah, or exterior body, the "vehicle" or covering which contains the *hidden soul*— their highest secret knowledge. The priests of the ancient nations never imparted their real philosophical secrets to the masses. They allotted to the latter only the husks. Northern Buddhism has its Greater and its Lesser Vehicle, known as the Mahâyâna, the esoteric, and the Hînayâna, the exoteric, schools. Nor can you blame them for such secrecy; for surely you would not think of feeding your flock of sheep on learned dissertations on botany instead of on grass. Pythagoras called his Gnôsis "the knowledge of things that are," or ἡ γνῶσις τῶν ὄντων, and preserved that Knowledge for his pledged disciples only—for those who could digest such mental food and feel satisfied; whom he pledged to silence and secrecy. Occult alphabets and secret ciphers are the development of the old Egyptian hieratic writings, the secret of which was, in the days of old, in the possession only of the Hierogrammatists, or initiated Egyptian priests. Ammonius Saccas, as his biographers tell us, bound his pupils by oath not to divulge his *higher doctrines* except to those who had already been instructed in preliminary knowledge, and who were also bound by a pledge. Finally, do we not find the same also in early Christianity, among the Gnostics, and even in the teachings of Christ? Did he not speak to the multitudes in parables which had a twofold meaning, and explain his reasons only to his disciples? "Unto you," he says, "it is given to know the mystery of the kingdom of God: but unto them that are without, all these things are done in parables." * And the author of *New Platonism* tells us that—

The Essenes of Judea and Carmel made similar distinctions, dividing their adherents into neophytes, brethren, and the perfect [or those initiated].

---

* Mark iv. 11.

Examples might be brought from every country to this effect.

INQ.—*Can you attain the "Secret Wisdom" simply by study?, Encyclopedias define* Theosophy *pretty much as Webster's Dictionary does, i.e., as "supposed intercourse with God and superior spirits, and consequent attainment of super-human knowledge by physical . . . or . . . chemical processes." Is this so?*

THEO.—I think not. Nor is there any lexicographer capable of explaining, whether to himself or others, how *su-perhuman* knowledge can be attained by physical or chemical processes. Had Webster said by metaphysical and alchemi-cal processes, the definition would be approximately cor-rect; as it is, it is absurd. Ancient Theosophists claimed, and so do the modern, that the Infinite cannot be known by the finite—i.e., sensed by the finite self—but that the divine essence could be communicated to the higher spiritual Self in a state of ecstasy. This condition can hardly be attained, like hypnotism, by "physical and chemical processes."

INQ.—*What is your explanation of it?*

THEO.—Real ecstasy was defined by Plotinus as "the liberation of the mind from its finite consciousness, becom-ing one and identified with the Infinite." This is the high-est condition, says Dr. A. Wilder, but not one of permanent duration, and it is reached only by the very, *very* few. It is, indeed, identical with that state which is known in India as Samâdhi. The latter is practised by the Yogîs, who facilitate it physically by the greatest abstinence in food and drink, and mentally by an incessant endeavor to purify and elevate the mind. Meditation is silent and *un-uttered* prayer, or, as Plato expressed it:

The ardent turning of the soul toward God; not to ask any particu-lar good [as in the common meaning of prayer], but for good itself—

for the universal Supreme Good [of which we are a part on earth, and out of the essence of which we have all emerged]. . . . Therefore remain silent in the presence of the *divine ones*, till they remove the clouds from thy eyes and enable thee to see, by the light which issues from themselves, not what appears as good to thee, but what is intrinsically good.

This is what the scholarly author of *New Platonism*, Dr. A. Wilder, describes as "spiritual photography":

The soul is the camera in which facts and events, future, past, and present, are alike fixed; and the mind becomes conscious of them. Beyond our every-day world of limits, all is one day or state—the past and future comprised in the present. . . . [Death is the last *ecstasis* on earth.] Then the soul is freed from the constraint of the body, and its nobler part is united to higher Nature and becomes partaker in the wisdom and foreknowledge of the higher beings.

Real Theosophy is, for the mystics, that state which Apollonius of Tyana was made to describe thus:

I can see the present and the future as in a clear mirror. The sage need not wait for the vapors of the earth and the corruption of the air to foresee [events]. . . . The *theoi*, or Gods, see the future; common men, the present; sages, that which is about to take place.

The Theosophy of the sages he speaks of is well expressed in the assertion, "The kingdom of God is within us."

INQ.—*Theosophy, then, is not, as held by some, a newly devised scheme?*

THEO.—Only ignorant people can thus refer to it. It is as old as the world, in its teachings and ethics, if not in name, as it is also the broadest and most catholic system among all.

INQ.—*How comes it, then, that Theosophy has remained so unknown to the nations of the western hemisphere? Why should it have been a sealed book to races confessedly the most cultured and advanced?*

THEO.—We believe there were nations as cultured in days of old, and certainly more spiritually " advanced," than we are. But there are several reasons for this willing ignorance. One of them was given by St. Paul to the cultured Athenians—a loss, for long centuries, of real spiritual insight, and even interest, owing to their too great devotion to things of sense and their long slavery to the dead letter of dogma and ritualism. But the strongest reason for it lies in the fact that real Theosophy has ever been kept secret.

INQ.—*You have brought forward proofs that such secrecy has existed; but what was the real cause for it?*

THEO.—The causes for it were: Firstly, the perversity of average human nature, and its selfishness, always tending to the gratification of *personal* desires to the detriment of neighbors and next of kin. Such people could never be intrusted with *divine* secrets. Secondly, their unreliability to keep the sacred and divine knowledge from desecration. It is the latter which led to the perversion of the most sublime truths and symbols, and to the gradual transformation of things spiritual into anthropomorphic, concrete, and gross imagery—in other words, to the dwarfing of the God-idea and to idolatry.

THEOSOPHY IS NOT BUDDHISM.

INQ.—*You are often spoken of as " Esoteric Buddhists." Are you, then, all followers of Gautama Buddha?*

THEO.—No more than musicians are all followers of Wagner. Some of us are Buddhists by religion; yet there are far more Hindûs and Brâhmans than Buddhists among us, and more Christian-born Europeans and Americans than converted Buddhists. The mistake has arisen from a misunderstanding of the real meaning of the title of Mr. A. P. Sinnett's excellent work, *Esoteric Buddhism.* The last word ought to have been spelled with one instead of two *d's*, for then *Budhism* would have meant what it was intended for, namely, "Wisdom-Religion" (from *bodha, bodhi,* "intelligence," "wisdom"), instead of *Buddhism,* Gautama's religious philosophy. Theosophy, as already said, is the Wisdom-Religion.

INQ.—*What is the difference between* Buddhism, *the religion founded by the Prince of Kapilavastu, and* Budhism, *the "Wisdom-Religion" which you say is synonymous with Theosophy?*

THEO.—Just the same difference as there is between the later ritualism and dogmatic theology of the churches and sects, and the secret teachings of Christ, which are called "the mysteries of the kingdom of heaven." Buddha means the "Enlightened" by Bodha, or Understanding, Wisdom. This has passed root and branch into the *esoteric* teachings that Gautama imparted to his chosen Arhats only.

INQ.—*But some Orientalists deny that Buddha ever taught any esoteric doctrine at all.*

THEO.—They may as well deny that Nature has any hidden secrets for men of science. Further on I will prove it by Buddha's conversation with his disciple Ânanda. His esoteric teachings were simply the Gupta-Vidyâ, or secret knowledge, of the ancient Brâhmans, the key to which their modern successors have, with few exceptions, completely lost. And this Vidyâ has passed into what is now known as the *inner* teachings of the Mahâyâna school of Northern Buddhism. Those who deny it are simply ignorant pretenders to Orientalism. I advise you to read the Rev. Mr. Edkins's *Chinese Buddhism*—especially the chapters on the exoteric and *esoteric* schools and teachings—and then compare the testimony of the whole ancient world upon the subject.

INQ.—*But are not the ethics of Theosophy identical with those taught by Buddha?*

THEO.—Certainly; because these ethics are the soul of the Wisdom-Religion, and were once the common property of the Initiates of all nations. But Buddha was the first to embody these lofty ethics in his public teachings, and to make them the foundation and the very essence of his public system. It is herein that lies the immense difference between exoteric Buddhism and every other religion. For while in other religions ritualism and dogma hold the first and most important place, in Buddhism it is the ethics which have always been the most insisted upon. This accounts for the resemblance, amounting almost to identity, between the ethics of Theosophy and those of the religion of Buddha.

INQ.—*Are there any great points of difference?*

THEO.—One great distinction between Theosophy and *exoteric* Buddhism is that the latter, represented by the Southern Church, entirely denies (*a*) the existence of any Deity, and (*b*) any conscious post-mortem life, or even any self-conscious surviving individuality in man. Such, at least, is the teaching of the Siamese sect, now considered as the *purest* form of exoteric Buddhism. And it is so, if we refer only to Buddha's public teachings; the reason for such reticence on his part I will give further on. But the schools of the Northern Buddhist Church, established in those countries to which his initiated Arhats retired after the Master's death, teach all that is now called Theosophical doctrines, because they form part of the knowledge of the Initiates—thus proving how the truth has been sacrificed to the dead letter by the too-zealous orthodoxy of Southern Buddhism. But how much grander and more noble, more philosophical and scientific, even in its dead letter, is this teaching than that of any other church or religion! Yet Theosophy is not Buddhism.

II.

EXOTERIC AND ESOTERIC THEOSOPHY.

WHAT THE MODERN THEOSOPHICAL SOCIETY IS NOT.

INQ.—*Your doctrines, then, are not a revival of Buddhism, nor are they entirely copied from the Neoplatonic Theosophy?*

THEO.—They are not. But to these questions I cannot give you a better answer than by quoting from a paper read on "Theosophy" by Dr. J. D. Buck, F.T.S., before the last Theosophical Convention, at Chicago, Ill. (April, 1889). No living Theosophist has better expressed and understood the real essence of Theosophy than our honored friend Dr. Buck.

The Theosophical Society was organized for the purpose of promulgating the Theosophical doctrines, and for the promotion of the Theosophic life. The present Theosophical Society is not the first of its kind. I have a volume entitled *Theosophical Transactions of the Philadelphian Society*, published in London in 1697; and another with the following title: *Introduction to Theosophy ; or, The Science of the Mystery of Christ, that is, of Deity, Nature, and Creature ; embracing the Philosophy of all the Working Powers of Life, Magical and Spiritual, and forming a Practical Guide to the Sublimest Purity, Sanctity, and Evangelical Perfection ; also to the Attainment of Divine Vision, and the Holy Angelic Arts, Potencies, and other Prerogatives of the Regeneration ;* published in London in 1855. The following is the dedication of this volume:

" To the students of Universities, Colleges, and Schools of Chris-

15

tendom: To Professors of Metaphysical, Mechanical, and Natural
Science in all its forms: To men and women of education generally, of
fundamental orthodox Faith: To Deists, Arians, Unitarians, Sweden-
borgians, and other defective and ungrounded creeds, rationalists and
skeptics of every kind: To just-minded and enlightened Mohammedans,
Jews, and Oriental Patriarch-Religionists: but especially to the gospel
minister and missionary, whether to the barbaric or intellectual peoples,
this introduction to Theosophy, or the science of the ground and mystery of all things, is most humbly and affectionately dedicated."

In the following year (1856) another volume was issued, royal octavo,
of six hundred pages, diamond type, of *Theosophical Miscellanies.* Of
the last-named work five hundred copies only were issued, for gratu-
itous distribution to libraries and universities. These earlier movements, of which there were many, originated within the church, with
persons of great piety and earnestness, and of unblemished character;
and all of these writings were in orthodox form, using the Christian
expressions, and, like the writings of the eminent churchman William
Law, would only be distinguished by the ordinary reader for their
great earnestness and piety. These were one and all but attempts to
derive and explain the deeper meanings and original import of the
Christian Scriptures, and to illustrate and unfold the Theosophic life.
These works were soon forgotten, and are now generally unknown.
They sought to reform the clergy and revive genuine piety, and were
never welcomed. That one word "heresy" was sufficient to bury
them in the limbo of all such Utopias. At the time of the Reformation
John Reuchlin made a similar attempt with the same result, though he
was the intimate and trusted friend of Luther. Orthodoxy never de-
sired to be informed and enlightened. These reformers were informed,
as was Paul by Festus, that too much learning had made them mad,
and that it would be dangerous to go further. Passing by the verbiage
—which was partly a matter of habit and education with these writers,
and partly due to religious restraint through secular power—and coming to the core of the matter, these writings were Theosophical in the
strictest sense, and pertained solely to man's knowledge of his own
nature and the higher life of the soul. The present Theosophical
movement has sometimes been declared to be an attempt to convert
Christendom to Buddhism, which means simply that the word
"heresy" has lost its terrors and relinquished its power. Individuals in every age have more or less clearly apprehended the Theosophical doctrines and wrought them into the fabric of their lives.
These doctrines belong exclusively to no religion, and are confined to
no society or time. They are the birthright of every human soul. Such

a thing as orthodoxy must be wrought out by each individual according to his nature and his needs, and according to his varying experience. This may explain why those who have imagined Theosophy to be a new religion have hunted in vain for its creed and its ritual. Its creed is Loyalty to Truth, and its ritual "To honor every truth by use."

How little this principle of Universal Brotherhood is understood by the masses of mankind, how seldom its transcendent importance is recognized, may be seen in the diversity of opinion and fictitious interpretations regarding the Theosophical Society. This society was organized on this one principle, the essential Brotherhood of Man, as herein briefly outlined and imperfectly set forth. It has been assailed as Buddhistic and antichristian, as though it could be both these together, when both Buddhism and Christianity, as set forth by their inspired founders, make Brotherhood the one essential of doctrine and of life. Theosophy has been also regarded as something new under the sun, or at best as old mysticism masquerading under a new name. While it is true that many societies founded upon and united to support the principles of altruism or essential Brotherhood have borne various names, it is also true that many have also been called Theosophic, and with principles and aims as the present society bearing that name. With these societies, one and all, the essential doctrine has been the same, and all else has been incidental, though this does not obviate the fact that many persons are attracted to the incidentals who overlook or ignore the essentials.

No better or more explicit answer—by a man who is one of our most esteemed and earnest Theosophists—could be given to your questions.

INQ.—*Which system do you prefer or follow, in that case, besides Buddhistic ethics?*

THEO.—None, and all. We hold to no religion and to no philosophy in particular; we cull the good we find in each. But here, again, it must be stated that, like all other ancient systems, Theosophy is divided into exoteric and esoteric sections.

INQ.—*What is the difference?*

THEO.—The members of the Theosophical Society at large are free to profess whatever religion or philosophy

they like—or none, if they so prefer—provided they are in
sympathy with, and ready to carry out one or more of, the
three objects of the association. The Society is a philanthropic and scientific body for the propagation of the idea
of brotherhood on practical instead of theoretical lines.
The Fellows may be Christians or Mussulmans, Jews or
Parsîs, Buddhists or Brâhmans, Spiritualists or materialists
—it does not matter; but every member must be either a
philanthropist or a scholar, a searcher into Âryan and other
old literature or a psychic student. In short, he has to help,
if he can, in the carrying out of at least one of the objects
of the program. Otherwise he has no reason for becoming
a Fellow. Such are the majority of the exoteric Society,
composed of "attached" and "unattached" members.*
These may or may not become Theosophists *de facto.*
Members they are, by virtue of their having joined the Society; but the latter cannot make a Theosophist of one who
has no sense for the divine fitness of things, or of him who
understands Theosophy in his own—if the expression may
be used—sectarian and egotistic way. "Handsome is as
handsome does" could be paraphrased in this case, and
made to run, "Theosophist is who Theosophy does."

THEOSOPHISTS AND MEMBERS OF THE THEOSOPH-
ICAL SOCIETY.

INQ.—*This applies to lay members, as I understand. And
what of those who pursue the esoteric study of Theosophy—
are they the real Theosophists?*

THEO.—Not necessarily, until they have proven themselves to be such. They have entered the inner group and

---

* An "attached" member means one who has joined some particular Branch of
the Theosophical Society. An "unattached," one who belongs to the Society at
large, has his diploma from the Headquarters (Adyar, Madras), but is connected with
no Branch or Lodge.

pledged themselves to carry out, as strictly as they can, the rules of the occult body. This is a difficult undertaking, as the foremost rule of all is the entire renunciation of one's personality—i.e., a pledged member has to become a thorough altruist, never to think of himself, and to forget his own vanity and pride in the thought of the good of his fellow-creatures, besides that of his fellow-brothers in the esoteric circle. He has to live, if the esoteric instructions shall profit him, a life of abstinence in everything, of self-denial and strict morality, doing his duty by all men. The few real Theosophists in the Theosophical Society are among these members. This does not imply that outside of the Theosophical Society and the inner circle there are no Theosophists; for there are, and more than people know of—certainly far more than are found among the lay members of the Theosophical Society.

Inq.—*Then what is the good of joining the so-called Theosophical Society in that case? Where is the incentive?*

Theo.—None, except the advantage of getting esoteric instructions, the genuine doctrines of the Esoteric Philosophy, and, if the real program is carried out, deriving much help from mutual aid and sympathy. Union is strength and harmony, and well-regulated simultaneous efforts produce wonders. This has been the secret of all associations and communities since mankind existed.

Inq.—*But why could not a man of well-balanced mind and singleness of purpose, one, say, of indomitable energy and perseverance, become an Occultist, and even an Adept, if he works alone?*

Theo.—He may; but there are ten thousand chances against one that he will fail. For one reason out of many others, no books on Occultism or Theurgy exist in our day which give out the secrets of Alchemy or medieval Theosophy in plain language. All are symbolical or in parables; and as the key to these has been lost for ages in the West, how can a man learn the correct meaning of what he is reading and studying? Therein lies the greatest danger —one that leads to unconscious black magic or the most helpless mediumship. He who has not an Initiate for a Master had better leave the dangerous study alone. Look around you and observe. While two thirds of " civilized " society ridicule the mere notion that there is anything in Theosophy, Occultism, Spiritualism, or in the Kabalah, the other third is composed of the most heterogeneous and opposite elements. Some believe in the mystical and even in the supernatural (!), but each believes in his own way. Others will rush single-handed into the study of the Kabalah, Psychism, Mesmerism, Spiritualism, or some form or another of Mysticism. Result: no two men think alike, no two are agreed upon any fundamental occult principles, though many are those who claim for themselves the *Ultima Thule* of knowledge, and would make outsiders believe that they are full-blown Adepts. Not only is there no scientific and accurate knowledge of Occultism accessible in the West— not even of true Astrology, the only branch of Occultism which, in its *exoteric* teachings, has definite laws and a definite system—but no one has any idea of what real Occultism means. Some limit ancient wisdom to the Kabalah and the Jewish *Zohar,* which each interprets in his own way according to the dead letter of the rabbinical methods. Others regard Swedenborg or Böhme as the ultimate expressions of the highest wisdom; while others, again, see in Mesmerism the great secret of ancient magic. One and all of those who put their theory into practice are rapidly drifting, through ignorance, into black magic. Happy are those who escape from it, as they have neither test nor criterion by which they can distinguish between the true and the false.

INQ.—*Are we to understand that the inner group of the Theosophical Society claims to learn what it does from real Initiates or Masters of Esoteric Wisdom?*

THEO.—Not directly. The personal presence of such Masters is not required. Suffice it if they give instructions to some of those who have studied under their guidance for years and devoted their whole lives to their service. Then, in turn, these can give out the knowledge so imparted to others who had no such opportunity. A portion of the true sciences is better than a mass of undigested and misunderstood learning. An ounce of gold is worth a ton of dust.

INQ.—*But how is one to know whether the ounce is real gold or only a counterfeit?*

THEO.—A tree is known by its fruit, a system by its results. When our opponents are able to prove to us that any solitary student of Occultism throughout the ages has become a saintly Adept like Ammonius Saccas, or even a Plotinus, or a Theurgist like Iamblichus, or achieved feats such as are claimed to have been done by St. Germain, without any Master to guide him, and all this without being a medium, a self-deluded psychic, or a charlatan, then shall we confess ourselves mistaken. But till then Theosophists prefer to follow the proven natural law of the tradition of the Sacred Science. There are mystics who have made great discoveries in chemistry and physical sciences, almost bordering on Alchemy and Occultism; others who, by the sole aid of their genius, have rediscovered portions, if not the whole, of the lost alphabets of the "mystery language," and are therefore able to read correctly Hebrew scrolls; others still who, being seers, have caught wonderful glimpses of the hidden secrets of Nature. But all these are *specialists*. One is a theoretical inventor, another a Hebrew —i.e., a sectarian Kabalist—a third a Swedenborg of modern times, denying all and everything outside of his own particular science or religion. . Not one of them can boast of having produced a universal or even a national benefit thereby, or a benefit even to himself. With the exception of a few healers—of that class which the Royal College of Physicians or Surgeons would call quacks—none have helped with their science humanity, or even a number of men of the same community. Where are the Chaldees of old— those who wrought marvelous cures, "not by charms, but by simples "? Where is an Apollonius of Tyana, who healed the sick and raised the dead under any climate and circumstances? We know some specialists of the former class even in Europe, but of the latter only in Asia, where the secret of the Yogî—" to live in death "—is still preserved.

INQ.—*Is the production of such healing Adepts the aim of Theosophy ?*

THEO.—Its aims are several; but the most important are those which are likely to lead to the relief of human suffering under any or every form, moral as well as physical. And we believe the former to be far more important than the latter. Theosophy has to inculcate ethics; it has to purify the soul if it would relieve the physical body, whose ailments, save cases of accidents, are all hereditary. It is not by studying Occultism for selfish ends—for the gratification of one's personal ambition, pride, or vanity—that one can ever reach the true goal of helping suffering mankind. Nor is it by studying one single branch of the Esoteric Philosophy that a man becomes an Occultist, but by studying, if not mastering, them all.

INQ.—*Is help, then, to reach this most important aim given only to those who study the esoteric sciences ?*

THEO.—Not at all. Every lay member is entitled to general instruction if he only wants it; but few are willing to become what is called " working members," and most prefer to remain the "drones" of Theosophy. Let it be understood that private research is encouraged in the Theosophical Society, provided it does not infringe the limit which separates the exoteric from the esoteric, the *blind* from the *conscious* magic.

THE DIFFERENCE BETWEEN THEOSOPHY AND OCCULTISM.

Inq.—*You speak of Theosophy and Occultism; are they identical?*

Theo.—By no means. A man may be a very good Theosophist indeed, whether in or outside of the Society, without being in any way an Occultist. But no one can be a true Occultist without being a real Theosophist; otherwise he is simply a black magician, whether conscious or unconscious.

Inq.—*What do you mean?*

Theo.—I have said already that a true Theosophist must put in practice the loftiest moral ideal; must strive to realize his unity with the whole of humanity, and work ceaselessly for others. Now, if an Occultist does not do all this, he must act selfishly for his own personal benefit; and if he has acquired more practical power than other ordinary men, he becomes forthwith a far more dangerous enemy to the world and those around him than the average mortal. This is clear.

Inq.—*Then is an Occultist simply a man who possesses more power than other people?*

Theo.—Far more—if he is a practical and really learned Occultist, and not one only in name. Occult sciences are *not*, as described in encyclopedias, "those *imaginary* sciences of the middle ages which related to the *supposed* action or influence of occult qualities or supernatural powers, as alchemy, magic, necromancy, and astrology," for they are real, actual, and very dangerous sciences. They teach the secret potency of things in Nature, developing and cultivating the hidden powers "latent in man," thus giving him tremendous advantages over more ignorant mortals. Hypnotism—now become so common, and a subject of serious scientific inquiry—is a good instance in point. Hypnotic power has been discovered almost by accident, the way to it having been prepared by Mesmerism. And now an able hypnotizer can do almost anything with it, from forcing a man, unconsciously to himself, to play the fool, to making him commit a crime—often by proxy for the hypnotizer, and for the latter's benefit. Is not this a terrible power if left in the hands of unscrupulous persons? And please to remember that this is only one of the minor branches of Occultism.

INQ.—*But are not all these occult sciences, magic, and sorcery considered by the most cultured and learned people as relics of ancient ignorance and superstition ?*

THEO.—Let me remind you that this remark of yours cuts both ways. The "most cultured and learned" among you regard also Christianity and every other religion as a relic of ignorance and superstition. People begin to believe now, at any rate, in Hypnotism, and some—even of the most cultured—in Theosophy and phenomena. But who among them, except preachers and blind fanatics, will confess to a belief in biblical miracles? And this is where the point of difference comes in. There are very good and pure Theosophists who may believe in the supernatural— divine "miracles" included—but no Occultist will do so. For an Occultist practises *scientific* Theosophy, based on accurate knowledge of Nature's secret workings; but a Theosophist, practising the powers called abnormal, *minus* the light of Occultism, will simply tend toward a dangerous form of mediumship; because, although holding to Theosophy and its highest conceivable code of ethics, he practises it in the dark, on sincere but blind faith. Any one, Theosophist or Spiritualist, who attempts to cultivate one of the branches of occult science—e.g., Hypnotism, Mesmerism, or even the secrets of producing physical phenomena—without the knowledge of the philosophic *rationale* of those powers, is like a rudderless boat launched on a stormy ocean.

THE DIFFERENCE BETWEEN THEOSOPHY AND SPIRITUALISM.

INQ.—*But do you not believe in Spiritualism?*

THEO.—If by "Spiritualism" you mean the explanation which Spiritualists give of some abnormal phenomena, then decidedly we do not. They maintain that these manifestations are all produced by the "spirits" of departed mortals —generally their relatives—who return to earth, they say, to communicate with those they have loved or to whom they are attached. We deny this point-blank. We assert that the spirits of the dead cannot return to earth, save in rare and exceptional cases, of which I may speak later; nor do they communicate with men except by entirely *subjective* means. That which appears *objectively* is only the phantom of the ex-physical man. But in psychic and, so to say, *spiritual* Spiritualism we do believe most decidedly.

INQ.—*Do you reject the phenomena also?*

THEO.—Assuredly not—save cases of conscious fraud.

INQ.—*How do you account for them, then?*

THEO.—In many ways. The causes of such manifestations are by no means so simple as the Spiritualists would like to believe. Foremost of all, the *deus ex machinâ* of the so-called "materializations" is usually the astral body or "double" of the medium or of some one present. This astral body is also the producer or operating force in the manifestations of slate-writing, "Davenport"-like manifestations, and so on.

INQ.—*You say " usually"; then what is it that produces the rest ?*

THEO.—That depends on the nature of the manifestations. Sometimes the astral remains, the kâmalokic "shells" of the vanished *personalities* that were; at other times, elementals. "Spirit" is a word of manifold and wide significance. I really do not know what Spiritualists mean by the term; but what we understand them to claim is that the physical phenomena are produced by the reincarnating Ego, the spiritual and immortal *individuality*. And this hypothesis we entirely reject. The conscious *individuality* of the disembodied *cannot materialize*, nor can it return from its own mental devachanic sphere to the plane of terrestrial objectivity.

INQ.—*But many of the communications received from the "spirits" show not only intelligence, but a knowledge of facts not known to the medium, and sometimes even not consciously present to the mind of the investigator or any of those who compose the audience.*

THEO.—This does not necessarily prove that the intelligence and knowledge you speak of belong to spirits, or emanate from *disembodied* souls. Somnambulists have been known to compose music and poetry and to solve mathematical problems while in their trance state, without having ever learned music or mathematics. Others answered intelligently questions put to them, and even, in several cases, spoke languages, such as Hebrew and Latin, of which they were entirely ignorant when awake—all this in a state of profound sleep. Will you, then, maintain that this was caused by "spirits"?

INQ.—*But how would you explain it?*

THEO.—We assert that, the divine spark in man being one and identical in its essence with the Universal Spirit, our "spiritual Self" is practically omniscient, but that it cannot manifest its knowledge, owing to the impediments of matter. Now the more these impediments are removed —in other words, the more the physical body is paralyzed as to its own independent activity and consciousness, as in deep sleep or deep trance, or, again, in illness—the more fully can the *inner* Self manifest on this plane. This is our explanation of those truly wonderful phenomena of a higher order in which undeniable intelligence and knowledge are exhibited. As to the lower order of manifestations—such 'as physical phenomena and the platitudes and common talk of the general "spirit"—to explain even the most important of the teachings we hold upon the subject would take up more space and time than can be allotted to it at present. We have no desire to interfere with the belief of the Spirit-ualists any more than with any other belief. The *onus pro-bandi* must fall on the believers in "spirits." And at the present moment, while still convinced that the higher kind of manifestations occur through disembodied souls, the leaders of the Spiritualists, and the most learned and intelli-gent among them, are the first to confess that not *all* the phenomena are produced by spirits. Gradually they will come to recognize the whole truth; but meanwhile we have no right nor desire to proselytize them to our views—the less so, as in the cases of purely *psychic and spiritual mani-festations* we believe in the intercommunication of the spirit of the living man with that of disembodied personalities.

We say that in such cases it is not the spirits of the dead who *descend* on earth, but the spirits of the living that *ascend* to the pure spiritual souls. In truth there is neither *ascending* nor *descending*, but a change of *state* or *condition* for the medium. The body of the latter becoming paralyzed or entranced, the spiritual Ego is free from its trammels, and finds itself on the same plane of consciousness as the disembodied spirits. Hence, if there is any spiritual attraction between the two, *they can communicate*, as often occurs in dreams. The difference between a mediumistic and a non-sensitive nature is this : the liberated spirit of a medium has the opportunity and facility of influencing the passive organs of its entranced physical body, and making them act, speak, and write at its will. The Ego can make it repeat, echo-like, and in human language, the thoughts and ideas of the disembodied entity as well as its own. But the non-receptive or non-sensitive organism of one who is very positive cannot be so influenced. Hence, although there is hardly a human being whose Ego does not hold free intercourse, during the sleep of its body, with those whom it loved and lost, yet, on account of the positiveness and non-receptivity of its physical envelope and brain, no recollection, or a very dim, dreamlike remembrance, lingers in the memory of the person when once awake.

INQ.—*This means that you reject the philosophy of Spiritualism in toto ?*

THEO.—If by " philosophy " you mean its crude theories, we do. But it has no philosophy, in truth. The best, the most intellectual and earnest defenders of Spiritualism say so. Their fundamental and only unimpeachable truth— namely, that phenomena occur through mediums controlled by invisible forces and intelligences—no one, except a blind materialist of the Huxley " big-toe " school, will or *can* deny. With regard to their philosophy, however, let me quote to you what the able editor of *Light*—than whom the Spiritualists will find no wiser or more devoted champion—says

of them and their philosophy.   This is what " M.A. Oxon.,"
one of the very few philosophical Spiritualists, writes, with
respect to their lack of organization and blind bigotry :

, It is worth while to look steadily at this point, for it is of vital moment. We have an experience and a knowledge beside which all other
knowledge is comparatively insignificant.   The ordinary Spiritualist
waxes wroth if any one ventures to impugn his assured knowledge of
the future and his absolute certainty of the life to come.   Where other
men have stretched forth feeble hands groping into the dark future, he
walks boldly as one who has a chart and knows his way.   Where other
men have stopped short at a pious aspiration, or have been content with
a hereditary faith, it is his boast that he knows what they only believe,
and that out of his rich stores he can supplement the fading faiths built
only upon hope.   He is magnificent in his dealings with man's most
cherished expectations. "You hope," he seems to say, " for that which
I can demonstrate.   You have accepted a traditional belief in what I
can experimentally prove according to the strictest scientific method.
The old beliefs are fading; come out from them and be separate.
They contain as much falsehood as truth.   Only by building on a sure
foundation of demonstrated fact can your superstructure be stable. All
round you old faiths are toppling. Avoid the crash and get you out."
   When one comes to deal with this magnificent person in a practical
way, what is the result? Very curious and very disappointing.   He
is so sure of his ground that he takes no trouble to ascertain the interpretation which others put upon his facts.   The wisdom of the ages
has concerned itself with the explanation of what he rightly regards as
proven; but he does not turn a passing glance on its researches.   He
does not even agree altogether with his brother Spiritualist.   It is the
story over again of the old Scotch body who, together with her husband, formed a "kirk."   They had exclusive keys to heaven, or rather
she had, for she was "na certain aboot Jamie."   So the infinitely
divided and subdivided and re-subdivided sects of Spiritualists shake
their heads, and are " na certain aboot" one another. Again, the collective experience of mankind is solid and unvarying on this point that
union is strength and disunion a source of weakness and failure.
Shoulder to shoulder, drilled and disciplined, a rabble becomes an
army, each man a match for a hundred of the untrained men that may
be brought against it.   Organization in every department of man's
work means success, saving of time and labor, profit and development.
Want of method, want of plan, haphazard work, fitful energy, undis-

ciplined effort—these mean bungling failure. The voice of humanity
attests the truth. Does the Spiritualist accept the verdict and act on
the conclusion? Verily, no. He refuses to organize. He is a law
unto himself, and a thorn in the side of his neighbors.*

INQ.—*I was told that the Theosophical Society was originally founded to crush Spiritualism and belief in the survival
of the individuality in man.*

THEO.—You are misinformed. Our beliefs are all
founded on that immortal individuality. But then, like
so many others, you confuse *personality* with *individuality*.
Your Western psychologists do not seem to have established
any clear distinction between the two. Yet it is precisely
that difference which gives the key-note to the understanding of Eastern philosophy, and which lies at the root of
the divergence between the Theosophical and Spiritualistic
teachings. And though it may draw upon us still more
the hostility of some Spiritualists, yet I must state here that
it is Theosophy which is the true and unalloyed spiritualism, while the modern scheme of that name is, as now
practised by the masses, simply transcendental materialism.

INQ.—*Please explain your idea more clearly.*

THEO.—What I mean is that, though our teachings insist
upon the identity of spirit and matter, and though we say
that spirit is potential matter, and matter simply crystallized
spirit, just as ice is solidified steam, yet, since the original
and eternal condition of the ALL is not spirit, but "superspirit," so to speak—visible and solid matter being simply
its periodical manifestation—we maintain that the term
"spirit" can only be applied to the *true individuality*.

INQ.—*But what is the distinction between this "true individuality" and the "I" or "Ego" of which we are all
conscious?*

---

* *Light,* June 22, 1889.

THEO.—Before I can answer you, we must agree upon what you mean by "I" or "Ego." We distinguish between the simple fact of self-consciousness—the simple feeling that "I am I"—and the complex thought that "I am Mr. Smith or Mrs. Brown." Believing as we do in a series of births for the same Ego, or reincarnation, this distinction is the fundamental pivot of the whole idea. You see "Mr. Smith" really means a long series of daily experiences strung together by the thread of memory, and forming what "Mr. Smith" calls "himself." But none of these "experiences" are really the "I" or the Ego, nor do they give "Mr. Smith" the feeling that he is himself, for he forgets the greater part of his daily experiences, and they produce the feeling of *egoity* in him only while they last. We Theosophists, therefore, distinguish between this bundle of "experiences," which we call the *false* (because so finite and evanescent) *personality*, and that element in man to which the feeling of "I am I" is due. It is this "I am I" which we call the *true individuality;* and we say that this Ego or individuality, like an actor, plays many parts on the stage of life.* Let us call every new life on earth of the same Ego a night on the stage of a theater. One night the actor, or Ego, appears as Macbeth, the next as Shylock, the third as Romeo, the fourth as Hamlet or King Lear, and so on, until he has run through the whole cycle of incarnations. The Ego begins his life-pilgrimage as a sprite, an Ariel, or a Puck; he plays the part of a "super"—is a soldier, a servant, one of the chorus; rises then to "speaking parts," playing leading rôles, interspersed with insignificant parts, till he finally retires from the stage as Prospero, the *magician.*

INQ.—*I understand. You say, then, that this true Ego cannot return to earth after death. But surely the actor is at*

---

* See further, Section VIII., "On Individuality and Personality."

liberty, if he has preserved the sense of his individuality, to return, if he likes, to the scene of his former actions?

THEO.—We say not; simply because such a return to earth would be incompatible with any state of *unalloyed* bliss after death, as I am prepared to prove. We say that man suffers so much unmerited misery during his life, through the fault of others with whom he is associated, or because of his environment, that he is surely entitled to perfect rest and quiet, if not bliss, before taking up again the burden of life. However, we can discuss this in detail later.

WHY IS THEOSOPHY ACCEPTED?

INQ.—*I understand to a certain extent; but I see that your teachings are far more complicated and metaphysical than either Spiritualism or current religious thought. Can you tell me, then, what has caused this system of Theosophy which you support to arouse so much interest and so much animosity at the same time?*

THEO.—There are several reasons for it, I believe. Among other causes that may be mentioned are: (1) The great reaction from the crassly materialistic theories now prevalent among scientific teachers. (2) General dissatisfaction with the artificial theology of the various Christian churches and the number of daily increasing and conflicting sects. (3) An ever-growing perception of the fact that the creeds which are so obviously self- and mutually contradictory *cannot* be true, and that claims which are unverified cannot be real. This natural distrust of conventional religions is only strengthened by their complete failure to preserve morals and to purify society and the masses. (4) A conviction on the part of many, and *knowledge* by a few, that there must be somewhere a philosophical and religious system which shall be scientific and not merely speculative.

(5) Finally, perhaps, a belief that such a system must be sought for in teachings far antedating any modern faith.

INQ.—*But how did this system come to be put forward just now ?*

THEO.—Just because the time was found to be ripe—a fact shown by the determined effort of so many earnest students to reach the truth, at whatever cost and wherever it may be concealed. Seeing this, its custodians permitted that some portions at least of that truth should be proclaimed. Had the formation of the Theosophical Society been postponed a few years longer, one half of the civilized nations would have become by this time rank materialists, and the other half anthropomorphists and phenomenalists.

INQ.—*Are we to regard Theosophy in any way as a revelation ?*

THEO.—In no way whatever, nor even in the sense of a new and direct disclosure from some higher, supernatural, or, at least, *superhuman* beings; but only in the sense of an "unveiling" of old—very old—truths to minds hitherto ignorant of them—ignorant even of the existence and preservation of any such archaic knowledge.

It has become fashionable, especially of late, to deride the notion that there ever was in the Mysteries of great and civilized peoples, such as the Egyptians, Greeks, or Romans, anything but priestly imposture. Even the Rosicrucians were no better than half lunatics, half knaves. Numerous books have been written on them; and tyros, who had hardly heard the name a few years before, sallied out as profound critics and gnostics on the subject of Alchemy, the fire-philosophers, and Mysticism in general. Yet a long series of Hierophants of Egypt, India, Chaldæa, and Arabia, together with the greatest philosophers and sages of Greece and the West, are known to have included under the designation of Wisdom and Divine Science all knowledge; for they considered the base and origin of every art and science as *essentially* divine. Plato regarded the Mysteries as most sacred; and Clemens Alexandrinus, who had been himself initiated into the Eleusinian Mysteries, has declared that "the doctrines taught therein contained in them the end of all human knowledge." Were Plato and Clemens two knaves or two fools, we wonder, or—both?

INQ.—*You spoke of "animosity." If truth is as represented by Theosophy, why has it met with such opposition, and with no general acceptance?*

THEO.—For many and various reasons again, one of which is the hatred felt by men for "innovations," as they call them. Selfishness is essentially conservative, and hates being disturbed. It prefers an easy-going, unexacting lie to the greatest truth, if the latter requires the sacrifice of one's smallest comfort. The power of mental inertia is great in anything that does not promise immediate benefit and reward. Our age is preëminently unspiritual and matter-of-fact. Moreover, there is the unfamiliar character of Theosophic teachings; the highly abstruse nature of the doctrines, some of which contradict flatly many of the human vagaries cherished by sectarians, which have eaten into the very core of popular beliefs. If we add to this the personal efforts and great purity of life exacted of those who would become the disciples of the inner circle, and the very limited class to which an entirely unselfish code appeals, it will be easy to perceive the reason why Theosophy is doomed to such slow, uphill work. It is essentially the philosophy of those who suffer, and have lost all hope of being helped out of the mire of life by any other means. Moreover, the history of any system of belief or morals newly introduced into a foreign soil shows that its beginnings were impeded by every obstacle that obscurantism and selfishness could suggest. "The crown of the innovator is a crown of thorns" indeed! No pulling down of old, worm-eaten buildings can be accomplished without some danger.

INQ.—*All this refers rather to the ethics and philosophy of Theosophy. Can you give me a general idea of the Theosophical Society, its objects and statutes ?*

THEO.—This has never been made secret. Ask, and you shall receive accurate answers.

INQ.—*But I heard that you were bound by pledges.*

THEO.—Only in the arcane or esoteric section.

INQ.—*And also, that some members after leaving did not regard themselves bound by them. Are they right ?*

THEO.—This shows that their idea of honor is an imperfect one. How can they be right ? As well said in the *Path*, our Theosophical organ at New York, treating of such a case: "Suppose that a soldier is tried for infringement of oath and discipline, and is dismissed from the service. In his rage at the justice he has called down, and of whose penalties he was distinctly forewarned, the soldier turns to the enemy with false information—a spy and traitor—as a revenge upon his former chief, and claims that his punishment has released him from his oath of loyalty to a cause." Is he justified, think you ? Do not you think he deserves being called a dishonorable man, a coward?

INQ.—*I believe so; but some think otherwise.*

THEO.—So much the worse for them. But we will talk on this subject later, if you please.

III.

THE WORKING SYSTEM OF THE THEOSOPHICAL SOCIETY.

THE OBJECTS OF THE SOCIETY.

INQ.—*What are the objects of the Theosophical Society?*

THEO.—They are three, and have been so from the beginning. (1) To form the nucleus of a Universal Brotherhood of Humanity without distinction of race, color, sex, caste, or creed. (2) To promote the study of Âryan and other Scriptures, of the world's religions and sciences, and to vindicate the importance of old Asiatic literature, such as that of the Brâhmanical, Buddhist, and Zoroastrian philosophies. (3) To investigate the hidden mysteries of Nature under every aspect possible, and the psychic and spiritual powers latent in man especially. These are, broadly stated, the three chief objects of the Theosophical Society.

INQ.—*Can you give me some more detailed information upon these?*

THEO.—We may divide each of the three objects into as many explanatory clauses as may be found necessary.

INQ.—*Then let us begin with the first. What means would you resort to in order to promote such a feeling of*

Brotherhood among races that are known to be of the most diversified religions, customs, beliefs, and modes of thought ?

THEO.—Allow me to add that which you seem unwilling to express. Of course we know that, with the exception of two remnants of races—the Parsîs and the Jews—every nation is divided, not merely against all other nations, but even against itself. This is found most prominently among the so-called civilized Christian nations. Hence your wonder, and the reason why our first object appears to you a Utopia. Is it not so?

INQ.—*Well, yes; but what have you to say against it ?*

THEO.—Nothing against the fact, but much about the necessity of removing the causes which make Universal Brotherhood a Utopia at present.

INQ.—*What are, in your view, these causes ?*

THEO.—First and foremost, the natural selfishness of human nature. This selfishness, instead of being eradicated, is daily strengthened and stimulated into a ferocious and irresistible feeling by the present religious education, which tends not only to encourage, but positively to justify it. People's ideas about right and wrong have been entirely perverted by the literal acceptance of the Jewish Bible. All the unselfishness of the altruistic teachings of Jesus has become merely a theoretical subject for pulpit oratory; while the precepts of practical selfishness taught in the Mosaic Bible, against which Christ so vainly preached, have become ingrained into the innermost life of the Western nations. "An eye for an eye, and a tooth for a tooth," has come to be the first maxim of your law. Now, I state openly and fearlessly that the perversity of this doctrine and of so many others Theosophy *alone* can eradicate.

THE COMMON ORIGIN OF MAN.

INQ.—*How?*

THEO.—Simply by demonstrating on logical, philosophical, metaphysical, and even scientific grounds that: (*a*) All men have spiritually and physically the same origin, which is the fundamental teaching of Theosophy. (*b*) As mankind is essentially of one and the same essence, and that essence is one—infinite, uncreate, and eternal, whether we call it God or Nature—nothing, therefore, can affect one nation or one man without affecting all other nations and all other men. This is as certain and as obvious as that a stone thrown into a pond will, sooner or later, set in motion every single drop of water therein.

INQ.—*But this is not the teaching of Christ, but rather a pantheistic notion.*

THEO.—That is where your mistake lies. It is purely Christian, although *not* Judaic, and therefore, perhaps, your biblical nations prefer to ignore it.

INQ.—*This is a wholesale and unjust accusation. Where are your proofs for such a statement?*

THEO.—They are ready at hand. Christ is alleged to have said, "Love one another," and "Love your enemies"; "for if ye love them [only] which love you, what reward [or merit] have ye? do not even the publicans * the same? And if ye salute your brethren only, what do ye more than others? do not even the publicans so?" These are Christ's words. But Genesis (ix. 25) says: "Cursed be Canaan; a

---

* Publicans—regarded as so many thieves and pickpockets in those days. Among the Jews the name and profession of a publican was the most odious thing in the world. They were not allowed to enter the Temple, and Matthew (xviii. 17) speaks of a heathen and a publican as identical. Yet they were only Roman tax-gatherers, occupying the same position as the British officials in India and other conquered countries.

servant of servants shall he be unto his brethren." And, therefore, not Christians, but biblical people prefer the law of Moses to Christ's law of love. It is upon the Old Testament, which panders to all their passions, that they base their laws of conquest, annexation, and tyranny over races which they call "inferior." What crimes have been committed on the strength of this—if taken in its dead-letter sense—infernal passage in Genesis, history alone gives us an idea, however inadequate.*

INQ.—*I have heard you say that the identity of our physical origin is proved by science, that of our spiritual origin by the Wisdom-Religion. Yet we do not find Darwinists exhibiting great fraternal affection.*

THEO.—Just so. This is what shows the deficiency of the materialistic systems, and proves that we Theosophists are in the right. The identity of our physical origin makes no appeal to our higher and deeper feelings. Matter, deprived of its soul and spirit, or its divine essence, cannot

---

* " At the close of the middle ages, slavery, under the power of moral forces, had mainly disappeared from Europe; but two momentous events occurred which overbore the moral power working in European society, and let loose a swarm of curses upon the earth such as mankind had scarcely ever known. One of these events was the first voyaging to a populated and barbarous coast where human beings were a familiar article of traffic; and the other the discovery of a new world, where mines of glittering wealth were open, provided labor could be imported to work them. For four hundred years men and women and children were torn from all whom they knew and loved, and were sold on the coast of Africa to foreign traders; they were chained below decks—the dead often with the living—during the horrible 'middle passage,' and, according to Bancroft, an impartial historian, two hundred and fifty thousand out of three and a quarter millions were thrown into the sea on that fatal passage, while the remainder were consigned to nameless misery in the mines, or under the lash in the cane and rice fields. The guilt of this great crime rests on the Christian church. ' In the name of the Most Holy Trinity' the Spanish government concluded more than ten treaties authorizing the sale of five hundred thousand human beings; in 1562 Sir John Hawkins sailed on his diabolical errand of buying slaves in Africa and selling them in the West Indies in a ship which bore the sacred name of Jesus; while Elizabeth, the Protestant queen, rewarded him for his success in this first adventure of Englishmen in that inhuman traffic by allowing him to wear as his crest ' a demi-Moor in his proper color, bound with a cord,' or, in other words, a manacled negro slave."—*Conquests of the Cross,* quoted from the *Agnostic Journal.*

speak to the human heart. But the identity of the soul and spirit, of real, immortal man, as Theosophy teaches us, once proven and become deep-rooted in our hearts, would lead us far on the road of real charity and brotherly good will.

INQ.—*But how does Theosophy explain the common origin of man?*

THEO.—By teaching that the root of all Nature, objective and subjective, and everything else in the universe, visible and invisible, is, was, and ever will be one absolute essence, from which all starts, and into which everything returns. This is Âryan philosophy, fully represented only by the Vedânta and the Buddhist system. With this object in view, it is the duty of all Theosophists to promote in every practical way, and in all countries, the spread of non-sectarian education.

INQ.—*What else is to be done besides this?—on the physical plane, I mean.*

THEO.—The organization of society depicted by Edward Bellamy in his magnificent work *Looking Backward* admirably represents the Theosophical idea of what should be the first great step toward the full realization of Universal Brotherhood. The state of things he depicts falls short of perfection, because selfishness still exists and operates in the hearts of men. But in the main, selfishness and individualism have been overcome by the feeling of solidarity and mutual brotherhood; and the scheme of life there described reduces the causes tending to create and foster selfishness to a minimum.

INQ.—*Then as a Theosophist you will take part in an effort to realize such an ideal?*

THEO.—Certainly; and we have proved it by action. Have not you heard of the Nationalist party and clubs

which have sprung up in America since the publication of
Bellamy's book? They are now coming prominently to
the front, and will do so more and more as time goes on.
Well, this party and these clubs were started in the first instance by Theosophists. One of the first, the Nationalist
Club of Boston, Mass., has Theosophists for president and
secretary, and the majority of its executive belong to the
Theosophical Society. In the constitution of all their
clubs, and of the party they are forming, the influence of
Theosophy and of the Society is plain; for they all take
as their basis—their first and fundamental principle—the
Brotherhood of Humanity as taught by Theosophy. In
their declaration of principles they state: "The principle of
the Brotherhood of Humanity is one of the eternal truths
that govern the world's progress on lines which distinguish
human nature from brute nature." What can be more
Theosophical than this? But it is not enough. What is
also needed is to impress men with the idea that, if the root
of mankind is one, then there must also be one truth which
finds expression in all the various religions—except in the
Jewish, as you do not find it *expressed* even in the Kabalah.

INQ.—*This refers to the common origin of religions, and
you may be right there. But how does it apply to practical
brotherhood on the physical plane?*

THEO.—First, because that which is true on the metaphysical plane must be also true on the physical. Secondly,
because there is no more fertile source of hatred and strife
than religious differences. When one party or another
thinks itself the sole possessor of absolute truth, it becomes
only natural that it should think its neighbor absolutely in
the clutches of error or the "devil." But once get a man
to see that none of them has the *whole* truth, but that they
are mutually complementary; that the complete truth can
be found only in the combined views of all, after that which

is false in each of them has been sifted out—then true brotherhood in religion will be established. The same applies in the physical world.

INQ.—*Please explain further.*

THEO.—Take an instance. A plant consists of a root, a stem, and many shoots and leaves. As humanity, as a whole, is the stem which grows from the spiritual root, so is the stem the unity of the plant. Injure the stem and it is obvious that every shoot and leaf will suffer. So it is with mankind.

INQ.—*Yes ; but if you injure a leaf or a shoot, you do not injure the whole plant.*

THEO.—And therefore you think that by injuring *one* man you do not injure humanity ? But how do *you* know ? Are you aware that even materialistic science teaches that any injury to a plant, however slight, will affect the whole course of its future growth and development ? Therefore you are mistaken, and the analogy is perfect. If, however, you overlook the fact that a cut on the finger may often make the whole body suffer, and react on the whole nervous system, I would all the more remind you that there may well be other spiritual laws, operating on plants and animals as well as on mankind, although, as you do not recognize their action on plants and animals, you may deny their existence.

INQ.—*What laws do you mean ?*

THEO.—We call them karmic laws; but you will not understand the full meaning of the term unless you study Occultism. However, my argument does not rest on the assumption of these laws, but really on the analogy of the plant. Expand the idea, carry it out to a universal application, and you will soon find that in true philosophy every physical action has its moral and everlasting effect. Injure a man by doing him bodily harm : you may think that his

pain and suffering cannot spread by any means to his neighbors, least of all to men of other nations. We affirm *that
it will, in good time.* Therefore we say that unless every
man is brought to understand, and accept *as an axiomatic
truth,* that by wronging one man we wrong not only
ourselves, but the whole of humanity in the long run,
no brotherly feelings such as preached by all the great reformers—preëminently by Buddha and Jesus—are possible
on earth.

OUR OTHER OBJECTS.

INQ.—*Will you now explain the methods by which you
propose to carry out the second object ?*

THEO.—To collect for the library of our Headquarters at
Adyar, Madras, and by the Fellows of the Branches for their
local libraries, all the good works upon the world's religions that we can; to put into written form correct information upon the various ancient philosophies, traditions,
and legends, and disseminate the same in such practicable
ways as the translation and publication of original works
of value, and extracts from and commentaries upon the
same, or the oral instructions of persons learned in their
respective departments.

INQ.—*And what about the third object, to develop in man
his latent spiritual or psychic powers ?*

THEO.—This has to be achieved also by means of publi-
cations in those places where no lectures and personal
teachings are possible. Our duty is to keep alive in man
his spiritual intuitions; to oppose and counteract—after
due investigation and proof of its irrational nature—bigotry
in every form, religious, scientific, or social, and "cant"
above all, whether as religious sectarianism or as belief in
miracles or anything supernatural. What we have to do

is to seek to obtain knowledge of all the laws of Nature, and to diffuse it; to encourage the study of those laws least understood by modern people—the so-called Occult Sciences, based on the true knowledge of Nature, instead of, as at present, on superstitious beliefs based on blind faith and authority. Popular folk-lore and traditions, however fanciful at times, when sifted, may lead to the discovery of long-lost but important secrets of Nature. The Society, therefore, aims at pursuing this line of inquiry, in the hope of widening the field of scientific and philosophical observation.

ON THE SACREDNESS OF THE PLEDGE.

INQ.—*Have you any ethical system that you carry out in the Society?*

THEO.—The ethics are there, ready and clear enough for whomsoever would follow them. They are the essence and cream of the world's ethics, gathered from the teachings of all the world's great reformers. Therefore you will find represented therein Confucius and Zoroaster, Lao-Tze and the *Bhagavad-Gîtâ*, the precepts of Gautama Buddha and Jesus of Nazareth, of Hillel and his school, as also of Pythagoras, Socrates, Plato, and their schools.

INQ.—*Do the members of your Society carry out these precepts? I have heard of great dissensions and quarrels among them.*

THEO.—Very naturally, since, although the reform in its present shape may be called new, the men and women to be reformed are the same human, sinning natures as of old. As already said, the earnest *working* members are few; but many are the sincere and well-disposed persons who try their best to live up to the Society's and their own ideals. Our duty is to encourage and assist individual Fellows in self-improvement, intellectual, moral, and spiritual; not to blame or condemn those who fail. We have, strictly speaking, no right to refuse admission to any one—especially in the Esoteric Section of the Society, wherein " he who enters is as one newly born." But if any member—his sacred pledges on his word of honor and Immortal Self notwithstanding—chooses, after that " new birth," to continue with the new man the vices or defects of his old life, and to indulge in them still in the Society, then, of course, he is more than likely to be asked to resign and withdraw, or, in case of his refusal, to be expelled. We have the strictest rules for such emergencies.

INQ.—*Can some of them be mentioned?*

THEO.—They can. To begin with, no Fellow in the Society, whether exoteric or esoteric, has a right to force his personal opinions upon another Fellow. This is one of the offenses in the Society at large. As regards the inner section, now called the Esoteric, the following rules were laid down and adopted so far back as 1880: " No Fellow shall put to his selfish use any knowledge communicated to him by any member of the first section [now a higher " degree "], violation of the rule being punished by expulsion." Now, however, before any such knowledge can be imparted, the applicant has to bind himself by a solemn oath not to use it for selfish purposes, nor to reveal anything said except by permission.

INQ.—*But is a man expelled or resigning from the section free to reveal anything he may have learned, or to break any clause of the pledge he has taken?*

THEO.—Certainly not. His expulsion or resignation only relieves him from the obligation of obedience to the teacher, and from that of taking an active part in the work of the Society, but surely not from the sacred pledge of secrecy.

INQ.—*But is this reasonable and just?*

THEO.—Most assuredly. To any man or woman with the slightest honorable feeling a pledge of secrecy taken even on one's word of honor, much more to one's Higher Self—the God within—is binding till death. And though he may leave the section and the Society, no man or woman of honor will think of attacking or injuring a body to which he or she has been so pledged.

INQ.—*But is not this going rather far?*

THEO.—Perhaps so, according to the low standard of the present time and morality. But if it does not bind as far as this, what use is a pledge at all? How can any one expect to be taught secret knowledge if he is to be at liberty to free himself from all the obligations he had taken whenever he pleases? What security, confidence, or trust would ever exist among men if pledges such as this were to have no really binding force at all? Believe me, the law of retribution (Karma) would very soon overtake one who so broke his pledge; perhaps even as soon as the contempt of every honorable man would, even on this physical plane. As well expressed in the *Path*, July, 1889, just cited on this subject:

A pledge, once taken, is forever binding in both the moral and the occult worlds. If we break it once and are punished, that does not justify us in breaking it again; and so long as we do, so long will the mighty lever of the Law [of Karma] react upon us.

IV.

THE RELATIONS OF THE THEOSOPHICAL SOCI-
ETY TO THEOSOPHY.

ON SELF-IMPROVEMENT.

INQ.—*Is moral elevation, then, the principal thing insisted upon in the Society ?*

THEO.—Undoubtedly. He who would be a true Theosophist must bring himself to live as one.

INQ.—*If so, then, as I remarked before, the behavior of some members strangely belies this fundamental rule.*

THEO.—Indeed it does. But this cannot be helped among us, any more than among those who call themselves Christians and act like fiends. This is no fault of our statutes and rules, but that of human nature. Even in some exoteric public Branches the members pledge themselves on their Higher Self to live the life prescribed by Theosophy. They have to bring their Divine Self to guide their every thought and action every day and at every moment of their lives. A true Theosophist ought " to deal justly and walk humbly."

INQ.—*What do you mean by this ?*

THEO.—Simply this : the one *Self* has to forget itself for the many *selves*. . Let me answer you in the words of a true

Philaletheian, a Fellow of the Theosophical Society, who has beautifully expressed it in the *Theosophist:*

What every man needs first is to find himself, and then take an honest inventory of his subjective possessions; and, bad or bankrupt as it may be, it is not beyond redemption if we set about it in earnest.

But how many do? All are willing to work for their own development and progress; very few for those of others. To quote the same writer again:

Men have been deceived and deluded long enough; they must break their idols, put away their shams, and go to work for themselves—nay, there is one little word too much or too many, for he who works for himself had better not work at all; rather let him work himself for others, for all. For every flower of love and charity he plants in his neighbor's garden a loathsome weed will disappear from his own, and so this garden of the gods—humanity—shall blossom as a rose. In all Bibles, all religions, this is plainly set forth; but designing men have at first misinterpreted and finally emasculated, materialized, besotted them. It does not require a new revelation. Let every man be a revelation unto himself. Let once man's immortal spirit take possession of the temple of his body, drive out the money-changers and every unclean thing, and his own divine humanity will redeem him; for when he is thus at one with himself he will know the " builder of the temple."

INQ.—*This is pure altruism, I confess.*

THEO.—It is. And if only one Fellow of the Theosophical Society out of ten would practise it, ours would be a body of elect indeed. But there are those among the outsiders who will always refuse to see the essential difference between Theosophy and the Theosophical Society, the idea and its imperfect embodiment. Such would visit every sin and shortcoming of the vehicle—the human body—on the pure spirit which sheds thereon its divine light. Is this just to either? They throw stones at an association that tries to work up to, and for the propagation of, its ideal with most tremendous odds against it. Some vilify the Theosophical Society only because it presumes to attempt to do that in which other systems—church and state Christianity pre-eminently—have failed most egregiously; others because they would fain preserve the existing state of things; Pharisees and Sadducees in the seat of Moses, and publicans and sinners reveling in high places, as under the Roman empire during its decadence. Fair-minded people, at any rate, ought to remember that the man who does all he can does as much as he who has achieved the most in this world of relative possibilities. This is a simple truism —an axiom supported for believers in the Gospels by the parable of the talents, given by their Master: the servant who doubled his two talents was rewarded as much as the other fellow-servant who had received five. To every man it is given "according to his several ability."

INQ.—*Yet it is rather difficult to draw the line of demarcation between the abstract and the concrete in this case, as we have only the latter by which to form our judgment.*

THEO.—Then why make an exception for the Theosophical Society? Justice, like charity, ought to begin at home. Will you revile and scoff at the Sermon on the Mount because your social, political, and even religious laws have, so far, not only failed to carry out its precepts in their spirit, but even in their dead letter? Abolish the oath in courts, parliament, army, and everywhere, and do as the Quakers do, if you will call yourselves Christians. Abolish the courts themselves; for if you would follow the commandments of Christ, you have to give away your cloak to him who deprives you of your coat, and turn your left cheek to the bully who smites you on the right. "Resist not evil," "love your enemies, bless them that curse you, do good to them that hate you;" for "whosoever shall break one of the least of these commandments, and shall teach men so, he shall be called the least in the kingdom of heaven," and "whosoever shall say, Thou fool, shall be in danger of hell-fire." And why should you judge, if you would not be judged in your turn? Insist that between Theosophy and the Theosophical Society there is no difference, and forthwith you lay the system of Christianity and its very essence open to the same charges, only in a more serious form.

INQ.— *Why* more *serious ?*

THEO.—Because, while the leaders of the Theosophical movement, recognizing fully their shortcomings, try all they can to amend their ways and uproot the evil existing in the Society, and while their rules and by-laws are framed in the spirit of Theosophy, the legislators and the churches of nations and countries which call themselves Christian do the reverse. Our members—even the worst among them—are no worse than the average Christian. Moreover, if the Western Theosophists experience so much difficulty in leading the true Theosophical life, it is because they are all the children of their generation. Every one of them was a Christian, bred and brought up in the sophistry of his church, his social customs, and even his paradoxical laws. He was this before he became a Theosophist—or rather a member of the Theosophical Society, as it cannot be too often repeated that between the abstract ideal and its vehicle there is a most important difference.

THE ABSTRACT AND THE CONCRETE.

INQ.—*Please elucidate this difference a little more.*

THEO.—The Society is a great body of men and women, composed of the most heterogeneous elements. Theosophy in its abstract meaning is Divine Wisdom, or the aggregate of the knowledge and wisdom that underlie the universe— the homogeneity of Eternal Good ; and in its concrete sense it is the sum total of the same as allotted to man by Nature on this earth, and no more. Some members earnestly endeavor to realize and, so to speak, to objectivize Theosophy in their lives; while others desire only to know of, not to practise it; and others still may have joined the Society merely out of curiosity or a passing interest, or perhaps, again, because some of their friends belong to it. How, then, can the system be judged by the standard of those who would assume the name without any right to it ? Is poetry or its muse to be measured only by those would-be poets who afflict our ears ? The Society can be regarded as the embodiment of Theosophy only in its abstract motives; it can never presume to call itself its concrete vehicle so long as human imperfections and weaknesses are all represented in its body; otherwise the Society would be only repeating the great error and the overflowing sacrileges of the so-called churches of Christ. If Eastern comparisons may be permitted, Theosophy is the shoreless ocean of universal truth, love, and wisdom, reflecting its radiance on the earth; while the Theosophical Society is only a visible bubble on that reflection. Theosophy is divine nature, visible and invisible, and its Society human nature trying to ascend to its divine parent. Theosophy, finally, is the fixed, eternal sun, and its Society the evanescent comet trying to settle in an orbit to become a planet, ever revolving within the attraction of the sun of truth. It was formed to assist in showing to men that such a thing as Theosophy exists, and to help them to ascend toward it by studying and assimilating its eternal verities.

INQ.—*I thought you said you had no tenets or doctrines of your own ?*

THEO.—Nor have we. The Society has no wisdom of its own to support or teach. It is simply the storehouse of all the truths uttered by the great seers, Initiates, and prophets of historic and even prehistoric ages—at least, as many as it can get. Therefore it is merely the channel through which more or less of truth found in the accumulated utterances of humanity's great teachers is poured out into the world.

INQ.—*But is such truth unreachable outside of the Society ? Does not every church claim the same ?*

THEO.—Not at all. The undeniable existence of great Initiates—true "Sons of God"—shows that such wisdom was often reached by isolated individuals; never, however, without the guidance of a Master at first. But most of the followers of such, when they became Masters in their turn, have dwarfed the catholicism of these teachings into the narrow groove of their own sectarian dogmas. The commandments of *a* chosen Master alone were then adopted and followed, to the exclusion of all others—if followed at all, note well, as in the case of the Sermon on the Mount. Each religion is thus a bit of the divine truth, made to focus a vast panorama of human fancy which claims to represent and replace that truth.

INQ.—*But Theosophy, you say, is not a religion ?*

THEO.—Most assuredly it is not, since it is the essence of all religion and of absolute truth, a drop of which only underlies every creed. To resort once more to metaphor, Theosophy on earth is like the white ray of the spectrum, and every religion only one of the seven prismatic colors. Ignoring all the others, and cursing them as false, every special colored ray claims not only priority, but to be that white ray itself, and anathematizes even its own tints from light to dark as heresies. Yet as the sun of truth rises higher and higher on the horizon of man's perception, and each colored ray gradually fades out until it is finally reabsorbed in its turn, humanity will at last be cursed no

longer with artificial polarizations, but will find itself bath-
ing in the pure, colorless sunlight of eternal truth. And
this will be Theosophia.

INQ.—*Your claim is, then, that all the great religions are
derived from Theosophy, and that it is by assimilating it that
the world will be finally saved from the curse of its great illusions and errors ?*

THEO.—Precisely so. And we add that our Theosophical Society is the humble seed which, if watered and let
live, will finally produce the Tree of Knowledge of Good
and Evil which is grafted on the Tree of Life Eternal.
For it is only by studying the various great religions and
philosophies of humanity, by comparing them dispassion-
ately and with an unbiased mind, that men can hope to
arrive at the truth. It is especially by finding out and not-
ing their various points of agreement that we may achieve
this result. For no sooner do we arrive—either by study
or by being taught by some one who knows—at their inner
meaning than we find, almost in every case, that it expresses
some great truth in Nature.

INQ.—*We have heard of a golden age that was, and what
you describe would be a golden age to be realized at some future day. When shall it be ?*

THEO.—Not before humanity as a whole feels the need
of it. A maxim in the Persian *Javidan Khirad* says:
"Truth is of two kinds—one manifest and self-evident,
the other demanding incessantly new demonstrations and
proofs." It is only when this latter kind of truth becomes
as universally obvious as it is now dim and therefore liable
to be distorted by sophistry and casuistry—it is only when
the two kinds will have become once more one, that all
people will be brought to see alike.

INQ.—*But surely those few who have felt the need of such
truths must have made up their minds to believe in something*

definite ?   You tell me that, the Society having no doctrines of its own, every member may believe as he chooses and accept what he pleases.   This looks as if the Theosophical Society were bent upon reviving the confusion of languages and beliefs of the Tower of Babel of old.   Have you no beliefs in common ?

THEO.—What is meant by the Society having no tenets or doctrines of its own is that no special doctrines or beliefs are *obligatory* on its members; but of course this applies only to the body as a whole.   The Society, as you were told, is divided into an outer and an inner body.   Those who belong to the latter have, of course, a philosophy or, if you so prefer it, a religious system of their own.

INQ.—*May we be told what it is ?*

THEO.—We make no secret of it.   It was outlined a few years ago in the *Theosophist* and *Esoteric Buddhism*, and may be found still more elaborated in *The Secret Doctrine.* It is based on the oldest philosophy of the world, called the Wisdom-Religion or the Archaic Doctrine.   If you like, you may ask questions and have them explained.

V

THE FUNDAMENTAL TEACHINGS OF THE-OSOPHY.

ON GOD AND PRAYER.

INQ.—*Do you believe in God?*

THEO.—That depends upon what you mean by the term.

INQ.—*I mean the God of the Christians, the Father of Jesus, and the Creator—the biblical God of Moses, in short.*

THEO.—In such a God we do not believe. We reject the idea of a personal or an extracosmic and anthropomorphic God, who is but the gigantic shadow of man, and not even of man at his best. The God of theology, we say —and prove it—is a bundle of contradictions and a logical impossibility. Therefore we will have nothing to do with him.

INQ.—*State your reasons, if you please.*

THEO.—They are many, and cannot all receive attention. But here are a few. This God is called by his devotees infinite and absolute, is he not?

INQ.—*I believe he is.*

THEO.—Then, if infinite—i.e., limitless—and especially if absolute, how can he have a form and be a Creator of

anything ?   Form implies limitation, and a beginning as
well as an end ; and in order to create, a Being must think
and plan.   How can the Absolute be supposed to think—
i.e., have any relation whatever to that which is limited,
finite, and conditioned ?   This is a philosophical and a
logical absurdity.   Even the Hebrew Kabalah rejects such
an idea, and therefore makes of the one and the Absolute
Deific Principle an Infinite Unity called Ain Suph.*   In
order to create, the Creator has to become active ; and as
this is impossible for Absoluteness, the Infinite Principle had
to be shown becoming the cause of evolution (not creation)
in an indirect way—i.e., through the emanation from itself
(another absurdity, due this time to the translators of the
Kabalah) † of the Sephiroth.

INQ.—*How about those Kabalists who, while being such,
still believe in Jehovah, or the Tetragrammaton ?*

THEO.—They are at liberty to believe in what they
please, as their belief or disbelief ·can hardly affect a self-
evident fact.   The Jesuits tell us that two and two are not
always four to a certainty, since it depends on the will of
God to make $2 \times 2 = 5$.   Shall we accept their sophistry
for all that ?

INQ.—*Then you are atheists ?*

THEO.—Not that we know of, and not unless the epithet
of "atheist" is to be applied to all those who disbelieve
in an anthropomorphic God.   We believe in a Universal
Divine Principle, the root of all, from which all proceeds,

---

* Ain Suph, אֵין סוֹף,=τὸ πᾶν=ἄπειρον, the Endless, or Boundless, in and
with Nature, the Non-existent which IS, but is not *a* Being.

† How can the non-active eternal principle emanate or emit ? The Parabrahman
of the Vedântins does nothing of the kind ; nor does the Ain Suph of the Chaldæan
Kabalah.   It is an eternal and periodical law which causes an active and creative
force (the Logos) to emanate from the ever-concealed and incomprehensible one principle at the beginning of every Mahâmanvantara, or new cycle of life. •

and within which all shall be absorbed at the end of the great cycle of Being.

INQ.—*This is the old, old claim of pantheism. If you are pantheists, you cannot be deists; and if you are not deists, then you have to answer to the name of atheists.*

THEO.—Not necessarily so. The term "pantheism" is, again, one of the many abused terms whose real and primitive meaning has been distorted by blind prejudice and a one-sidedness of view. If you accept the Christian etymology of this compound word, and form it of *pan* (πᾶν), "all," and *theos* (θεός), "god," and then imagine and teach that this means that every stone and every tree in Nature is a God or the One God, then, of course, you will be right, and make of pantheists fetish-worshipers, in addition to their legitimate name. But you will hardly be as successful if you etymologize the word "pantheism" esoterically, and as we do.

INQ.—*What is, then, your definition of it?*

THEO.—Let me ask you a question in my turn. What do you understand by Pan, or Nature?

INQ.—*Nature is, I suppose, the sum total of things existing around us; the aggregate of causes and effects in the world of matter, the creation or universe.*

THEO.—Hence the personified sum and order of known causes and effects; the total of all finite agencies and forces, as utterly disconnected from an intelligent Creator or Creators, and perhaps "conceived of as a single and separate force"—as in your cyclopedias?

INQ.—*Yes, I believe so.*

THEO.—Well, we neither take into consideration this objective and material nature, which we call an evanescent illusion, nor do we mean by Pan, Nature, in the sense of its

accepted derivation from the Latin *natura*, "becoming,"
from *nasci*, "to be born." When we speak of the Deity
and make it identical—hence coeval—with Nature, the
eternal and uncreate Nature is meant, and not your aggregate of flitting shadows and finite unrealities. We leave it
to the hymn-makers to call the visible sky or heaven God's
throne, and our earth of mud his footstool. Our Deity is
neither in a paradise nor in a particular tree, building, or
mountain; it is everywhere, in every atom of the visible as
of the invisible cosmos; in, over, and around every invisible atom and divisible molecule; for IT is the mysterious
power of evolution and involution, the omnipresent, omnipotent, and even omniscient creative potentiality.

INQ.—*Stop! Omniscience is the prerogative of something
that thinks, and you deny to your Absoluteness the power of
thought.*

THEO.—We deny it to the Absolute, since thought is
something limited and conditioned. But you evidently forget that in philosophy absolute unconsciousness is also absolute consciousness, as otherwise it would not be absolute.

INQ.—*Then your Absolute thinks?*

THEO.—No, IT does not—for the simple reason that it
is Absolute Thought itself. Nor does it exist, for the same
reason, as it is absolute existence, and "Be-ness," not a
Being. Read the superb Kabalistic poem by Solomon ben-
Yehudah Ibn Gebirol, in the *Kether Malchuth*, and you
will understand:

Thou art one, the root of all numbers, but not as an element of
numeration; for unity admits not of multiplication, change, or form.
Thou art one, and in the secret of Thy unity the wisest of men are
lost, because they know it not. Thou art one, and Thy unity is never
diminished, never extended, and cannot be changed. Thou art one,
and no thought of mine can fix for Thee a limit, or define Thee.
Thou ART, but not as one existent, for the understanding and vision

of mortals cannot attain to Thy existence, nor determine for Thee the where, the how, and the why.

In short, our Deity is the eternal, incessantly evolving, not creating, builder of the universe; that universe itself unfolding out of its own essence, not being made. It is a sphere, without circumference, in its symbolism, which has but one ever-acting attribute embracing all other existing or thinkable attributes—Itself. It is the one law, giving the impulse to manifested, eternal, and immutable laws, within that never-manifesting, because absolute, Law which in its manifesting periods is The Ever-Becoming.

INQ.—*I once heard one of your members remark that Universal Deity, being everywhere, was in vessels of dishonor, as in those of honor, and therefore was present in every atom of my cigar-ash! Is this not rank blasphemy?*

THEO.—I do not think so, as simple logic can hardly be regarded as blasphemy. Were we to exclude the Omnipresent Principle from one single mathematical point of the universe, or from a particle of matter occupying any conceivable space, could we still regard it as infinite?

IS IT NECESSARY TO PRAY?

INQ.—*Do you believe in prayer, and do you ever pray?*

THEO.—We do not. We act instead of talk.

INQ.—*You do not offer prayers even to the Absolute Principle?*

THEO.—Why should we? Being well-occupied people, we can hardly afford to lose time in addressing verbal prayers to a pure abstraction. The Unknowable is capable of relations only in its parts one to another, but is non-existent as regards any finite relations. The visible universe depends for its existence and phenomena on its mutually acting forms and their laws, not on prayer or prayers.

INQ.—*Do you not believe at all in the efficacy of prayer?*

THEO.—Not in prayer taught in so many words and repeated externally, if by prayer you mean the outward petition to an unknown God as the addressee, which was inaugurated by the Jews and popularized by the Pharisees.

INQ.—*Is there any other kind of prayer?*

THEO.—Most decidedly; we call it *will-prayer*, and it is rather an internal command than a petition.

INQ.—*To whom, then, do you pray when you do so?*

THEO.—To "our Father in heaven"—in its esoteric meaning.

INQ.—*Is that different from the one given to it in theology?*

THEO.—Entirely so. An Occultist or a Theosophist addresses his prayer to his "Father" *which is in secret* (read, and try to understand, Matthew vi. 6), not to an extracosmic and therefore finite God; and that "Father" is in man himself.

INQ.—*Then you make of man a God?*

THEO.—Please say "God" and not "a God." In our sense, the inner man is the only God of whom we can have cognizance. And how can this be otherwise? Grant us our postulate that God is a universally diffused, infinite principle, and how can man alone escape from being soaked through by and in the Deity? We call our "Father in heaven" that deific essence of which we are cognizant within us, in our heart and spiritual consciousness, and which has nothing to do with the anthropomorphic conception we may form of it in our physical brain or its fancy: "Know ye not that ye are the temple of God, and that

the Spirit of [the absolute] God dwelleth in you ? " * Yet
let no man anthropomorphize that essence in us. Let no
Theosophist, if he would hold to divine, not human truth,
say that this " God in secret " listens to, or is distinct from,
either finite man or the infinite essence; for all are one.
Nor, as just remarked, that a prayer is a petition. It is a
mystery, rather; an occult process by which finite and conditioned thoughts and desires, unable to be assimilated by
the absolute Spirit which is unconditioned, are translated
into spiritual wills and the will; such process being called
"spiritual transmutation." The intensity of our ardent
aspirations changes prayer into the "philosopher's stone,"
or that which transmutes lead into pure gold. The only
homogeneous essence, our "will-prayer," becomes the active or creative force, producing effects according to our
desire.

INQ.—*Do you mean to say that prayer is an occult process
bringing about physical results ?*

THEO.—I do. *Will-power* becomes a living power. But
woe unto those Occultists and Theosophists who, instead
of crushing out the desires of the lower personal *ego* or
physical man, and saying—addressing their Higher Spiritual Ego, immersed in Âtmâ-Buddhic light—"Thy will be
done, not mine," send up waves of will-power for selfish or
unholy purposes ! For this is black magic, abomination,

---

* One often finds in Theosophical writings conflicting statements about the Christos
principle in man. Some call it the sixth principle (Buddhi), others the seventh
(Âtman). If Christian Theosophists wish to make use of such expressions, let them
be made philosophically correct by following the analogy of the old Wisdom-Religion
symbols. We say that Christos is not only one of the three higher principles, but all
the three regarded as a Trinity. This Trinity represents the Holy Ghost, the Father,
and the Son, as it answers to abstract spirit, differentiated spirit, and embodied spirit.
Krishna and Christ are philosophically the same principle under its triple aspect of
manifestation. In the *Bhagavad-Gîtâ* we find Krishna calling himself indifferently
Âtman, the Abstract Spirit, Kshetrajna, the Higher or reincarnating Ego, and the
Universal SELF—all names which, when transferred from the universe to man, answer to Âtmâ, Buddhi, and Manas. The *Anugîtâ* is full of the same doctrine.

and spiritual sorcery. Unfortunately, all this is the favorite occupation of our Christian statesmen and generals, especially when the latter are sending two armies to murder each other. Both before action indulge in a bit of such sorcery, when severally offering prayers to the same God of hosts, each entreating his help to cut his enemies' throats.

INQ.—*David prayed to the Lord of hosts to help him smite the Philistines and slay the Syrians and the Moabites, and " the Lord preserved David whithersoever he went." In that we only follow what we find in the* Bible.

THEO.—Of course you do. But since you delight in calling yourselves Christians, not Israelites or Jews, as far as we know, why do you not rather follow that which Christ says ? And he distinctly commands you not to follow " them of old times," or the Mosaic law, but bids you do as he tells you, and warns those who would take the sword that they too will perish by the sword. Christ has given you one prayer, of which you have made a lip-prayer and a boast, and which none but the *true* Occultist understands. In it you say, in your dead-sense meaning, " Forgive us our debts, as we forgive our debtors "—which you never do. Again, he told you to love your enemies and do good to them that hate you. It is surely not the " meek prophet of Nazareth " who taught you to pray to your " Father " to slay and give you victory over your enemies ! This is why we reject what you call " prayers."

INQ.—*But how do you explain the universal fact that all nations and peoples have prayed to and worshiped a God or Gods ? Some have adored and propitiated devils and harmful spirits, but this only proves the universality of the belief in the efficacy of prayer.*

THEO.—It is explained by the fact that prayer has several other meanings besides that given to it by the Christians. It means not only a pleading or petition, but in days of old meant far more an invocation and incantation. The *mantra*, or the rhythmically chanted prayer of the Hindûs, has precisely such a meaning, for the Brâhmans hold themselves higher than the common Devas or " Gods." A prayer may be an appeal or an incantation for malediction and a curse—as in the case of two armies praying simultaneously for mutual destruction—as much as for blessing. And as the great majority of people are intensely selfish, and pray only for themselves, asking to be given their "daily bread" instead of working for it, and begging God not to lead them "into temptation," but to deliver them (the memorialists only) from evil, the result is that prayer, as now understood, is doubly pernicious: (*a*) it kills in man self-reliance; (*b*) it develops in him a still more ferocious selfishness and egotism than he is already endowed with by nature. I repeat that we believe in "communion" and simultaneous action in unison with our "Father in secret"; and, in rare moments of ecstatic bliss, in the mingling of our higher soul with the universal essence, attracted as it is toward its origin and center—a state called during life Samâdhi, and after death Nirvâna. We refuse to pray to created finite beings—i.e., gods, saints, angels, etc.— because we regard it as idolatry; we cannot pray to the Absolute for reasons explained before; therefore we try to replace fruitless and useless prayer by meritorious and good-producing actions.

Inq.—*Christians would call this pride and blasphemy. Are they wrong?*

Theo.—Entirely so. It is they, on the contrary, who show satanic pride in their belief that the Absolute or the Infinite—even if there were such a thing as the possibility of any relation between the unconditioned and the conditioned—will stoop to listen to every foolish or egotistical prayer. And it is they, again, who virtually blaspheme in teaching that an Omniscient and Omnipotent God needs uttered prayers to know what he has to do ! This, understood esoterically, is corroborated by both Buddha and Jesus. The one says: "Seek naught from the helpless Gods—pray not ! but rather act; for darkness will not brighten. Ask naught from silence, for it can neither speak nor hear." And the other—Jesus—recommends: "Whatsoever ye shall ask in my name [that of Christos], that will I do." Of course this quotation, if taken in its literal sense, goes against our argument. But if we accept it esoterically, with the full knowledge of the meaning of the term Christos—which to us represents Âtmâ-Buddhi-Manas, the SELF—it comes to this: the only God we must recognize and pray to, or rather act in unison with, is that Spirit of God of which our body is the temple, and in which it dwelleth.

PRAYER KILLS SELF-RELIANCE.

INQ.—*But did not Christ himself pray and recommend prayer ?*

THEO.—It is so recorded; but those prayers are precisely of that kind of communion just mentioned with one's "Father in secret." Otherwise, and if we identify Jesus with the Universal Deity, there would be something too absurdly illogical in the inevitable conclusion that he, the "very God himself," prayed to himself, and separated the will of that God from his own !

INQ.—*One argument more ; an argument, moreover, much used by some Christians. They say, " I feel that I am not able to conquer my passions and weaknesses in my own strength. But when I pray to Jesus Christ I feel that he gives me strength, and that in his power I am able to conquer."*

THEO.—No wonder. If "Christ Jesus" is God, and one independent and separate from him who prays, of course everything is, and *must* be, possible to "Almighty God." But, then, where is the merit, or justice either, of such a conquest? Why should the pseudo-conqueror be rewarded for something done which has cost him only prayers? Would you, even a simple mortal man, pay your laborer a full day's wage if you did most of his work for him, he sitting under an apple-tree and praying to you to do so all the while? This idea of passing one's whole life in moral idleness, and having one's hardest work and duty done by another—whether God or man—is most revolting to us, as it is most degrading to human dignity.

INQ.—*Perhaps so; yet it is the idea of trusting in a personal Saviour to help and strengthen in the battle of life which is the fundamental idea of modern Christianity. And there is no doubt that, subjectively, such belief is efficacious; that is, that those who believe do feel themselves helped and strengthened.*

THEO.—Nor is there any more doubt that some patients of "Christian" and "Mental Scientists"—the great "Deniers" *—are also sometimes cured; nor that hypnotism and suggestion, psychology and even mediumship, will produce such results as often, if not oftener. You take into consideration, and string on the thread of your argument, successes alone. And how about ten times the number of failures? Surely you will not presume to say that failure is unknown, even with a sufficiency of blind faith, among fanatical Christians?

INQ.—*But how can you explain those cases which are followed by full success? Where does a Theosophist look for power to subdue his passions and selfishness?*

---

* A new sect of healers, who, by disavowing the existence of anything but spirit, which can neither suffer nor be ill, claim to cure all and every disease, provided the patient has faith that what he denies can have no existence. A new form of self-hypnotism.

THEO.—To his Higher Self, the divine spirit or the God in him, and to his Karma. How long shall we have to repeat over and over again that the tree is known by its fruit, the nature of the cause by its effects? You speak of subduing passions and becoming good through and with the help of God or Christ. We ask, where do you find more virtuous, guiltless people, abstaining from sin and crime—in Christendom or Buddhism; in Christian countries or in heathen lands? Statistics are there to give the answer and corroborate our claims. According to the last census in Ceylon and India, in the comparative table of crimes committed by Christians, Mussulmans, Hindûs, Eurasians, Buddhists, etc., in two millions of population taken at random from each, and covering the misdemeanors of several years, the proportion of crimes committed by the Christian stands at about fifteen to four committed by the Buddhist population.* No Orientalist, no historian of any note, or traveler in Buddhist lands, from Bishop Bigandet and Abbé Huc to Sir William Hunter and every fair-minded official, will fail to give the palm of virtue to Buddhists before Christians. Yet the former—not the true Buddhist Siamese sect, at all events—do not believe in either God or a future reward outside of this earth. They do not pray—neither priests nor laymen. "Pray!" they would exclaim in wonder; "to whom, or to what?"

INQ.—*Then they are truly atheists.*

THEO.—Most undeniably; but they are also the most virtue-loving and virtue-keeping men in the whole world. Buddhism says: Respect the religions of other men and remain true to your own; but church Christianity, denouncing all the gods of other nations as devils, would doom every non-Christian to eternal perdition.

INQ.—*Does not the Buddhist priesthood do the same?*

---

* See *Lucifer* for April, 1888, p. 147, art. "Christian Lectures on Buddhism."

THEO.—Never. They hold too much to the wise precept found in the *Dhammapada* to do so, for they know that:

If any man, whether he be learned or not, consider himself so great as to despise other men, he is like a blind man holding a candle—blind himself, he illumines others.

ON THE SOURCE OF THE HUMAN SOUL.

INQ.—*How, then, do you account for man being endowed with a spirit and soul? Whence these?*

THEO.—From the Universal Soul; certainly not bestowed by a Personal God. Whence the moist element in the jellyfish? From the ocean which surrounds it, in which it lives and breathes and has its being, and whither it returns when dissolved.

INQ.—*So you reject the teaching that soul is given, or breathed into man, by God?*

THEO.—We are obliged to. The "soul" spoken of in Genesis (ii. 7) is, as therein stated, the "living soul" or *nephesh*, the vital, animal soul with which God—we say Nature and immutable Law—endows man like every animal. It is not at all the thinking soul or mind; least of all is it the immortal spirit.

INQ.—*Well, let us put it otherwise : is it God who endows man with a human rational soul and immortal spirit?*

THEO.—Again, in the way you put the question, we must object to it. Since we believe in no Personal God, how can we believe that he endows man with anything ? But granting, for the sake of argument, a God who takes upon himself the risk of creating a new soul for every newborn babe, all that can be said is that such a God can hardly be regarded as himself endowed with any wisdom or prevision. Certain other difficulties, and the impossibility of reconciling this with the claims made for the mercy, justice, equity, and omniscience of that God, are so many deadly reefs on which this theological dogma is daily and hourly broken.

INQ.—*What do you mean?   What difficulties?*

THEO.—I am thinking of an unanswerable argument offered once in my presence by a Cingalese Buddhist priest, a famous preacher, to a Christian missionary—one in no way ignorant or unprepared for the public discussion during which it was advanced. It was near Colombo, and the missionary had challenged the priest Megittawatti to give his reasons why the Christian God should not be accepted by the "heathen." Well, the missionary came out of that memorable discussion second-best, as usual.

INQ.—*I should be glad to learn in what way.*

THEO.—Simply this: the Buddhist priest premised by asking the *padre* whether his God had given commandments to Moses for men only to keep, but to be broken by God himself. The missionary denied the supposition indignantly. "Well," said his opponent, "you tell us that God makes no exceptions to this rule, and that no soul can be born without his will. Now God forbids adultery, among other things, and yet you say in the same breath that it is he who creates every babe born, and he who endows it with a soul. Are we then to understand that the millions of children born in crime and adultery are your God's work? that your God forbids and punishes the breaking of his laws, and that, nevertheless, he creates daily and hourly souls for just such children? According to the simplest logic, your God is an accomplice in the crime; since, but for his help and interference, no such children of lust could be born. Where is the justice of punishing not only the guilty parents, but even the innocent babe, for

that which is done by that very God, whom yet you exon-
erate from any guilt himself ? " The missionary looked at
his watch and suddenly found it was getting too late for
further discussion.

INQ.—*You forget that all such inexplicable cases are mysteries, and that we are forbidden by our religion to pry into
the mysteries of God.*

THEO.—No, we do not forget, but simply reject such
impossibilities. Nor do we want you to believe as we do.
We only answer the questions you ask. We have, however, another name for your "mysteries."

THE BUDDHIST TEACHINGS ON THE ABOVE.

INQ.—*What does Buddhism teach with regard to the soul ?*

THEO.—It depends whether you mean exoteric, popular
Buddhism, or its esoteric teachings. The former explains
itself in the *Buddhist Catechism* in this wise:

"Soul" it considers a word used by the ignorant to express a false
idea. If everything is subject to change, then man is included, and every
material part of him must change. That which is subject to change
is not permanent; so there can be no immortal survival of a changeful
thing.

This seems plain and definite. But when we come to
the question that the new personality in each succeeding
rebirth is the aggregate of *skandhas*, or the attributes of
the old personality, and ask whether this new aggregation
of *skandhas* is a new being likewise, in which nothing has
remained of the last, we read that:

In one sense it is a new being, in another it is not. During this
life the *skandhas* are continually changing; and while the man A B
of forty is identical, as regards personality, with the youth A B of
eighteen, yet by the continual waste and reparation of his body, and
change of mind and character, he is a different being. Nevertheless

the man in his old age justly reaps the reward or suffering consequent upon his thoughts and actions at every previous stage of his life. So the new being of a rebirth, being the same individuality as before [but not the same personality], with but a changed form, or new aggregation of *skandhas*, justly reaps the consequences of his actions and thoughts in the previous existence.

This is abstruse metaphysics, and plainly does not express disbelief in soul by any means.

INQ.—*Is not something like this spoken of in* esoteric Budhism?

THEO.—It is; for this teaching belongs both to esoteric Budhism, or Secret Wisdom, and to exoteric Buddhism, or the religious philosophy of Gautama Buddha.

INQ.—*But we are distinctly told that most of the Buddhists do not believe in the soul's immortality.*

THEO.—Nor do we, if you mean by soul the *personal* Ego, or life-soul—*nephesh*. But every learned Buddhist believes in the individual or divine Ego. Those who do not, err in their judgment; they are as mistaken on this point as those Christians who mistake the theological interpolations of the later editors of the Gospels about damnation and hell-fire for verbatim utterances of Jesus. Neither Buddha nor Christ ever wrote anything themselves, but both spoke in allegories and used "dark sayings," as all true Initiates did, and will do for a long time yet to come. Both Scriptures treat of all such metaphysical questions very cautiously, and both Buddhist and Christian records sin by that excess of exotericism, the dead-letter meaning far overshooting the mark in both cases.

INQ.—*Do you mean to suggest that neither the teachings of Buddha nor those of Christ have been heretofore rightly understood?*

THEO.—What I mean is just as you say. Both gospels —the Buddhist and the Christian—were preached with the

same object in view. Both reformers were ardent philanthropists and practical altruists, preaching most unmistak-
ably socialism of the noblest and highest type, self-sacrifice
to the bitter end. "Let the sins of the whole world fall
upon me, that I may relieve man's misery and suffering!"
cries Buddha. "I would not let one cry whom I could
save!" exclaims the prince-beggar, clad in the refuse rags
of the burial-grounds. "Come unto me, all ye that labor
and are heavy-laden, and I will give you rest," is the appeal to the poor and the disinherited made by the "Man
of Sorrows," who had not where to lay his head. The
teachings of both are boundless love for humanity, charity,
forgiveness of injury, forgetfulness of self, and pity for the
deluded masses; both show the same contempt for riches,
and make no difference between *meum* and *tuum*. Their
desire was, without revealing to all the sacred mysteries of
initiation, to give the ignorant and the misled, whose burden in life was too heavy for them, hope enough and an
inkling into the truth sufficient to support them in their
heaviest hours. But the object of both reformers was
frustrated, owing to excess of zeal of their later followers.
The words of the Masters having been misunderstood and
misinterpreted, behold the consequences!

INQ.—*But surely Buddha must have repudiated the soul's
immortality if all the Orientalists and his own priests say
so?*

THEO.—The Arhats began by following the policy of
their Master, and the majority of the priests who followed
them were not initiated, just as in Christianity; and so,
little by little, the great esoteric truths became almost lost.
A proof in point is that, out of the two existing sects in
Ceylon, the Siamese believes death to be the absolute annihilation of individuality and personality, and the other explains Nirvâna as we Theosophists do.

INQ.—*But why, in that case, do Buddhism and Christianity represent the two opposite poles of such belief?*

THEO.—Because the conditions under which they were preached were not the same. In India the Brâhmans, jealous of their superior knowledge, and excluding from it every caste save their own, had driven millions of men into idolatry and almost fetishism. Buddha had to give the death-blow to an exuberance of unhealthy fancy and fanatical superstition resulting from ignorance, such as has rarely been known before or after. Better a philosophical atheism than such ignorant worship for those

> Who cry upon their gods and are not heard
> Or are not heeded,

and who live and die in mental despair. He had to arrest first of all this muddy torrent of superstition; to uproot errors before he gave out the truth. And as he could not give out all, for the same good reason as Jesus—who reminds his disciples that the mysteries of heaven are not for the unintelligent masses, but for the elect alone, and therefore he spoke to the people in parables (Matt. xiii. 10, 11) —so his caution led Buddha to conceal too much. He even refused to say to the monk Vacchagotta whether there was or was not an Ego in man. When pressed to answer, "the exalted one maintained silence."

Buddha gives his initiated disciple Ânanda, who inquires for the reason of this silence, a plain and unequivocal answer in the dialogue translated by Oldenburg from the *Samyuttaka Nikaya:*

If I, Ânanda, when the wandering monk Vacchagotta asked me, "Is there the Ego?" had answered, "The Ego is," then that, Ânanda, would have confirmed the doctrine of the Sâmanas and Brâhmanas, who believed in permanence. If I, Ânanda, when the wandering monk Vacchagotta asked me, "Is there not the Ego?" had answered, "The Ego is not," then that, Ânanda, would have confirmed the doctrine of those who believed in annihilation. If I, Ânanda, when the wandering monk Vacchagotta asked me, " Is there the Ego?" had answered, " The Ego is," would that have served my end, Ânanda, by producing in him the knowledge, all existences (*dhamma*) are non-ego? But if I, Ânanda, had answered,'" The Ego is not," then that, Ânanda, would only have caused the wandering monk Vacchagotta to be thrown from one bewilderment to another : " My Ego, did it not exist before? But now it exists no longer!"

This shows better than anything that Gautama Buddha withheld such difficult metaphysical doctrines from the masses in order not to perplex them more. What he meant was the difference between the personal temporary Ego and the Higher Self, which sheds its light on the imperishable Ego, the spiritual " I " of man.

INQ.—*This refers to Gautama, but in what way does it touch the Gospels ?*

THEO.—Read history and think over it. At the time the events narrated in the Gospels are alleged to have happened there was a similar intellectual fermentation taking place in the whole civilized world, only with opposite results in the East and the West. The old gods were dying out. While the civilized classes drifted, in the train of the unbelieving Sadducees, into materialistic negations and mere dead-letter Mosaic form in Palestine, and into moral dissolution in Rome, the lowest and poorest classes ran after sorcery and strange gods, or became hypocrites or worse. Once more the time for a spiritual reform had arrived. The cruel, anthropomorphic, and jealous God of the Jews, with his sanguinary laws of " an eye for an eye, and a tooth for a tooth," of the shedding of blood and animal sacrifice, had to be relegated to a secondary place and replaced by the merciful " Father in secret." The latter had to be shown, not as an extracosmic God, but as a divine Saviour of the man of flesh, enshrined in his own heart and soul, in the poor as in the rich. No more here than in India could the secrets of initiation be divulged, lest by giving that which is holy to the dogs, and casting pearls before swine, both the revealer and the things revealed should be trodden underfoot. Thus the reticence of both Buddha and Jesus—whether the latter lived out the historic period allotted to him or not—led in the one case to the blank negations of Southern Buddhism, and in the other to the three clashing forms of the Christian church and the two hundred sects in Protestant England alone.

VI.

THEOSOPHICAL TEACHINGS AS TO NATURE AND MAN.

THE UNITY OF ALL IN ALL.

INQ.—*Having·told me what God, the soul, and man are not, in your views, can you inform me what they* are, *according to your teachings ?*

THEO.—In their origin and in eternity the three, like the universe and all therein, are one with the absolute unity, the unknowable deific essence I spoke about some time·back. We believe in no creation, but in the periodical and consecutive appearances of the universe from the subjective on to the objective plane of being, at regular intervals of time, covering periods of immense duration.

INQ.—*Can you elaborate the subject ?*

THEO.—Take as a first comparison, and a help toward a more correct conception, the solar year; and as a second, the two halves of that year, producing each a day and a night of six months' duration at the north pole. Now ·imagine, if you can, instead of a solar year of 365 days, eternity. Let the sun represent the universe, and the polar days and nights of six months each days and nights lasting each 182 trillions and quadrillions of years, instead of 182

75

days each. As the sun rises every morning on our objective horizon out of its (to us) subjective and antipodal space, so does the universe emerge periodically on the plane of objectivity, issuing from that of subjectivity—the antipodes of the former. This is the "Cycle of Life." And as the sun disappears from our horizon, so does the universe disappear at regular periods, when the "Universal Night" sets in. The Hindûs call such alternations the "Days and Nights of Brahmâ," or the times of *manvantara* and *pralaya* (dissolution). The Westerns may call them Universal Days and Nights if they prefer. During the latter (the Nights) All is in All; every atom is resolved into one homogeneity.

EVOLUTION AND ILLUSION.

INQ.—*But who is it that each time creates the universe?*

THEO.—No one creates it. Science would call the process evolution; the pre-Christian philosophers and the Orientalists called it emanation; we Occultists and Theosophists see in it the only universal and eternal Reality casting a periodical reflection of Itself on the infinite spatial depths. This reflection, which you regard as the objective material universe, we consider as a temporary "illusion" and nothing else. That alone which is eternal is real.

INQ.—*At that rate, you and I are also "illusions."*

THEO.—As flitting personalities—to-day one person, to-morrow another—we are. Would you call the sudden flashes of the aurora borealis—the northern lights—a "reality," though it is as real as can be while you look at it? Certainly not; it is the cause that produces it, if permanent and eternal, which is the only reality, while the effect is but a passing illusion.

INQ.—*All this does not explain to me how this "illusion" called the universe originates ; how the conscious to be proceeds to manifest itself from the unconsciousness that is.*

THEO.—It is "unconsciousness" only to our finite consciousness. Verily may we paraphrase St. John (i. 5), and say, "And the [absolute] light [which is darkness to us] shineth in darkness [which is illusionary material light]; and the darkness comprehended it not." This absolute light is also absolute and immutable Law. Whether by radiation or emanation—we need not quarrel over terms—the universe passes out of its homogeneous subjectivity on to the first plane of manifestation; of which planes there are seven, we are taught. With each plane it becomes more dense and material until it reaches this our plane, on which the only world approximately known and understood in its physical composition by science is the planetary or solar system—one *sui generis*, we are told.

INQ.—*What do you mean by* sui generis ?

THEO.—I mean that though the fundamental law and the universal working of laws of Nature are uniform, still our solar system—like every other such system in the millions of others in cosmos, and even our earth—has its own program of manifestations, differing from the respective programs of all others. We speak of the inhabitants of other planets, and imagine that if they are men—i.e., thinking entities—they must be as we are. The fancy of poets and painters and sculptors never fails to represent even the angels as a beautiful copy of man—plus wings. We say that all this is an error and a delusion; because, if on this little earth alone one finds such a diversity in its flora, fauna, and mankind—from the seaweed to the cedar of Lebanon, from the jellyfish to the elephant, from the Bushman and negro to the Apollo Belvedere—alter the conditions, cosmic and planetary, and there must be as a result quite a different flora, fauna, and mankind. The same laws will fashion quite a different set of things and beings even on this our plane, including in it all our planets. How much more different, then, must be external Nature in other solar systems; and how foolish is it to judge of other stars and worlds and human beings by our own, as physical science does !

INQ.—*But what are your data for this assertion ?*

THEO.—What science in general will never accept as proof—the cumulative testimony of an endless series of seers who have testified to this fact. Their spiritual visions —real explorations by and through psychic and spiritual senses untrammeled by blind flesh—have been systematically checked and compared one with the other, and their nature sifted. All that was not corroborated by unanimous and collective experience was rejected, while that only was recorded as established truth which, in various ages, under different climes, and throughout an untold series of incessant observations, was found to agree and receive constantly further corroboration. The methods used by our scholars and students of the psychospiritual sciences do not differ from those of students of the natural and physical sciences, as you may see. Only our fields of research are on two different planes, and our instruments are made by no human hands; for which reason, perchance, they are but the more reliable. The retorts, accumulators, and microscopes of the chemist and naturalist may get out of order; the telescope and the astronomer's horological instruments may get spoiled; our recording instruments are beyond the influence of weather or the elements.

INQ.—*And therefore you have implicit faith in them ?*

THEO.—Faith is a word not to be found in Theosophical dictionaries; we say knowledge based on observation and experience. There is this difference, however: that while the observation and experience of physical science lead the scientists to about as many working hypotheses as there are minds to evolve them, our knowledge consents to add to its lore only those facts which have become undeniable and which are fully and absolutely demonstrated. We have no two beliefs or hypotheses on the same subject.

INQ.—*Is it on such data that you came to accept the strange theories we find in* esoteric Budhism ?

THEO.—Just so. These theories may be slightly incorrect in their minor details, and even faulty in their exposition by lay students; they are facts in Nature, nevertheless, and come nearer the truth than any scientific hypothesis.

ON THE SEPTENARY CONSTITUTION OF OUR PLANET.

INQ.—*I understand that you describe our earth as forming part of a chain of earths ?*

THEO.—We do. But the other six " earths " or globes are not on the same plane of objectivity as our earth is; therefore we cannot see them.

INQ.—*Is that on account of the great distance ?*

THEO.—Not at all; for we see with our naked eye not only planets, but even stars at immeasurably greater distances; but it is owing to these six globes being outside our physical means of perception or plane of being. It is not only that their material density, weight, and fabric are entirely different from those of our earth and the other known planets; but they are (to us) in an entirely different layer of space, so to speak—a layer not to be perceived or felt by our physical senses. And when I say "layer," please do not allow your fancy to suggest to you layers like strata or beds laid one over the other; for this would only lead to another absurd misconception. What I mean by "layer" is that plane of infinite space which by its nature

cannot fall under our ordinary waking perceptions, whether
mental or physical, but which exists in Nature outside of
our normal mentality or consciousness, outside of our three-
dimensional space, and outside of our division of time.
Each of the seven fundamental planes or layers in space—
of course as a whole, as the pure space of Locke's definition, not as our finite space—has its own objectivity and
subjectivity, its own space and time, its own consciousness
and set of senses. But all this will be hardly comprehensible to one trained in the modern ways of thought.

INQ.—*What do you mean by a different set of senses ? Is
there anything on our human "plane" that you could bring as
an illustration of what you say, just to give a clearer idea of
what you may mean by this variety of senses, spaces, and respective perceptions ?*

THEO.—None, except, perhaps, that which for science
would be rather a handy peg on which to hang a counter-
argument. We have a different set of senses in dream-life,
have we not? We feel, talk, hear, see, taste, and function
in general on a different plane, the change of state of our
consciousness being evidenced by the fact that a series of
acts and events embracing years, as we think, passes ideally
through our mind in one instant. Well, that extreme rapid-
ity of our mental operations in dreams, and the perfect
naturalness, for the time being, of all the other functions,
show us that we are on quite another plane. Our philosophy teaches us that as there are seven fundamental forces
in Nature, and seven planes of being, so there are seven
states of consciousness in which man can live, think, remember, and have his being. To enumerate these here is
impossible, and for this one has to turn to the study of
Eastern metaphysics. But in these two states—the waking
and the dreaming—every ordinary mortal, from a learned
philosopher down to a poor untutored savage, has a good
proof that such states differ.

INQ.—*You do not accept, then, the well-known explanations of biology and physiology to account for the dream-state?*

THEO.—We do not. We reject even the hypotheses of your psychologists, preferring the teachings of Eastern Wisdom. Believing in seven planes of cosmic being and states of consciousness with regard to the universe or the macrocosm, we stop at the fourth plane, finding it impossible to go with any degree of certainty beyond. But with respect to the microcosm, or man, we speculate freely on his seven states and principles.

INQ.—*How do you explain these?*

THEO.—We find, first of all, two distinct beings in man—the spiritual and the physical; the man who thinks and the man who records as much of these thoughts as he is able to assimilate. Therefore we divide him into two distinct natures—the upper or the spiritual being, composed of three "principles" or aspects; and the lower or the physical quaternary, composed of four—seven in all.

THE SEPTENARY NATURE OF MAN.

INQ.—*Is this the same as the division we call spirit and soul, and the man of flesh?*

THEO.—It is not. That is the old Platonic division. Plato was an Initiate, and therefore could not go into forbidden details; but he who is acquainted with the archaic doctrine finds the seven in Plato's various combinations of soul and spirit. He regarded man as constituted of two parts—one eternal, formed of the same essence as the Absoluteness; the other mortal and corruptible, deriving its constituent parts from the minor "created" Gods. Man is composed, he shows, of (1) a mortal body; (2) an immortal principle; and (3) a "separate mortal kind of soul." It is that which we respectively call the physical man, the spiritual soul or spirit (*nous*), and the animal soul (*psuche*). This is the division adopted by Paul, another Initiate, who maintains that there is a psychical body which is sown in the corruptible (astral or physical body), and a spiritual body that is raised in incorruptible substance. Even James (iii. 15) corroborates the same by saying that the "wisdom" (of our lower soul) descendeth not from above, but is terrestrial, "psychical," "demoniacal" (*vide* Greek text), while the other is heavenly wisdom. Now, so plain is it that Plato and even Pythagoras, while speaking but of three "principles," give them seven separate functions in their various combinations, that if we contrast our teachings this will become quite plain. Let us take a cursory view of these seven aspects by drawing a table.

THEOSOPHICAL DIVISION.

	Sanskrit Terms.	Exoteric Meaning.	Explanatory.
The Lower Quaternary.	(a) Rûpa, or Sthûla Sharîra.	(a) Physical body.	(a) Is the vehicle of all the other "principles" during life.
	(b) Prâna.	(b) Life, or vital principle.	(b) Necessary only to a, c, d, and the functions of the lower Manas, which embrace all those limited to the *physical* brain.
	(c) Linga Sharîra.	(c) Astral body.	(c) The double, the phantom body.
	(d) Kâma Rûpa.	(d) The seat of animal desires and passions.	(d) This is the center of the animal man, where lies the line of demarcation which separates the mortal man from the immortal entity.
The Upper Imperishable Triad.	(e) Manas—a dual principle in its functions.	(e) Mind, intelligence; the higher human mind, whose light, or radiation, links the Monad, for the lifetime, to the mortal man.	(e) The future state and the karmic destiny of man depend on whether Manas gravitates more downward to Kâma Rûpa, the seat of the animal passions, or upward to Buddhi, the spiritual Ego. In the latter case, the higher consciousness of the individual spiritual aspirations of mind (Manas), assimilating Buddhi, is absorbed by it and forms the Ego, which goes into devachanic bliss.*
	(f) Buddhi.	(f) The spiritual soul.	(f) The vehicle of pure universal spirit.
	(g) Âtmâ.	(g) Spirit.	(g) One with the Absolute, as its radiation.

* In Mr. Sinnett's *Esoteric Buddhism*, d, e, and f are respectively called the animal, the human, and the spiritual souls, which answers as well. Though the principles in *Esoteric Buddhism* are numbered, this is, strictly speaking, useless. The dual

Now what does Plato teach ? He speaks of the interior man as constituted of two parts—one immutable and always the same, formed of the same substance as Deity, and the other mortal and corruptible. These two parts are found in the upper triad and the lower quaternary of our table. He explains that when the soul (*psuche*) "allies herself to the *nous* (divine spirit or substance *), she does everything aright and felicitously"; but the case is otherwise when she attaches herself to *anoia* (folly, or the irrational animal soul). Here, then, we have Manas, or the soul in general, in its two aspects: when attaching itself to *anoia* (our Kâma Rûpa, or the "animal soul" in *Esoteric Buddhism*) it runs toward entire annihilation, as far as the personal Ego is concerned; when allying itself to the *nous* (Âtmâ-Buddhi) it merges into the immortal, imperishable Ego, and then its spiritual consciousness of the personal Ego that was becomes immortal.

THE DISTINCTION BETWEEN SOUL AND SPIRIT.

INQ.—*Do you really teach, as you are accused of doing by some Spiritualists and French Spiritists, the annihilation of every personality ?*

THEO.—We do not. Our opponents have started the nonsensical charge because this question of duality—the *individuality* of the divine Ego and the *personality* of the

---

Monad alone (Âtmâ-Buddhi) is susceptible of being thought of as the two highest numbers (the 6th and 7th) As to all others, since that "principle" only which is predominant in man has to be considered as the first and foremost, no numeration is possible as a general rule. In some men it is the higher intelligence (Manas, or the 5th) which dominates the rest; in others it is the animal soul (Kâma Rûpa) that reigns supreme, exhibiting the most bestial instincts, etc

* Paul calls Plato's *nous* "spirit"; but as this spirit is "substance," then, of course, Buddhi and not Âtmâ is meant, as the latter cannot philosophically be called "substance" under any circumstance. We include Âtmâ among the human "principles" in order not to create additional confusion. In reality it is no *human* principle, but the Universal Absolute Principle of which Buddhi, the soul-spirit, is the car-

human animal—involves that of the possibility of the real
immortal Ego appearing in séance-rooms as a "materialized spirit," which we deny, as already explained.

INQ.—*You have just spoken of psuche running toward its
entire annihilation if it attaches itself to anoia. What did
Plato, and what do you, mean by this ?*

THEO.—The entire annihilation of the *personal* consciousness, as an exceptional and rare case, I think. The
general and almost invariable rule is the merging of the
personal into the individual or immortal consciousness of
the Ego—a transformation or a divine transfiguration—
and the entire annihilation only of the lower quaternary.
Would you expect the man of flesh (or the temporary personality), his shadow (the astral), his animal instincts, and
even physical life, to survive with the spiritual Ego and
become sempiternal ? Naturally all this ceases to exist,
either at or soon after corporeal death. It becomes in
time entirely disintegrated and disappears from view, being
annihilated as a whole.

INQ.—*Then you also reject resurrection in the flesh ?*

THEO.—Most decidedly we do. Why should we, who
believe in the archaic Esoteric Philosophy of the ancients,
accept the unphilosophical speculations of the later Christian theology, borrowed from the Egyptian and Greek exoteric systems of the Gnostics ?

INQ.—*The Egyptians revered nature-spirits, and deified
even onions ; your Hindûs are idolaters to this day ; the Zoroastrians worshiped, and do still worship, the sun ; and the
best Greek philosophers were either dreamers or materialists—
witness Plato and Democritus. How can you compare !*

THEO.—It may be so in your modern theological and
even scientific catechisms ; it is not so for unbiased minds.
The Egyptians revered the "One-Only-One" as Nout ; and

it is from this word that Anaxagoras got his denomination *nous*, or, as he calls it, νοῦς αὐτοκρατής, "the mind or spirit self-potent;" ἀρχή τῆς κινήσεως, "the leading motor" or *primum mobile* of all. With him the *nous* was God, and the *logos* was man, his emanation. The *nous* is the spirit (whether in cosmos or in man), and the *logos*, whether universe or astral body, the emanation of the former, the physical body being merely the animal. Our external powers perceive *phenomena;* our *nous* alone is able to recognize their *noumena.* It is the *logos* alone, or the *noumenon*, that survives, because it is immortal in its very nature and essence; and the *logos* in man is the eternal Ego, that which reincarnates and lasts forever. But how can the evanescent or external shadow, the temporary clothing of that divine *emanation* which returns to the source whence it proceeded, be that which is "raised in incorruptibility"?

INQ.—*Still you can hardly escape the charge of having invented a new division of man's spiritual and psychic constituents; for no philosopher speaks of them, though you believe that Plato does.*

THEO.—And I support the belief. Not only Plato, but also Pythagoras followed the same division.* He described the soul as a self-moving unit (*monas*) composed of three elements—the *nous* (spirit), the *phren* (mind), and the *thumos* (life, breath, or the *nephesh* of the Kabalists), which three correspond to our Âtmâ-Buddhi (higher spirit-soul), to Manas (the Ego), and to Kâma Rûpa in conjunction with the lower reflection of Manas. That which the ancient

---

* "Plato and Pythagoras," says Plutarch, "distribute the soul into two parts, the rational [noëtic] and irrational soul [*agnoia*], that that part of the soul of man which is rational is eternal—for though it be not God, yet it is the product of an eternal Deity—but that part of the soul which is divested of reason [the *agnoia*] dies." The modern term *agnostic* comes from *a-gnosticos*, a word cognate with *agnoia* We wonder why Mr. Huxley, the author of the word, should have connected his great intellect with "the soul . . . divested of reason," which dies? Is it the exaggerated humility of the modern materialist?

Greek philosophers termed soul, in general, we call spirit, or spiritual soul—Buddhi, as the vehicle of Âtmâ; the *To Agathon*, or Plato's Supreme Deity. The fact that Pythagoras and others state that *phren* and *thumos* are shared by us with the brutes proves that in this case the lower mânasic reflection (instinct) and Kâma Rûpa (animal living passions) are meant. And as Socrates and Plato accepted the clue and followed it, if to these five—namely, *To Agathon* (Deity or Âtmâ), *psuche* (soul in its collective sense), *nous* (spirit or mind), *phren* (physical mind), and *thumos* (Kâma Rûpa or passions)—we add the *eidolon* of the Mysteries (the shadowy form or human double), and the *physical body*, it will be easy to demonstrate that the ideas of both Pythagoras and Plato were identical with ours. Even the Egyptians held to the septenary division. They taught that the soul (Ego) in its exit had to pass through its seven chambers or principles—both those it left behind and those it took along with itself. The only difference is that, ever bearing in mind the penalty of revealing Mystery-doctrines, which was death, they gave out the teaching in broad outline, while we elaborate it and explain it in its details. But though we do give out to the world as much as is lawful, even in our doctrine more than one important detail is withheld, which those who study the Esoteric Philosophy and are pledged to silence are alone entitled to know.

THE GREEK TEACHINGS.

INQ.—*We have magnificent Greek and Latin, Sanskrit and Hebrew scholars. How is it that we find nothing in their translations that would afford us a clue to what you say?*

THEO.—Because your translators, their great learning notwithstanding, have made of the philosophers—the Greeks especially—misty instead of mystic writers. Take as an instance Plutarch, and read what he says of the " principles" of man. What he describes is accepted literally and attributed to metaphysical superstition and ignorance. Let me give you an illustration in point from this author:

> Man is compound; and they are *mistaken who think him to be compounded of two parts only.* For they imagine that the understanding [brain-intellect] is a part of the soul [the upper triad]; but they err in this no less than those who make the soul to be a part of the body [i.e., those who make of the *triad* part of the corruptible mortal *quaternary*]. For the understanding [*nous*] as far exceeds the soul as the soul is better and diviner than the body. Now this composition of the soul [*psuche*] with the understanding [*nous*] makes reason, and with the body [or *thumos*, the animal soul] passion; of which the one is the beginning or principle of pleasure and pain, and the other of virtue and vice. Of these three parts conjoined and compacted together, the earth has given the body, the moon the soul, and the sun the understanding, to the generation of man.

This last sentence is purely allegorical, and will be comprehended only by those who are versed in the esoteric science of correspondences and know what planet is related to every principle. Plutarch divides the principles into three groups, and makes of the body a compound of *physical frame, astral shadow*, and *breath*, or the triple lower part, which "from earth was taken and to earth returns"; of the middle principle and the *instinctual soul* the second part, derived from and through, and ever influenced by, the moon;* and only of the higher part, or the *spiritual soul* (Buddhi), with the *âtmic* and *mânasic* elements in it, does he make a direct emanation of the sun, who stands here for *To Agathon*, the Supreme Deity. This is proven by what he says further as follows:

> Now of the deaths we die, the one makes man two of three and the other one of [out of] two. The former is in the region and jurisdiction of Demeter; whence the name given to the Mysteries, τελεῖν, resembled that given to death, τελευτᾶν. The Athenians also heretofore

---

* The Kabalists who know the relation of Jehovah, the life and children giver, to the moon, and the influence of the latter on generation, will again see the point as much as will some astrologers.

called the deceased sacred to Demeter. As for the other death, it is in the moon or region of Persephone.

Here you have our doctrine, which shows man a septenary during life; a quintile just after death, in Kâmaloka; and a triad, Ego, spirit-soul, and consciousness in Devachan. This separation, first in the "Meadows of Hades," as Plutarch calls the Kâmaloka, then in Devachan, was part and parcel of the performances during the Sacred Mysteries, when the candidates for initiation enacted the whole drama of death and the resurrection as a glorified spirit, by which name we mean *consciousness*. This is what Plutarch means when he says:

And as with the one, the terrestrial, so with the other, celestial, Hermes doth dwell. This suddenly and with violence plucks the soul from the body; but Proserpina mildly and in a long time disjoins the understanding from the soul.* For this reason she is called *monogenes*, only begotten, or rather begetting one alone; for the better part of man becomes alone when it is separated by her. Now both the one and the other happens thus according to nature. It is ordained by Fate [Fatum or Karma] that every soul, whether with or without understanding [mind], when gone out of the body, should wander for a time—though not all for the same—in the region lying between the earth and moon [Kâmaloka].† For those who have been unjust and dissolute suffer then the punishment due to their offenses; but the good and virtuous are there detained till they are purified and have, by expiation, purged out of them all the infections they might have contracted from the contagion of the body, as if from foul health—living in the mildest part of the air, called the Meadows of Hades, where they must remain for a certain prefixed and appointed time. And then, as if they were returning from a wandering pilgrimage or long exile into their country, they have a taste of joy, such as they principally receive who are initiated into Sacred Mysteries, mixed with trouble, admiration, and each one's proper and peculiar hope.

---

* Proserpina, or Persephone, stands here for post-mortem Karma, which is said to regulate the separation of the lower from the higher "principles"—the soul, as *nephesh*, the breath of animal life, which remains for a time in Kâmaloka, from the higher compound Ego, which goes into the state of Devachan, or bliss.

† Until the separation of the higher, spiritual "principle" from the lower principles, which remain in Kâmaloka until disintegrated.

This is nirvânic bliss, and no Theosophist could describe in plainer though esoteric language the mental joys of Devachan, where every man has his paradise around him, created by his consciousness. But you must beware of the general error into which too many even of our Theosophists fall. Do not imagine that because man is called septenary, then quintuple and a triad, he is a compound of seven, five, or three entities; or, as well expressed by a Theosophical writer, of skins to be peeled off like the skins of an onion. The "principles," as already said—save the body, the life, and the astral *eidolon*, all of which disperse at death—are simply *aspects* and *states of consciousness*. There is but one *real* man, enduring through the cycle of life and immortal in essence, if not in form, and this is Manas, the mind-man or embodied consciousness. The objection made by the materialists, who deny the possibility of mind and consciousness acting without matter, is worthless in our case. We do not deny the soundness of their argument, but we simply ask our opponents: Are you acquainted *with all the states of matter*—you who knew hitherto but of three? And how do you know whether that which we refer to as Absolute Consciousness or Deity, forever invisible and unknowable, be not that which, though it forever eludes our human finite conception, is still universal spirit-matter or matter-spirit in its absolute infinitude? It is then one of the lowest, and in its manvantaric manifestations fractioned, aspects of this spirit-matter which is the conscious Ego that creates its own paradise—a fools' paradise, it may be, still a state of bliss.

INQ.—*But what is Devachan?*

THEO.—The "land of Gods," literally; a condition, a state of mental bliss. Philosophically, a mental condition analogous to, but far more vivid and real than, the most vivid dream. It is the state after death of most mortals.

VII.

ON THE VARIOUS POST-MORTEM STATES.

THE PHYSICAL AND THE SPIRITUAL MAN.

INQ.—*I am glad to hear you believe in the immortality of the soul.*

THEO.—Not of the soul, but of the divine spirit; or rather in the immortality of the reincarnating Ego.

INQ.—*What is the difference?*

THEO.—A very great one in our philosophy; but this is too abstruse and difficult a question to touch lightly upon. We shall have to analyze them separately, and then in conjunction. We may begin with spirit.

We say that the spirit—the "Father in secret" of Jesus —or Âtman is no individual property of any man, but is the divine essence which has no body, no form, which is imponderable, invisible, and indivisible, that which does not *exist* and yet *is*, as the Buddhists say of Nirvâna. It only overshadows the mortal, that which enters into him and pervades the whole body being but its omnipresent rays, or light, radiated through Buddhi, its vehicle and direct emanation. This is the secret meaning of the assertions of almost all the ancient philosophers when they said that "the *rational* part of man's soul " * never enters wholly into the man, but only overshadows him more or less through the *irrational* spiritual soul, or Buddhi.†

INQ.—*I labored under the impression that the "animal soul" alone was irrational, and not the "divine soul."*

THEO.—You have to learn the difference between that which is negatively or *passively* irrational, because undifferentiated, and that which is irrational because too *active* and positive. Man is a correlation of spiritual powers, as well as a correlation of chemical and physical forces, brought into function by what we call "principles."

INQ.—*I have read a good deal upon the subject, and it seems to me that the notions of the older philosophers differed a great deal from those of the medieval Kabalists, though they do agree in some particulars.*

THEO.—The most substantial difference between them and us is this: while we believe, with the Neoplatonists and the Eastern teachings, that the spirit (Âtmâ) never descends hypostatically into the living man, but only showers more or less its radiance on the *inner* man—the psychic and spiritual compound of the astral principles—the Kabalists maintain that the human spirit, detaching itself from the ocean of light and universal spirit, enters man's soul, where it remains throughout life imprisoned in the astral capsule. All Christian Kabalists still maintain the same, as they are unable to break quite loose from their anthropomorphic and biblical doctrines.

INQ.—*And what do you say ?*

---

* In its generic sense, the word "rational" meaning something emanating from the Eternal Wisdom

† Irrational in the sense that as a *pure* emanation of the Universal Mind it can have no individual reason of its own on this plane of matter, but, like the moon, who borrows her light from the sun and her life from the earth, so Buddhi, receiving its light of wisdom from Âtmâ, gets its rational qualities from Manas. As something homogeneous, however, it is devoid of attributes *per se.*

· THEO.—We say that we only allow the presence of the radiation of spirit, or Âtmâ, in the astral capsule, and so far only as that spiritual radiancy is concerned. We say that man and soul have to conquer their immortality by ascending toward the unity with which, if successful, they will be finally linked, and into which they are finally, so to speak, absorbed. The individualization of man after death depends on the spirit, not on his soul and body. Although the word "personality," in the sense in which it is usually understood, is an absurdity if applied literally to our immortal essence, still the latter is, as our individual Ego, a distinct entity, immortal and eternal *per se*. It is only in the case of black magicians or of criminals beyond redemption—criminals who have been such during a long series of lives—that the shining thread which links the spirit to the personal soul from the moment of the birth of the child is violently snapped, and the disembodied entity becomes divorced from the personal soul, the latter being annihilated without leaving the smallest impression of itself on the former. If this union between the lower or personal Manas and the individual reincarnating Ego has not been effected during life, then the former is left to share the fate of the lower animals—to gradually dissolve into ether and have its personality annihilated. But even then the spiritual Ego remains a distinct being. It only loses—after that special, and in that case, indeed, useless life—one devachanic state which it would otherwise have enjoyed as that idealized personality, and is reincarnated almost immediately, after enjoying for a short time its freedom as a planetary spirit.

INQ.—*It is stated in Isis Unveiled that such planetary spirits or angels, " the gods of the pagans or the archangels of the Christians," will never be men on our planet.*

THEO.—Quite right. Not "*such* planetary spirits," but *some* classes of higher planetary spirits. They will never

be men on this planet, because they are liberated spirits
from a previous; earlier world, and as such they cannot re-
become men on this earth. Yet all these will live again in
the next and far higher *mahâmanvantara*, after this "Great
Age" and its Brahmic *pralaya* (a little period of sixteen
figures or so) are over. For you must have heard, of
course, that Eastern philosophy teaches us that mankind
consists of such "spirits" imprisoned in human bodies.
The difference between animals and men is this: the
former are ensouled by the "principles" *potentially*, the
latter *actually*.* Do you now understand the difference?

INQ.—*Yes; but this specialization has been in all ages the
stumbling-block of metaphysicians.*

THEO.—It has. The whole esotericism of the Buddhistic
philosophy is based on this mysterious teaching, understood by so few, and so totally misrepresented by many of
the most learned modern scholars. Even metaphysicians
are too inclined to confound the effect with the cause.
An Ego who has won his immortal life as spirit will remain
the same Inner Self throughout all his rebirths on earth;
but this does not imply necessarily that he must either
remain the Mr. Smith or Mr. Brown he was on earth, or
lose his individuality. Therefore the astral soul and the
terrestrial body of a man may, in the dark hereafter, be
absorbed into the cosmical ocean of sublimated elements,
and he may cease to feel his last *personal* Ego (if it did not
deserve to soar higher); and yet his *divine* Ego may still
remain the same unchanged entity, though this terrestrial
experience of its emanation may be totally obliterated at
the instant of separation from the unworthy vehicle.

INQ.—*If the spirit, or the divine portion of the soul, is preëxistent as a distinct being from all eternity, as Origen, Synesius,*

---

* This is fully explained in the Commentaries of the second volume of *The Secret
Doctrine.*

*and other semi-Christians and semi-Platonic philosophers
taught, and if it is the same, and nothing more than the metaphysically objective soul, how can it be otherwise than eternal?
And what matters it, in such a case, whether man leads a pure
or an animal life, if, do what he may, he can never lose his
individuality?*

THEO.—This doctrine, as you have stated it, is just as
pernicious in its consequences as that of vicarious atonement.   Had the latter dogma, in company with the false
idea that we are all immortal, been demonstrated to the
world in its true light, humanity would have been bettered
by its propagation.

Let me repeat to you again: Pythagoras, Plato, Timæus
of Locris, and the old Alexandrian school derived the soul
of man, or his higher "principles" and attributes, from the
Universal World-Soul, the latter being, according to their
teachings, Æther (Pater-Zeus).   Therefore none of these
"principles" can be the *unalloyed* essence of the Pythagorean *monas*, or our Âtmâ, because the *anima mundi* is but
the effect—the subjective emanation or rather radiation—
of the *monas*.   Both the human spirit, or the individuality,
the reincarnating spiritual Ego, and Buddhi, the spiritual
soul, are preëxistent.   But while the former exists as a distinct entity, an individualization, the soul exists as preëxist-
ing breath, a nescient portion of an intelligent whole.   Both
were originally formed from the eternal ocean of light;
but as the Fire-Philosophers, the medieval Theosophists,
expressed it, there is a visible as well as invisible spirit in
fire.   They made a difference between the *anima bruta* and
the *anima divina*.   Empedocles firmly believed all men and
animals to possess two souls; and in Aristotle we find that
he calls one the reasoning soul (νοῦς) and the other the animal soul (ψυχή).   According to these philosophers, the
reasoning soul comes from *within* the Universal Soul, and
the other from *without*.

INQ.—*Would you call the soul, i.e., the human thinking soul, or what you call the Ego, matter ?*

THEO.—Not matter, but *substance*, assuredly ; nor would the word " matter," if prefixed with the adjective " primordial," be a word to avoid. This matter, we say, is coeternal with spirit, and is not our visible, tangible, and divisible matter, but its extreme sublimation. Pure spirit is but one remove from the *no*-spirit, or the absolute *All.* Unless you admit that man was evolved out of this primordial spirit-matter, and represents a regular progressive scale of " principles " from superspirit down to the grossest matter, how can we ever come to regard the *inner* man as immortal, and at the same time as a spiritual entity and a mortal man ?

INQ.—*Then why should you not believe in God as such an entity ?*

THEO.—Because that which is infinite and unconditioned can have no form, and cannot be a being—not in any Eastern philosophy worthy of the name, at any rate. An " entity " is immortal, but is so only in its ultimate essence, not in its individual form, when at the last point of its cycle it is absorbed into its primordial nature ; and it becomes spirit when it loses its name of entity.

Its immortality as a form is limited only to its life-cycle or the *mahâmanvantara*, after which it is one and identical with the Universal Spirit, and no longer a separate entity. As to the *personal* soul—by which we mean the spark of consciousness that preserves in the spiritual Ego the idea of the personal " I " of the last incarnation—this lasts, as a separate distinct recollection, only throughout the devachanic period, after which time it is added to the series of other innumerable incarnations of the Ego, like the remembrance in our memory of one of a series of days at the end of a year. Will you bind the infinitude you claim for your God to finite conditions ? That alone which is indissolubly cemented by Âtmâ—viz., Buddhi-Manas—is immortal. The soul of man—i.e., of the personality—*per se* is neither immortal, eternal, nor divine. Says the *Zohar:*

> The soul, when sent to this earth, puts on an earthly garment, to preserve herself here; so she receives above a shining garment, in order to be able to look without injury into the mirror, whose light proceeds from the Lord of Light.

Moreover, the *Zohar* teaches that the soul cannot reach the abode of bliss unless she has received the "holy kiss," or the reunion of the soul *with the substance from which she emanated*—spirit. All souls are dual; and while the latter is a feminine principle, the spirit is masculine. While imprisoned in body, man is a trinity, unless his pollution is such as to have caused his divorce from the spirit. "Woe to the soul which prefers to her divine husband [spirit] the earthly wedlock with her terrestrial body," records a text of the *Book of the Keys*—a Hermetic work. Woe indeed; for nothing will remain of that personality to be recorded on the imperishable tablets of the Ego's memory.

INQ.—*How can that which, if not breathed by God into man, is yet, on your own confession, of an identical substance with the divine, fail to be immortal?*

THEO.—Every atom and speck of matter, not of substance only, is *imperishable* in its essence, but not in its *individual consciousness*. Immortality is but one's unbroken consciousness, and the *personal* consciousness can hardly last longer than the personality itself. And such consciousness, as I have already told you, survives only throughout Devachan, after which it is reabsorbed, first in the *individual*, and then in the *universal* consciousness. Better inquire of your theologians how it is that they have so sorely jumbled up the Jewish Scriptures. Read the Bible, if you would have a good proof that the writers of the Pentateuch —Genesis especially—never regarded *nephesh*—that which

God breathes into Adam (Gen. ii. 7)—as the *immortal* soul. Here are some instances: "And God created . . . every life [*nephesh*] that moveth" (Gen. i. 21), meaning animal. "And man became a living soul [*nephesh*]" (Gen. ii. 7), which shows that the word *nephesh* was indifferently applied to *immortal* man and to *mortal* beast. "And surely your blood of your lives [*nepheshim*] will I require: at the hand of every beast will I require it, and at the hand of man" (Gen. ix. 5). "Escape for thy life [*nephesh*]" (Gen. xix. 17). "Let us not kill him" (Gen. xxxvii. 21). "Let us not kill his *nephesh*" is the Hebrew text. "*Nephesh* for *nephesh*," says Leviticus. "He that killeth any man shall surely be put to death" —literally, "He that smiteth the *nephesh* of a man" (Lev. xxiv. 17). "And he that killeth a beast [*nephesh*] shall make it good; beast for beast" (*ibid.*, 18), whereas the original text has it "*nephesh* for *nephesh*." How could man *kill* that which is immortal? This explains, also, why the Sadducees denied the immortality of the soul, and also affords another proof that very probably the Mosaic Jews—the uninitiated, at any rate—never believed in the soul's survival at all.

ON ETERNAL REWARD AND PUNISHMENT, AND ON NIRVÂNA.

INQ.—*It is hardly necessary, I suppose, to ask you whether you believe in the Christian dogmas of paradise and hell, or in future rewards and punishments as taught by the orthodox churches?*

THEO.—As described in your catechisms, we reject them absolutely; least of all would we accept their eternity. But we believe firmly in what we call the *Law of Retribution*, and in the absolute justice and wisdom guiding this law, or Karma. Hence we positively refuse to accept the cruel and unphilosophical belief in eternal reward or eternal punishment. We say with Horace:

> Let rules be fixed that may our rage contain,
> And punish faults *with a proportion'd pain;*
> But do not flay him who deserves alone
> A whipping for the fault that he has done.

This is a rule for all men, and a just one. Have we to believe that God, whom you make the embodiment of wisdom, love, and mercy, is less entitled to these attributes than mortal man?

INQ.—*Have you any other reasons for rejecting this dogma?*

THEO.—Our chief reason for so doing is the fact of reincarnation. As already stated, we reject the idea of a new soul created for every newly born babe. We believe that every human being is the bearer, or vehicle, of an Ego coeval with every other Ego; because all Egos are *of the same essence* and belong to the primeval emanation from one universal infinite Ego. Plato calls the latter the *Logos* (or the second manifested God); and we, the manifested Divine Principle, which is one with the Universal Mind or Soul—not the anthropomorphic, extracosmic, and personal God in which so many theists believe. Pray do not confuse.

INQ.—*But where is the difficulty, once you accept a manifested Principle, in believing that the soul of every new mortal is created by that Principle, as all the souls before it have been so created?*

THEO.—Because that which is impersonal can hardly create, plan, and think, at its own sweet will and pleasure. Being a universal Law, immutable in its periodical manifestations—those of radiating and manifesting its own essence at the beginning of every new cycle of life—It is not supposed to create men, only to repent a few years later of having created them. If we have to believe in a Divine

Principle at all, it must be in one which is as absolute harmony, logic, and justice, as it is absolute love, wisdom, and impartiality; and a God who would create every soul for the space of one brief span of life, regardless of the fact whether it has to animate the body of a wealthy, happy man or that of a poor suffering wretch, hapless from birth to death, though he has done nothing to deserve his cruel fate, would be rather a senseless fiend than a God.* Why, even the Jewish philosophers, believers in the Mosaic Bible (esoterically, of course), have never entertained such an idea. Moreover, they believed in reincarnation, as we do.

INQ.—*Can you give me some instances as a proof of this?*

THEO.—Most decidedly I can. Philo Judæus says:

The air is full of them [of souls]; . . . those which are nearest the earth, descending to be tied to mortal bodies, παλινδρομοῦσιν αὖθις, *return to other bodies, being desirous to live in them.*†

In the *Zohar* the soul is made to plead her freedom before God:

Lord of the universe! I am happy in this world, and do not wish to go into another world, where I shall be a handmaid, and be exposed to all kinds of pollutions.‡

The doctrine of fatal necessity, the everlasting immutable law, is asserted in the answer of the Deity:

Against thy will thou becomest an embryo, and against thy will thou art born.§

Light would be incomprehensible without darkness to make it manifest by contrast; good would be no longer good without evil to show the priceless nature of the boon; and so personal virtue could claim no merit unless it had passed through the furnace of temptation. Nothing is eter-

---

* See, further, "On the Reward and Punishment of the Ego "
† *De Gignat,* p. 222 C; *De Somniis,* 455 D
‡ *Zohar,* ii., 96.
§ *Mishna,* Aboth, iv., 29

nal and unchangeable save the concealed Deity. Nothing
that is finite—whether because it had a beginning or must
have an end—can remain stationary; it must either progress or recede; and a soul which thirsts after a reunion
with its spirit, which alone confers upon it immortality,
must purify itself through cyclic transmigrations onward
toward the only land of bliss and eternal rest, called in the
Zohar the "Palace of Love," היכל אהבה; in the Hindû
religion, "Moksha"; among the Gnostics, the "Plerôma
of Eternal Light"; and by the Buddhists, "Nirvâna." And
all these states are temporary, not eternal.

INQ.—*Yet there is no reincarnation spoken of in all this.*

THEO.—A soul which pleads to be allowed to remain
where she is must be preëxistent, and not have been created for the occasion. In the *Zohar*, however, there is a
still better proof. Speaking of the reincarnating Egos, the
rational souls, those whose last personality has to fade out
entirely, it is said:

All souls which are not guiltless in this world have already alienated
themselves in heaven from the Holy One (blessed be he); they have
thrown themselves into an abyss at their very existence, and have an-
ticipated the time when they are to descend (once more) on earth.*

The "Holy One" means here, esoterically, the Âtman, or
Âtmâ-Buddhi.

INQ.—*Moreover, it is very strange to find Nirvâna spoken
of as something synonymous with the kingdom of heaven, or
paradise, since according to every Orientalist of note Nirvâna
is a synonym of annihilation !*

THEO.—Taken literally, with regard to the personality
and differentiated matter; but not otherwise. These ideas
on reincarnation and the trinity of man were held by many

---

* iii, 61 *b* The above quotations are from K. R. H. Mackenzie's *Masonic Cyclopedia*, art. "Kabbalah."

of the early Christian fathers. It is the jumble made by
the translators of the New Testament and ancient philosophical treatises between soul and spirit that has occa-
sioned the many misunderstandings. It is also one of the
many reasons why Buddha, Plotinus, and so many other
Initiates are now accused of having longed for the total
extinction of their souls—"absorption into the Deity," or
"reunion with the Universal Soul," meaning, according to
modern ideas, annihilation. The personal soul must, of
course, be disintegrated into its particles before it is able
to link its purer essence forever with the immortal spirit.
But the translators of both the Acts and the Epistles, who
laid the foundation of the *kingdom of heaven*, and the
modern commentators on the Buddhist Sutta of the *foundation of the kingdom of righteousness*, have muddled the
sense of the great Apostle of Christianity as of the great
reformer of India. The former have smothered the word
psuchikos (ψυχικὸς) so that no reader imagines it to have any
relation with soul; and with this confusing together of soul
and spirit, Bible readers get only a perverted sense of anything on the subject. On the other hand, the interpreters
of Buddha have failed to understand the meaning and
object of the Buddhist four degrees of Dhyâna. Ask the
Pythagoreans: Can that spirit which gives life and motion
and partakes of the nature of light be reduced to nonentity?
Can even that sensitive spirit in brutes which exercises
memory—one of the rational faculties—die and become
nothing? observe the Occultists. In Buddhistic philosophy
"annihilation" means only a dispersion of matter, in whatever form or *semblance* of form it may be; for everything
that has form is temporary, and is, therefore, really an illusion. For in eternity the longest periods of time are as the
wink of an eye. So with form. Before we have time to
realize that we have seen it, it is gone like an instantaneous
flash of lightning, and passed forever. When the spiritual

entity breaks loose forever from every particle of matter, substance, or form, and re-becomes a spiritual breath, then only does it enter upon the eternal and unchangeable Nirvâna, lasting as long as the cycle of life has lasted—an eternity, truly. And then that Breath, existing *in spirit*, is *nothing* because it is *all;* as a form, a semblance, a shape, it is completely annihilated; as absolute spirit it still *is*, for it has become, to coin a word, *be-ness* itself. The very phrase "absorbed in the universal essence," when used of the soul as spirit, means *union with*. It can never mean annihilation, for that would mean eternal separation.

INQ.—*Do you not lay yourself open to the accusation of preaching annihilation by the language you yourself use? You have just spoken of the soul of man returning to its primordial elements.*

THEO.—But you forget that I have given you the differences between the various meanings of the word "soul," and shown the loose way in which the term "spirit" has been hitherto translated. We speak of an animal, a human, and a spiritual soul, and distinguish between them. Plato, for instance, calls "rational soul" that which we call Buddhi, adding to it the adjective of "spiritual," however; but that which we call the reincarnating Ego, Manas, he calls spirit, *nous*, etc., whereas we apply the term "spirit," when standing alone and without any qualification, to Âtmâ only. Pythagoras repeats our archaic doctrine when stating that the Ego (*nous*) was eternal with Deity; that the soul only passed through various stages to arrive at divine excellence; while *thumos* returned to the earth, and even the *phren*, the lower Manas, was eliminated. Again, Plato defines *soul* (Buddhi) as "the motion that is able to move itself." "Soul," he adds (*Laws*, x.), "is the most ancient of all things, and the commencement of motion"—thus calling Âtmâ-Buddhi soul, and Manas spirit, which we do not.

Soul was generated prior to body, and body is posterior and secondary, as being, according to Nature, ruled over by the ruling soul. . . . The soul which administers all things that are moved, in every way, administers likewise the heavens. . . .

Soul, then, leads everything in heaven, and on earth, and in the sea, by its movements—the names of which are, to will, to consider, to take care of, to consult, to form opinions true and false, to be in a state of joy, sorrow, confidence, fear, hate, love, together with all such primary movements as are allied to these. . . . Being a goddess herself, she ever takes as an ally *nous*, a god, and disciplines all things correctly and happily; but when with *anoia* [not *nous*] it works out everything the contrary.

In this language, as in the Buddhist texts, the negative is treated as essential existence. "Annihilation" comes under a similar exegesis. The positive state is essential being, but no manifestation as such. When the spirit, in Buddhistic parlance, enters Nirvâna, it loses objective existence, but retains subjective being. To objective minds this is becoming absolute "nothing"; to subjective, *no-thing*—nothing to be displayed to sense. Thus their Nirvâna means the certitude of individual immortality *in spirit*, not in soul, which, though "the most ancient of all things," is still—along with all the other Gods—a finite emanation in forms and individuality, if not in substance.

INQ.—*I do not quite seize the idea yet, and would be thankful to have you explain this to me by some illustrations.*

THEO.—No doubt it is very difficult to understand, especially to one brought up in the regular orthodox ideas of the Christian church. Moreover, I must tell you one thing; and this is that unless you have studied thoroughly well the separate functions assigned to all the human "principles," and the state of all these after death, you will hardly realize our Eastern philosophy.

ON THE VARIOUS "PRINCIPLES" IN MAN.

INQ.—*I have heard a good deal about this constitution of the "inner man," as you call it, but could never make "head or tail on't," as the translator of Le Comte de Gabalis expresses it.*

THEO.—Of course it is most difficult, and, as you say, puzzling to understand correctly and distinguish between the various aspects, called by us the "principles," of the real Ego. It is the more so as there exists a notable difference in the numbering of these principles by various Eastern schools, though at the bottom there is the same identical substratum of teaching.

INQ.—*Do you mean the Vedântins, as an instance? Do they not divide your seven "principles" into five only?*

THEO.—They do; but though I would not presume to dispute the point with a learned Vedântin, I may yet state as my private opinion that they have an obvious reason for it. With them it is only that compound spiritual aggregate which consists of various mental aspects that is called *man* at all, the physical body being, in their view, something beneath contempt, and merely an illusion. Nor is the Vedânta the only philosophy to reckon in this manner. Lao-Tze, in his *Tao-te-King*, mentions only five principles, because he, like the Vedântins, omits to include two principles, namely, the spirit (Âtmâ) and the physical body, the latter of which, moreover, he calls the "cadaver." Then there is the Târaka Râja Yoga school. Its teaching recognizes only three "principles," in fact; but then, in reality, their *sthûlopâdhi*, or physical body, in its waking, conscious state, their *sûkshmopâdhi*, the same body in *svapna*, or the dreaming state, and their *kâranopâdhi*, or "causal body," or that which passes from one incarnation to another, are all dual in their aspects, and thus make six. Add to this

Âtmâ, the impersonal Divine Principle or the immortal element in man, undistinguished from the Universal Spirit, and you have the same seven again.* They are welcome to hold to their division; we hold to ours.

INQ.—*Then it seems almost the same as the division made by the mystic Christians : body, soul, and spirit.*

THEO.—Just the same. We could easily make of the body the vehicle of the vital double; of the latter the vehicle of life, or Prâna; of Kâma Rûpa, or animal soul, the vehicle of the higher and the lower mind; and make of this six principles, crowning the whole with the one immortal spirit. In Occultism every qualificative change in the state of our consciousness gives to man a new aspect; and if it prevails and becomes part of the living and acting Ego, it must be (and is) given a special name, to distinguish the man in that particular state from the man he is when he places himself in another state.

INQ.—*It is just that which it is so difficult to understand.*

THEO.—It seems to me very easy, on the contrary, once that you have seized the main idea, i.e., that man acts on this or another plane of consciousness in strict accordance with his mental and spiritual condition. But such is the materialism of the age that the more we explain the less people seem capable of understanding what we say. Divide the terrestrial being called man into three chief aspects, if you like; and unless you make of him a pure animal you cannot do less. Take his objective body; the thinking principle in him—which is only a little higher than the instinctual element in the animal—or the vital conscious soul; and that which places him so immeasurably beyond and higher than the animal, i.e., his reasoning soul or spirit.

---

* See, for a clearer explanation, *The Secret Doctrine,* i., 157 (1st ed); i., 181 (3d ed.).

Well, if we take these three groups or representative entities, and subdivide them according to the occult teaching,
what do we get ?

First of all, spirit—in the sense of the absolute and therefore indivisible ALL—or Âtmâ. As this can neither be
located nor limited in philosophy, being simply that which
is in eternity, and which cannot be absent from even the
tiniest geometrical or mathematical point of the universe
of matter or substance, it ought not to be called, in truth,
a "human" principle at all.   Rather, and at best, it is, in
metaphysics, that point in space which the human monad
and its vehicle, man, occupy for the period of every life.
Now that point is as imaginary as man himself, and in
reality is an illusion, a *mâyâ;* but then for ourselves, as for
other personal Egos, we are a reality during that fit of illusion called life, and we have to take ourselves into account
—in our own fancy, at any rate—if no one else does.   To
make it more conceivable to the human intellect when first
attempting the study of Occultism, and to solve the a-b-c
of the mystery of man, Occultism calls this seventh principle the synthesis of the sixth, and gives it for vehicle the
spiritual soul (Buddhi). Now the latter conceals a mystery
which is never given to any one, with the exception of ir-
revocably pledged *chelâs*, or those, at any rate, who can be
safely trusted. Of course there would be less confusion
could it only be told; but as this is directly concerned
with the power of projecting one's double consciously and
at will, and as this gift, like the "ring of Gyges," would
prove very fatal to man at large and to the possessor of
this faculty in particular, it is carefully guarded. But let
us proceed with the "principles." This divine soul, or
Buddhi, then, is the vehicle of the spirit. In conjunction
these two are one, impersonal and without any attributes
(on this plane, of course), but make two spiritual "principles." If we pass on to the human soul, Manas or *mens*,
every one will agree that the intelligence of man is dual,

to say the least—e.g., the high-minded man can hardly become low-minded; the very intellectual and spiritual-minded man is separated by an abyss from the obtuse, dull, and material, if not animal-minded, man.

INQ.—*But why should not man be rather represented by two principles or two aspects?*

THEO.—Every man has these two principles in him, one more active than the other; and in rare cases one of them is entirely stunted in its growth, so to say, or paralyzed by the strength and predominance of the other aspect in every direction. These, then, are what we call the two principles or aspects of Manas, the higher and the lower; the former, the higher Manas, or the thinking, conscious Ego, gravitating toward the spiritual soul (Buddhi); and the latter, or its instinctual principle, attracted to Kâma, the seat of animal desires and passions in man. Thus we have four principles justified, the last three being (1) the double, which we have agreed to call protean or plastic soul, the vehicle of (2) the life principle; and (3) the physical body. Of course no physiologist or biologist will accept these principles, nor can he make head or tail of them. And this is why, perhaps, none of them to this day understand either the functions of the spleen, the physical vehicle of the protean double, or those of a certain organ on the right side of man, the seat of the above-mentioned desires; nor yet do they know anything of the pineal body, which is described as a gland with a little sand in it, whereas it is in truth the very seat of the highest and divinest consciousness in man —his omniscient, spiritual, and all-embracing mind. And this shows you still more plainly that we have neither invented these seven principles, nor are they new in the world of philosophy, as we can easily prove.

INQ.—*But what is it that reincarnates, in your belief?*

THEO.—The spiritual, thinking Ego, the permanent principle in man, or that which is the seat of Manas. It is not

Âtmâ, or even Âtmâ-Buddhi, regarded as the dual monad,
which is the individual or divine man, but Manas; for Âtman is the Universal ALL, and becomes the Higher Self of
man only in conjunction with Buddhi, its vehicle, which
links It to the individuality or divine man. For it is the
Buddhi-Manas—the united fifth and sixth principles—which
is called the Causal Body by the Vedântins, and which
is *consciousness*, that connects It with every personality It
inhabits on earth. Therefore, soul being a generic term,
there are in men three aspects of soul: (1) the terrestrial
or animal; (2) the human soul; and (3) the spiritual soul;
these, strictly speaking, are one soul in its three aspects.
Now of the first aspect nothing remains after death; of
the second, *nous* or Manas, only its divine essence, *if left
unsoiled*, survives; while the third, in addition to being immortal, becomes *consciously* divine, by the assimilation of
the higher Manas. But to make it clear we have to say a
few words first of all about reincarnation.

INQ.—*You will do well, as it is against this doctrine that
your enemies fight the most ferociously.*

THEO.—You mean the Spiritualists ? I know; and many
are the absurd objections laboriously spun by them over
the pages of their journals. So obtuse and malicious are
some of them that they will stop at nothing. One of them
recently found a contradiction—which he gravely dis-
cusses in a letter to *Light*—in two statements picked out
of Mr. Sinnett's lectures. He discovers this grave contradiction in the two sentences: " Premature returns to earth-
life, in the cases when they occur, may be due to karmic
complication ;" and " There is no *accident* in the supreme
act of divine justice guiding evolution." So profound a
thinker would surely see a contradiction of the law of
gravitation if a man stretched out his hand to stop a falling stone from crushing the head of a child !

VIII.

ON REINCARNATION OR REBIRTH.

WHAT IS MEMORY ACCORDING TO THEOSOPHICAL
TEACHING?

INQ.—*The most difficult thing for you will be to explain*
and give reasonable grounds for such a belief. No Theoso-
phist has ever yet succeeded in bringing forward a single valid
proof to shake my skepticism. First of all, you have against
this theory of reincarnation the fact that no single man has yet
been found to remember that he has lived, least of all who he
was during his previous life.

THEO.—Your argument, I see, tends to the same old
objection: the loss of memory in each of us of our previous incarnation. You think it invalidates our doctrine?
My answer is that it does not; or that, at any rate, such
an objection cannot be final.

INQ.—*I should like to hear your arguments.*

THEO.—They are short and few. Yet when you take
into consideration the utter inability of the best modern
psychologists to explain to the world the nature of mind,
and their complete ignorance of its potentialities and higher
states, you have to admit that this objection is based on
an *a priori* conclusion drawn from *prima facie* and circum-

109

stantial evidence more than anything else. Now, what is memory in your conception, pray ?

INQ.—*That which the generally accepted definition explains : the faculty in our mind of remembering and of retaining the knowledge of previous thoughts, deeds, and events.*

THEO.—Please add to it that there is a great difference between the three accepted forms of memory. Besides memory in general you have *remembrance, recollection,* and *reminiscence,* have you not ? Have you ever thought over the difference ? Memory, remember, is a generic name.

INQ.—*Yet, all these are only synonyms.*

THEO.—Indeed, they are not—not in philosophy, at all events. Memory is simply an innate power in thinking beings, and even in animals, of reproducing past impressions by an association of ideas principally suggested by objective things or by some action on our external sensory organs. Memory is a faculty depending entirely on the more or less healthy and normal functioning of our physical brain; and *remembrance* and *recollection* are the attributes and handmaidens of this memory. But *reminiscence* is an entirely different thing. Reminiscence is defined by the modern psychologist as something intermediate between remembrance and recollection, or:

A conscious process of recalling past occurrences, but *without that full and varied reference* to particular things which characterizes *recollection.*

Locke, speaking of recollection and remembrance, says:

When an idea again recurs without the operation of the like object on the external sensory, it is *remembrance ;* if it be sought after by the mind, and with pain and endeavor found and brought again into view, it is *recollection.*

But even Locke leaves reminiscence without any clear definition, because it is no faculty or attribute of our *phys-*

ical memory, but an intuitional perception apart from and outside our physical brain; a perception which, being called into action by the ever-present knowledge of our spiritual Ego, covers all those visions in man which are regarded as abnormal—from the pictures suggested by genius to the ravings of fever and even madness—and are classed by science as having no existence outside of our fancy. Occultism and Theosophy, however, regard reminiscence in an entirely different light. For us, while memory is physical and evanescent, and depends on the physiological conditions of the brain—a fundamental proposition with all teachers of mnemonics, who have the researches of modern scientific psychologists to back them—reminiscence is the memory of the soul. And it is *this* memory which gives the assurance to almost every human being, whether he understands it or not, of his having lived before and having to live again. Indeed, as Wordsworth has it:

> Our birth is but a sleep and a forgetting;
> The Soul that rises with us, our life's Star,
> Hath had elsewhere its setting,
> And cometh from afar.

INQ.—*If it is on this kind of memory—poetry and abnormal fancies, on your own confession—that you base your doctrine, then you will convince very few, I am afraid.*

THEO.—I did not confess it was a fancy. I simply said that physiologists and scientists in general regard such reminiscences as hallucinations and fancy, to which "learned" conclusion they are welcome. We do not deny that such visions of the past and glimpses far back into the corridors of time are abnormal, as contrasted with our normal daily life experience and physical memory. But we do maintain, with Professor W. Knight, that "the absence of memory of any action done in a previous state cannot be a conclusive argument against our having lived through it." And every fair-minded opponent must agree with what is said in Butler's *Lectures on Platonic Philosophy,* " that the feeling of extravagance with which it [preëxistence] affects us has its secret source in materialistic or semi-materialistic prejudices." Besides which, we maintain that memory is, as Olympiodorus called it, simply "fantasy," * and the most unreliable thing in us. Ammonius Saccas asserted that the only faculty in man directly opposed to prognostication, or looking into futurity, is memory. Furthermore, remember that memory is one thing and mind or thought is another: memory is a recording machine, a register which very easily gets out of order; but thoughts are eternal and imperishable. Would you refuse to believe in the existence of certain things or men only because your physical eyes have not seen them? Would not the collective testimony of past generations who have seen Julius Cæsar be a sufficient guaranty that he once lived? Why should not the same testimony of the psychic senses of the masses be taken into consideration?

INQ.—*But do you not think that these are too fine distinctions to be accepted by the majority of mortals?*

THEO.—Say, rather, by the majority of materialists. And to them we say: Behold, even in the short span of ordinary existence memory is too weak to register all the events of a lifetime. How frequently do even most important events lie dormant in our memory until awakened by some association of ideas, or aroused to function and activity by some other link! This is especially the case

---

* "The fantasy," says Olympiodorus, in Plato's *Phædo,* "is an impediment to our intellectual conceptions; and hence, when we are agitated by the inspiring influence of the Divinity, if the fantasy intervenes, the enthusiastic energy ceases; for enthusiasm and the ecstasy are contrary to each other. Should it be asked whether the soul is able to energize without the fantasy, we reply that its perception of universals proves that it is able. It has perceptions, therefore, independent of the fantasy; at the same time, however, the fantasy attends in its energies, just as a storm pursues him who sails on the sea."

with people of advanced age, who are always found suffering from feebleness of recollection. When, then, we bear in mind what we know about the physical and the spiritual principles in man, it is not the fact that our memory has failed to record our precedent life and lives that ought to surprise us, but the contrary, were it to happen.

WHY DO WE NOT REMEMBER OUR PAST LIVES?

INQ.—*You have given me a bird's-eye view of the seven principles. How do you account for our complete loss of any recollection of having lived before, in the light of what you have said concerning these principles ?*

THEO.—Very easily. Those principles which we call physical * are disintegrated after death together with their constituent elements, and *memory* along with the brain. This vanished memory of a vanished personality can consequently neither remember nor record anything in the subsequent reincarnation of the Ego. Reincarnation means that the Ego will be furnished with a *new* body, a *new* brain, and a *new* memory. Therefore it would be as absurd to expect this new memory to remember that which it has never recorded as it would be to examine under a microscope a shirt which had never been worn by a murderer, and seek on it for the stains of blood which are to be found only on the clothes he has worn. It is not the clean shirt that we have to question, but the clothes worn during the perpetration of the crime; and if these are burned and destroyed, how can you get at them?

---

* Namely, the body, life, passional and animal instincts, and the astral *eidolon* of every man, whether perceived in thought or our mind's eye, or objectively and separate from the physical body; which principles we call Sthûla Sharîra, Prâna, Kâma Rûpa, and Linga Sharîra. None of these is denied by science, though it calls them by different names.

ˈINQ.—*Aye, how can you get at the certainty that the crime was ever committed at all, or that the man in the clean shirt ever lived before?*

THEO.—Not by physical processes, most assuredly, nor by relying on the testimony of that which exists no longer. But there is such a thing as circumstantial evidence, since our wise laws accept it, more, perhaps, even than they should. To get convinced of the fact of reincarnation and past lives, one must put one's self *en rapport* with one's real permanent Ego, not with one's evanescent memory.

INQ.—*But how can people believe in that which they do not know, nor have ever seen, far less put themselves en rapport with it?*

THEO.—If people, and they the most learned, will believe in the " gravity," " ether," " force," and what not of science—abstractions and working hypotheses which they have neither seen, touched, smelled, heard, nor tasted—why should not other people believe, on the same principle, in the permanent Ego, a far more logical and important " working hypothesis " than any other?

INQ.—*What is, finally, this mysterious eternal principle? Can you explain its nature so as to make it comprehensible to all?*

THEO.—The Ego which reincarnates is the individual—not personal—and immortal " I "; the vehicle, in short, of the Âtmâ-Buddhic monad; that which is rewarded in Devachan and punished on earth; and that, finally, to which the reflection only of the *skandhas*, or attributes,* of every incarnation attaches itself.

---

* There are five *skandhas*, or attributes, in the Buddhist teachings: " *rûpa* [form or body], material qualities; *vedana*, sensation; *sanna*, abstract ideas; *samkhara*, tendencies of mind; *vinnana*, mental powers. Of these we are formed; by them we are conscious of existence; and through them communicate with the world about us."

INQ.—*What do you mean by* skandhas?

THEO.—Just what I said—" attributes," among which is memory. All of these perish like a flower, leaving behind them only a feeble perfume. Here is another paragraph from Colonel H. S. Olcott's *Buddhist Catechism*,* which bears directly upon the subject. It deals with the question as follows:

> The aged man remembers the incidents of his youth, despite his being physically and mentally changed. Why, then, is not the recollection of past lives brought over by us from our last birth into the present birth?
>
> Because memory is included within the *skandhas*, and the *skandhas* having changed with the new existence, a memory, the record of that particular existence, develops. Yet the record or reflection of all the past lives must survive; for, when Prince Siddhartha became Buddha, the full sequence of his previous births was seen by him. . . . And any one who attains to the state of *jhana* can thus retrospectively trace the line of his lives.

This proves to you that while the undying qualities of the personality—such as love, goodness, charity, etc.—attach themselves to the immortal Ego, photographing on it, so to speak, a permanent image of the divine aspect of the man who was, his material *skandhas*—those which generate the most marked karmic effects—are as evanescent as a flash of lightning, and cannot impress the new brain of the new personality; yet their failing to do so impairs in no way the identity of the reincarnating Ego.

INQ.—*Do you mean to infer that that which survives is only the soul-memory, as you call it, that soul or Ego being one and the same, while nothing of the personality remains?*

THEO.—Not quite; something of each personality—unless the latter was an *absolute* materialist, with not even a

---

* By Henry S. Olcott, president and founder of the Theosophical Society. The accuracy of the teaching is sanctioned by the Rev. H. Sumangala, high priest of the Sripada and Galle, and principal of the Widyodaya Parivena (College) at Colombo, as being in agreement with the Canon of the Southern Buddhist Church.

chink in his nature for a spiritual ray to pass through—must survive, as it leaves its eternal impress on the incarnating permanent Self or spiritual Ego.* The personality, with its *skandhas*, is ever changing with every new birth. It is, as said before, only the part played by the actor, the true Ego, for one night. This is why we preserve no memory on the physical plane of our past lives, though the *real* Ego has lived them over and knows them all.

INQ.—*Then how does it happen that the real or spiritual man does not impress his new personal "I" with this knowledge?*

THEO.—How is it that the servant-girls in a poor farmhouse could speak Hebrew and play the violin in their trance or somnambulic state, and knew neither when in their normal condition? Because, as every genuine psychologist of the old—not your modern—school will tell you, the spiritual Ego can act only when the personal Ego is paralyzed. The spiritual " I " in man is omniscient and has every knowledge innate in it, while the personal self is the creature of its environment and the slave of the physical memory. Could the former manifest itself uninterruptedly and without impediment, there would be no longer men on earth, but we should all be Gods.

INQ.—*Still there ought to be exceptions, and some ought to remember.*

THEO.—And so they do. But who believes in their report? Such sensitives are generally regarded as hallucinated hysteriacs, as crack-brained enthusiasts or humbugs, by modern materialists. Let them read, however, works on this subject, preëminently *Reincarnation : A Study of For-*

---

* Or the spiritual in contradistinction to the personal self. The student must not confuse this spiritual Ego with the HIGHER SELF, which is Âtmâ, the God within us, and inseparable from the Universal Spirit. (See Section IX., "On Post-mortem and Postnatal Consciousness.")

gotten Truth, by E. D. Walker, F.T.S., and see in it the mass of proofs which the able author brings to bear on this vexed question. Speak to some people of soul, and they ask, What is soul? Have you ever proved its existence? Of course it is useless to argue with those who are materialists. But even to them I would put the question, Can you remember what you were or what you did when a baby? Have you preserved the smallest recollection of your life, thoughts, or deeds, or that you lived at all during the first eighteen months or two years of your existence? Then why not deny that you have ever lived as a babe, on the same principle? When to all this we add that the reincarnating Ego, or individuality, retains during the devachanic period merely the essence of the experience of its past earth-life or personality, the whole physical experience involving into a state of *in potentiâ*, or being, so to speak, translated into spiritual formulæ; when we remember, further, that the term between two rebirths is said to extend from ten to fifteen centuries—during which the physical consciousness is totally and absolutely inactive, having no organs to act through, and therefore no *existence*—the reason for the absence of all remembrance in the purely physical memory is apparent.

INQ.—*You just said that the spiritual Ego was omniscient. Where, then, is that vaunted omniscience during its devachanic life, as you call it?*

THEO.—During that time it is latent and potential, because, first of all, the spiritual Ego, the compound of Buddhi-Manas, is *not* the Higher Self, which, being one with the Universal Soul or Mind, is alone omniscient; and, secondly, because Devachan is the idealized continuation of the terrestrial life just left behind, a period of retributive adjustment, and a reward for unmerited wrongs and sufferings undergone in that special life. The spiritual Ego is

omniscient only potentially in Devachan; it enjoys actual
omniscience in Nirvâna alone, when the Ego is merged in
the Universal Mind-Soul. Nevertheless the Ego re-becomes
quasi-omniscient during those hours on earth when certain
abnormal conditions and physiological changes in the body
make it free from the trammels of matter. Thus the examples cited above of somnambulists—a poor servant speaking Hebrew, and another playing the violin—give you an
illustration of the case in point. This does not mean that
the explanations of these two facts offered us by medical
science have no truth in them, for one girl had, years before, heard her master, a clergyman, read Hebrew works
aloud, and the other had heard an artist playing a violin at
their farm. But neither could have done so as perfectly as
they did had they not been ensouled by *That* which, owing
to the sameness of its nature with the Universal Mind, is
omniscient. In the former case the higher principle acted
on the *skandhas* and moved them; in the latter, the personality being paralyzed, the individuality manifested itself.
Pray do not confuse the two.

ON INDIVIDUALITY AND PERSONALITY.

Inq.—*But what is the difference between the two? I confess that I am still in the dark.*

Theo.—In his *Buddhist Catechism*, Colonel Olcott, forced
by the logic of Esoteric Philosophy, found himself obliged
to correct the mistakes of previous Orientalists who made
no such distinction, and gives the reader his reasons for it
as follows:

The successive appearances upon one or many earths, or " descents
into generation," of the *tanhaically* coherent parts (*skandhas*) of a
certain being are a succession of personalities. In each birth the
personality differs from that of the previous or next succeeding birth.
Karma, the *deus ex machinâ*, masks (or, shall we say, reflects?)

itself now in the personality of a sage, again as an artisan, and so on throughout the string of births. But though personalities ever shift, the one line of life along which they are strung like beads runs unbroken; it is ever that *particular line*, never any other. It is therefore individual, an individual vital undulation, which began in Nirvâna, or the subjective side of Nature, as the light or heat undulation through ether began at its dynamic source; is careering through the objective side of Nature under the impulse of Karma and the creative direction of *tanha* [the unsatisfied desire for existence]; and leads through many cyclic changes back to Nirvâna. Mr. Rhys-Davids calls that which passes from personality to personality along the individual chain " character " or " doing." Since " character " is not a mere metaphysical abstraction, but the sum of one's mental qualities and moral propensities, would it not help to dispel what Mr. Rhys-Davids calls " the desperate expedient of a mystery " (*Buddhism*, p. 101), if we regarded the life-undulation as individuality, and each of its series of natal manifestations as a separate personality? The perfect individual, Buddhistically speaking, is a Buddha, I should say; for Buddha is but the rare flower of humanity, without the least supernatural admixture. And as countless generations (" four *asankheyyas* and a hundred thousand cycles "—Fausboll and Rhys-Davids's *Buddhist Birth-Stories*, p. 13) are required to develop a man into a Buddha, and *the iron will to become one runs throughout all the successive births*, what shall we call that which thus wills and perseveres? Character? or individuality—an individuality but partly manifested in any one birth, but built up of fragments from all the births?

I have long tried to impress this distinction between the individuality and personality on people's minds; but alas! it is harder with some than to make them feel a reverence for childish impossibilities, only because they are orthodox, and because orthodoxy is respectable. To understand the idea well, you have to first study the dual sets of principles: the *spiritual*, or those which belong to the imperishable Ego; and the *material*, or those principles which make up the ever-changing bodies or the series of personalities of that Ego. Let us fix permanent names to these, and say that:

I. Âtmâ, the Higher Self, is neither your spirit nor mine, but, like sunlight, shines on all. It is the universally diffused Divine Principle, and is inseparable from its one and absolute superspirit, as the sunbeam is inseparable from sunlight.

II.   Buddhi, the spiritual soul, is only its vehicle. Neither Âtmâ nor Buddhi separately, nor the two collectively, are of any more use to the body of man than sunlight and its beams are for a mass of granite buried in the earth, unless the divine duad is assimilated by, and reflected in, *some consciousness.*   Neither Âtmâ nor Buddhi is ever reached by Karma, because the former is the highest aspect of Karma, *the working agent* of *Itself* in one aspect, and the latter is unconscious *on this plane.*   This consciousness or mind is

III.   Manas,* the derivation or product, in a reflected form, of *ahamkâra,* "the conception of I" or "Egoship."   It is therefore, when inseparably united to the first two, called the spiritual Ego, and *taijasa,* the radiant.   This is the real individuality, or the divine man.   It is this Ego which—having originally incarnated in the senseless human form animated by, but unconscious of, the presence in itself of the dual monad, since it had no consciousness—made of that human-like form a real *man.*   It is this Ego, this "causal body," which overshadows every personality into which Karma forces it to incarnate. It is this Ego which is held responsible for all the sins committed through and in every new body or personality—the evanescent masks which hide the true individual through the long series of rebirths.

---

* *Mahat,* or the universal mind, is the source of Manas. The latter is *mahat,* i.e., mind in man. Manas is also called *kshetrajña,* embodied spirit, because it is, according to our philosophy, the *mânasa-putras,* or "sons of the universal mind," who created, or rather produced, the thinking man, *manu,* by incarnating in the third race mankind in our Round. It is Manas, therefore, which is the real incarnating and permanent spiritual Ego, the individuality, and our various and numberless personalities only its external masks.

INQ.—*But is this just? Why should this Ego receive punishment as the result of deeds which it has forgotten?*

THEO.—It has not forgotten them; it knows and remembers its misdeeds as well as you remember what you did yesterday. Is it because the memory of that bundle of physical compounds called "body" does not recollect what its predecessor, the personality *that was*, did, that you imagine that the real Ego has forgotten them? As well say it is unjust that the new coat on the back of a boy who is flogged for stealing apples should be punished for that of which it knows nothing.

INQ.—*But are there no modes of communication between the spiritual and human consciousness or memory?*

THEO.—Of course there are; but they have never been recognized by your modern scientific psychologists. To what do you attribute intuition, the "voice of conscience," premonitions, vague, undefined reminiscences, etc., if not to such communications? Would that the majority of educated men, at least, had the fine spiritual perceptions of Coleridge, who shows how intuitional he is in some of his comments. Hear what he says with respect to the probability that "all thoughts are in themselves imperishable":

If the intelligent faculty [sudden "revivals" of memory] should be rendered more comprehensive, it would require only a different and appropriate organization—the *body celestial* instead of the *body terrestrial* —to bring before every human soul *the collective experience of its whole past existence* [*existences*, rather].

And this *body celestial* is our mânasic Ego.

ON THE REWARD AND PUNISHMENT OF THE EGO.

INQ.—*I have heard you say that the Ego, whatever the life of the person he incarnated in may have been on earth, is never visited with post-mortem punishment.*

THEO.—Never, save in very exceptional and rare cases, of which we will not speak here, as the nature of the "punishment" in no way approaches any of your theological conceptions of damnation.

INQ.—*But if the Ego is punished in this life for the misdeeds committed in previous lives, then it ought to be rewarded also, whether here or when disincarnated.*

THEO.—And so it is. If we do not admit of any punishment outside of this earth, it is because the only state the spiritual Self knows of hereafter is that of unalloyed bliss.

INQ.—*What do you mean ?*

THEO.—Simply this: *crimes and sins committed on a plane of objectivity and in a world of matter cannot receive punishment in a world of pure subjectivity.* We believe in no hell or paradise as localities; in no objective hell-fires and worms that never die, nor in any Jerusalems with streets paved with sapphires and diamonds. What we believe in is a post-mortem state or mental condition such as we are in during a vivid dream. We believe in an immutable law of absolute Love, Justice, and Mercy. And believing in it, we say: Whatever was the sin and whatever were the dire results of the original karmic transgression of the now incarnated Egos,* no man—or the outer material and peri-

---

* It is on this transgression that the cruel and illogical dogma of the "fallen angels" has been built, which is explained in the second volume of *The Secret Doctrine.* All our Egos are thinking and rational entities (*mânasa-putras*) who had lived, whether under human or other forms, in the precedent life-cycle (*manvantara*), and whose Karma it was to incarnate in the *man* of this one. It was taught in the Mysteries that, having delayed in complying with this law (or having "refused to create," as

odical form of the spiritual entity—can be held, with any
degree of justice, responsible for the consequences of his
birth. He does not ask to be born, nor can he choose the
parents that will give him life. In every respect he is a
victim to his environment, the child of circumstances over
which he has no control; and if each of his transgressions
were impartially investigated, it would be found that in
nine out of every ten cases he was the one sinned against,
rather than the sinner. Life is at best a heartless play, a
stormy sea to cross, and a heavy burden often too difficult
to bear. The greatest philosophers have tried in vain to
fathom and find out its *raison d'être*, and—except those
who had the key to it, namely, the Eastern sages—have
all failed. Life is, as Shakespeare describes it:

> . . . but a walking shadow—a poor player,
> That struts and frets his hour upon the stage,
> And then is heard no more. It is a tale
> Told by an idiot, full of sound and fury,
> Signifying nothing—

nothing in its separate parts, yet of the greatest importance
in its collectivity or series of lives. In any case, almost
every individual life is, in its full development, a sorrow.
And are we to believe that poor helpless man, after being
tossed about like a piece of rotten timber on the angry bil-
lows of life, is, if he proves too weak to resist them, to be
punished by a sempiternity of damnation, or even a temporary punishment ? Never ! Whether a great or an average sinner, good or bad, guilty or innocent, once delivered
of the burden of physical life, the tired and worn-out *manu*,
or "thinking Ego," has won the right to a period of abso-

Hindûism says of the *kumâras* and Christian legend of the archangel Michael)—i.e.,
having failed to incarnate in due time—the bodies predestined for them became defiled.
Hence the original sin of the senseless forms and the punishment of the Egos. What
is meant by the rebellious angels being hurled down into hell is simply explained by
these pure spirits or Egos being imprisoned in bodies of unclean matter, flesh.

lute rest and bliss. The same unerringly wise and just,
rather than merciful, Law which inflicts upon the incarnated
Ego the karmic punishment for every sin committed during the preceding life on earth has provided for the now
disembodied entity a long lease of mental rest, and the entire oblivion of every sad event—aye, to the smallest painful thought—that took place in its last life as a personality,
leaving in the soul-memory nothing but the reminiscence
of that which was bliss, or which led to happiness. Plotinus, who said that our body was the true river of Lethe,
for "souls plunged into it forget all," meant more than he
said. For, as our terrestrial body on earth is like Lethe,
so is our *celestial body* in Devachan, and much more.

INQ.—*Then am I to understand that the murderer, the
transgressor of law divine and human in every shape, is allowed to go unpunished ?*

THEO.—Who ever said that ? Our philosophy has a
doctrine of punishment as stern as that of the most rigid
Calvinist, only far more philosophical and consistent with
absolute justice. No deed, no sinful thought even, will
go unpunished. In fact, the latter are even more severely
punished than the former, as a thought is far more potent
in creating evil results than deeds.* We believe in an unerring law of retribution, called Karma, which asserts itself
in a natural concatenation of causes and their unavoidable
results.

INQ.—*And how, or where, does it act ?*

THEO.—Every laborer is worthy of his hire, saith Wisdom in the gospel; every action, good or bad, is a prolific
parent, saith the Wisdom of the Ages. Put the two together and you will find the "why." After allowing the

---

* "But I say unto you, That whosoever looketh on a woman to lust after her hath
committed adultery with her already in his heart." (Matt. v. 28.)

soul, when escaped from the pangs of personal life, a sufficient—aye, a hundredfold—compensation, Karma, with its
army of *skandhas*, waits at the threshold of Devachan,
whence the Ego reëmerges to assume a new incarnation.
It is at this moment that thê future destiny of the now
rested Ego trembles in the scales of just retribution, as *it*
now falls once again under the sway of active karmic law.
It is in this rebirth which is ready for *it*—a rebirth selected
and prepared by this mysterious, inexorable, but, in the
equity and wisdom of its decrees, infallible Law—that the
sins of the previous life of the Ego are punished.   Only it
is into no imaginary hell, with theatrical flames and ridiculous tailed and horned devils, that the Ego is cast, but
verily onto this earth, the plane and region of his sins,
where he will have to atone for every bad thought and
deed.   As he has sown, so will he reap.   Reincarnation
will gather round him all those other Egos who have suffered, whether directly or indirectly, at the hands, or even
through the unconscious instrumentality, of the past personality.   They will be thrown by Nemesis in the way of the
new man, concealing the *old*, the eternal Ego, and . . .

INQ.—*But where is the equity you speak of, since these* new
*personalities are not aware of having sinned or been sinned
against ?*

THEO.—Has the coat torn to shreds from the back of the
man who stole it, by another man who was robbed of it
and recognizes his property, to be regarded as fairly dealt
with ?   The new personality is no better than a fresh suit
of clothes, with its specific characteristics, color, form, and
qualities; but the real man who wears it is the same cul-
prit as of old.   It is the individuality which suffers through
its personality.   And it is this, and this alone, that can account for the terrible *seeming* injustice in the distribution of
lots in life to man.   When your modern philosophers will

have succeeded in showing us good reason why so many apparently innocent and good men are born only to suffer during a whole lifetime; why so many are born poor unto starvation in the slums of great cities, abandoned by fate and men; why, while these are born in the gutter, others open their eyes to the light in palaces; why a noble birth and fortune seem often given to the worst of men and only rarely to the worthy; why there are beggars whose *inner* selves are peers to the highest and noblest of men—when this, and much more, is satisfactorily explained by either your philosophers or theologians, then only, but not till then, you will have the right to reject the theory of reincarnation. The highest and grandest poets have dimly perceived this truth of truths. Shelley believed in it; Shakespeare must have thought of it when writing on the worthlessness of birth. Remember his words:

> Why should my birth keep down my mounting spirit?
> Are not all creatures subject unto time?
> There's legions now of beggars on the earth,
> That their original did spring from kings,
> And many monarchs now, whose fathers were
> The riffraff of their age.

Alter the word "fathers" into Egos, and you will have the truth.

IX

ON KÂMALOKA AND DEVACHAN.

ON THE FATE OF THE LOWER PRINCIPLES.

INQ.—*You spoke of Kâmaloka; what is it?*

THEO.—When the man dies his three lower principles leave him forever—i.e., body, life, and the vehicle of the latter, the astral body or the double of the *living* man. And then his four principles—the central or middle principle (the animal soul or Kâma Rûpa), with what it has assimilated from the lower Manas and the higher triad—find themselves in Kâmaloka. The latter is an astral locality, the *limbus* of scholastic theology, the *hades* of the ancients, and, strictly speaking, a *locality* only in a relative sense. It has neither a definite area nor boundary, but exists *within* subjective space, i.e., ᴑ beyond our sensuous perceptions. Still it exists, and it is there that the astral *eidolons* of all the beings that have lived, animals included, await their "second death." For the animals it comes with the disintegration and the entire fading out of their *astral* particles to the last. For the human *eidolon* it begins when the Âtmâ-Buddhi-Mânasic triad is said to "separate" itself from its lower principles, or the reflection of the ex-personality, by falling into the devachanic state.

INQ.—*And what happens after this?*

THEO.—Then the kâma-rûpic phantom, remaining bereft of its informing, thinking principle, the higher Manas, and the lower aspect of the latter, the animal intelligence, no longer receiving light from the higher mind, and no longer having a physical brain to work through, collapses.

INQ.—*In what way ?*

THEO.—Well, it falls into the state of the frog when certain portions of its brain are taken out by the vivisector. It can think no more, even on the lowest animal plane. Henceforth it is no longer even the lower Manas, since this "lower" is nothing without the "higher."

INQ.—*And is it this nonentity which we find materializing in séance-rooms with mediums ?*

THEO.—It is this nonentity—a true nonentity, however, only as to reasoning or cogitating powers; still an *entity*, however astral and fluidic. This is shown in certain cases when this entity, being magnetically and unconsciously drawn toward a medium, is revived for a time and lives in him by proxy, so to speak. This "spook," or the Kâma Rûpa, may be compared with the jellyfish, which has an ethereal gelatinous appearance so long as it is in its own element, or water (the medium's specific *aura*); no sooner is it thrown out of the water, however, than it dissolves in the hand or on the sand, especially in sunlight. In the medium's aura it lives a kind of vicarious life, and reasons and speaks either through the medium's brain or those of other persons present. But this would lead us too far, and upon other people's grounds, whereon I have no desire to trespass. Let us keep to the subject of reincarnation.

INQ.—*What of the latter ?   How long does the incarnating Ego remain in the devachanic state ?*

THEO.—This, we are taught, depends on the degree of spirituality and the merit or demerit of the last incarnation. The average time is from ten to fifteen centuries, as I have already told you.

INQ.—*But why could not this Ego manifest and communicate with mortals as Spiritualists will have it? What is there to prevent a mother from communicating with the children she left on earth, a husband with his wife, and so on? It is a most consoling belief, I must confess; nor do I wonder that those who believe in it are so averse to give it up.*

THEO.—Nor are they forced to, unless they happen to prefer truth to fiction, however "consoling." Uncongenial our doctrines may be to Spiritualists; yet nothing of what we believe in and teach is half as selfish and cruel as what they preach.

INQ.—*I do not understand you. What is selfish?*

THEO.—Their doctrine of the return of spirits, the real "personalities," as they say; and I will tell you why. If Devachan—call it "paradise," if you like; a "place of bliss and of supreme felicity," if it is anything—is such a place, or say *state*, logic tells us that no sorrow, nor even a shade of pain, can be experienced therein. "God shall wipe away all tears" from the eyes of those in paradise, we read in the book of many promises. And if the "spirits of the dead" are able to return and see all that is going on on earth, and especially *in their homes*, what kind of bliss can be in store for them?

WHY THEOSOPHISTS DO NOT BELIEVE IN THE RETURN OF PURE "SPIRITS."

INQ.—*What do you mean? Why should this interfere with their bliss?*

THEO.—It is quite simple; let us take an instance. A mother dies, leaving behind her little helpless children

whom she adores; perhaps a beloved husband also. We
say that her spirit or Ego—that individuality which is now
wholly impregnated, for the entire devachanic period, with
the noblest feelings held by its late personality, with love
for her children, pity for those who suffer, and so on—is
now entirely separated from the "vale of tears"; that its
future bliss consists in the blessed ignorance of all the woes
it left behind. Spiritualists, on the contrary, say that it
is as vividly aware of them, *and more so than before*, for
"spirits see more than mortals in the flesh do." We say
that the bliss of the Devachanî consists in its complete conviction that it has never left the earth, and that there is no
such thing as death at all; that the post-mortem spiritual
consciousness of the mother will cause her to think that
she lives surrounded by her children and all those whom
she loved; that no gap, no link, will be missing to make
her disembodied state the most perfect and absolute happiness. The Spiritualists deny this point-blank. According
to their doctrine, unfortunate man is not liberated even by
death from the sorrows of this life. Not a drop from the
life-cup of pain and suffering will miss his lips; and *nolens
volens*, since he sees everything then, shall he drink it to the
bitter dregs. Thus the loving wife, who during her lifetime
was ready to save her husband sorrow at the price of her
heart's blood, is now doomed to see, in utter helplessness,
his despair, and to register every hot tear he sheds for her
loss. Worse than that, she may see the tears dry too soon,
and another beloved face smile on him, the father of her
children; find another woman replacing her in his affections; doomed to hear her children give the holy name of
"mother" to one indifferent to them, and to see those little
ones neglected, if not ill treated. According to this doctrine, the "gentle wafting to immortal life" becomes the
way into a new path of mental suffering without any tran-
sition. And yet the columns of the *Banner of Light*, the

veteran journal of the American Spiritualists, are filled with messages from the dead, the "dear departed ones," who all write to say how very *happy* they are ! Is such a state of knowledge consistent with bliss ? Then "bliss" stands, in such a case, for the greatest curse, and orthodox damnation must be a relief in comparison to it !

INQ.—*But how does your theory avoid this ?   How can you reconcile the theory of the soul's omniscience with its blindness to that which is taking place on earth ?*

THEO.—Because such is the law of love and mercy. During every devachanic period the Ego, omniscient as it is *per se*, clothes itself, so to say, with the *reflection* of the personality that was. I have just told you that the *ideal* efflorescence of all the abstract, and therefore undying and eternal, qualities or attributes—such as love and mercy, the love of the good, the true, and the beautiful—which ever spoke in the heart of the living personality, after death cling to the Ego, and therefore follow it into Devachan. For the time being, then, the Ego becomes the ideal reflection of the human being it was when last on earth, and *that* is not omniscient. Were it that, it would never be in the state we call Devachan at all.

INQ.—*What are your reasons for it ?*

THEO.—If you want an answer on the strict lines of our philosophy, then I would say that it is because everything is "illusion" (*mâyâ*) outside of eternal truth, which has neither form, color, nor limitation. He who has placed himself beyond the veil of *mâyâ*—and such are the highest Adepts and Initiates—can have no Devachan. As to the ordinary mortal, his bliss in Devachan is complete. It is an *absolute* oblivion of all that gave it pain or sorrow in the past incarnation, and even oblivion of the fact that such things as pain or sorrow exist at all. The Devachani lives its intermediate cycle between two incarnations surrounded by everything it had aspired to in vain, and in the companionship of every one it loved on earth. It has reached the fulfilment of all its soul-yearnings. And thus it lives throughout long centuries an existence of *unalloyed* happiness, which is the reward for its sufferings in earth-life. In short, it bathes in a sea of uninterrupted felicity spanned only by events of still greater felicity in degree.

INQ.—*But this is more than simple delusion; it is an existence of insane hallucinations !*

THEO.—From your standpoint it may be; not so from that of philosophy. Besides, is not our whole terrestrial life filled with such delusions? Have you never met men and women living for years in a fools' paradise? And because you should happen to learn that the husband whom a wife adores, and believes herself loved in turn by him, is untrue to her, would you go and break her heart and beautiful dream by rudely awakening her to the reality? I think not. I say it again, such oblivion and hallucination, if you call it so, is only a merciful law of Nature and strict justice. At any rate, it is a far more fascinating prospect than the orthodox golden harp with a pair of wings. The assurance that "the soul that lives ascends frequently and runs familiarly through the streets of the heavenly Jerusalem, visiting the patriarchs and prophets, saluting the apostles, and admiring the army of martyrs," may seem of a more pious character to some. Nevertheless it is an hallucination of a far more delusive character, since mothers love their children with an immortal love, we all know, while the personages mentioned in the "heavenly Jerusalem" are still of a rather doubtful nature. But I would still rather accept the "new Jerusalem," with its streets paved like the show-windows of a jeweler's shop, than find consolation in the heartless doctrine of the Spiritualists. The idea alone that the *intellectual conscious souls* of one's father, mother, daughter, or brother find their bliss in a "summer-land"—only a little more natural, but just as ridiculous as the "new Jerusalem" in its description—would be enough to make one lose every respect for one's "departed ones." To believe that a pure spirit can feel happy while doomed to witness the sins, mistakes, treachery, and, above all, the sufferings of those from whom it is severed by death, and whom it loves best, without being able to help them, would be a maddening thought.

INQ.—*There is something in your argument. I confess to having never seen it in this light.*

THEO.—Just so; and one must be selfish to the core, and utterly devoid of the sense of retributive justice, to have ever imagined such a thing. We are with those whom we have lost in material form, and far, far nearer to them now than when they were alive. And it is not only in the fancy of the Devachanî, as some may imagine, but in reality. For pure divine love is not merely the blossom of a human heart, but has its roots in eternity. Spiritual holy love is immortal, and Karma sooner or later brings all those who loved each other with such a spiritual affection to incarnate once more in the same family group. Again we say that love beyond the grave, illusion though you may call it, has a magic and divine potency which reacts on the living. A mother's Ego filled with love for the imaginary children it sees near itself, living a life of happiness as real to *it* as when on earth, will ever cause that love to be felt by the children in flesh. It will manifest in their dreams, and often in various events—in " providential " protections and escapes; for love is a strong shield, and is not limited by space or time. As with this devachanic "mother," so with the rest of human relationships and attachments, save the purely selfish or material. Analogy will suggest to you the rest.

INQ.—*In no case, then, do you admit the possibility of the communication of the living with the* disembodied *spirit?*

THEO.—Yes; there are even two exceptions to the rule. The first case is during the few days that immediately follow the death of a person, and before the Ego passes into the devachanic state. But whether any living mortal has derived much benefit from the return of the spirit into the *objective* plane is another question. Perhaps it may be so in a few exceptional cases, when the intensity of the desire in the dying person to return for some purpose forced the higher consciousness *to remain awake,* and therefore it was really the *individuality,* the "spirit," that communicated. But in general the spirit is dazed after death, and falls very soon into what we call "pre-devachanic unconsciousness." The second exception is found in the *nirmânakâyas.*

INQ.—*What of them? What does the name signify for you?*

THEO.—It is the name given to those who, though they have won the right to Nirvâna and cyclic Rest,* yet, out of pity for mankind and those they have left on earth, renounce this nirvânic state. Such an Adept, or saint, or whatever you may call him, believing it a selfish act to rest in bliss while mankind groans under the burden of misery produced by ignorance, renounces Nirvâna, and determines to remain invisible *in spirit* on this earth. *Nirmânakâyas* have no material body, for they have left it behind; but otherwise they remain with all their principles, even *in astral life,* in our sphere. And such can and do communicate with a few elect ones, but surely not with ordinary mediums.

INQ.—*I have put you the question about* nirmânakâyas *because I read in some German and other works that it was the*

---

* *Not* Devachan, as the latter is an illusion of our consciousness, a happy dream, and as those who are fit for Nirvâna must have lost entirely every desire or possibility of desire for the world's illusions.

name given in Northern Buddhistic teachings to the terrestrial appearances or bodies assumed by Buddhas.

THEO.—This is so, only the Orientalists have confused this "terrestrial" body by understanding it to be objective and physical instead of purely astral and subjective.

INQ.—*And what good can these* nirmânakâyas *do on earth ?*

THEO.—Not much, as regards individuals, as they have no right to interfere with Karma, and can only advise and inspire mortals for the general good. Yet they do more beneficent actions than you imagine.

INQ.—*To this science would never subscribe, not even modern psychology. For science and psychology, no portion of intelligence can survive the physical brain. What would you answer to this ?*

THEO.—I would not even go to the trouble of answering, but would simply say, in the words given to " M.A. Oxon." :

Intelligence *is* perpetuated after the body is dead. Though it is not a question of the brain only. . . . It is reasonable to propound the indestructibility of the human spirit from what we know.*

INQ.—*But " M.A. Oxon." is a Spiritualist ?*

THEO.—Quite so, and the only true Spiritualist I know of, though we may still disagree from him on many a minor question. Apart from this, no Spiritualist comes nearer to the occult truths than he does. Like any one of us, he speaks incessantly " of the surface dangers that beset the ill-equipped, feather-headed muddler with the occult, who crosses the threshold without counting the cost." † Our only disagreement rests in the question of " spirit identity." Otherwise I, for one, almost entirely agree with him, and accept the three propositions he embodied in his address

---

* *Spirit Identity*, p. 69.
† " Some things that I *do* know of Spiritualism, and some that I do *not*."

of July, 1884. It is this eminent Spiritualist, rather, who disagrees from us, not we from him.

INQ.—*What were these propositions?*

THEO.—They are as follows:

1. That there is a life coincident with, and independent of, the physical life of the body.
2. That, as a necessary corollary, this life extends beyond the life of the body. [We say it extends throughout Devachan.]
3. That there is communication between the denizens of that state of existence and those of the world in which we now live.

All depends, you see, on the minor and secondary aspects of these fundamental propositions. Everything depends on the views we take of spirit and soul, or *individuality* and *personality*. Spiritualists confuse the two "into one"; we separate them, and say that, with the exceptions above enumerated, no spirit will revisit the earth, though the animal soul may. But let us return once more to our direct subject, the *skandhas*.

INQ.—*I begin to understand better now. It is the spirit, so to say, of those* skandhas *that are the most ennobling, which, attaching itself to the incarnating Ego, survives, and is added to the stock of its angelic experiences. And it is the attributes connected with the material* skandhas, *with selfish and personal motives, which, disappearing from the field of action between two incarnations, reappear at the subsequent incarnation as karmic results to be atoned for; and therefore the spirit will not leave Devachan. Is it so?*

THEO.—Very nearly so. If you add to this that the law of retribution, or Karma, rewarding the highest and most spiritual attributes in Devachan, never fails to reward them again on earth by giving them a further development, and by furnishing the Ego with a body fitted for it, then you will be quite correct.

A FEW WORDS ABOUT THE SKANDHAS.

INQ.—*What becomes of the other, the lower skandhas of the personality, after the death of the body? Are they quite destroyed?*

THEO.—They are and yet they are not—a fresh metaphysical and occult mystery for you. They are destroyed as the working stock in hand of the personality; they remain as *karmic effects*, as germs, hanging in the atmosphere of the terrestrial plane, ready to come to life, as so many avenging fiends, to attach themselves to the new personality of the Ego when it reincarnates.

INQ.—*This really passes my comprehension, and is very difficult to understand.*

THEO.—Not once that you have assimilated all the details. For then you will see that for logic, consistency, profound philosophy, divine mercy, and equity, this doctrine of reincarnation has not its equal on earth. It is a belief in a perpetual progress for each incarnating Ego, or divine soul, in an evolution from the outward into the inward, from the material to the spiritual, arriving at the end of each stage at absolute unity with the Divine Principle. From strength to strength, from the beauty and perfection of one plane to the greater beauty and perfection of another, with accessions of new glory, of fresh knowledge and power, in each cycle—such is the destiny of every Ego, which thus becomes its own savior in each world and incarnation.

INQ.—*But Christianity teaches the same. It also preaches progression.*

THEO.—Yes, only with the addition of something else. It tells us of the *impossibility* of attaining salvation without the aid of a miraculous savior, and, moreover, dooms to perdition all those who will not accept the dogma. This is just

the difference between Christian theology and Theosophy.
The former enforces belief in the descent of the spiritual
Ego into the lower *self;* the latter inculcates the necessity
of endeavoring to elevate one's self to the Christos or
Buddhi state.

INQ.—*By teaching the annihilation of consciousness in case
of failure, however, do you not think that this amounts to the
annihilation of* self, *in the opinion of the non-metaphysical?*

THEO.—From the standpoint of those who believe in
the resurrection of the body literally, and insist that every
bone, every artery and atom of flesh will be raised bodily
on the judgment-day, of course it does. If you still insist
that it is the perishable form and finite qualities that make
up *immortal* man, then we shall hardly understand each
other. And if you do not understand that, by limiting the
existence of every Ego to one life on earth, you make of
Deity an ever-drunken Indra of the Paurânic dead letter,
a cruel Moloch, a god who makes an inextricable mess on
earth, and yet claims thanks for it, then the sooner we drop
the conversation the better.

INQ.—*But let us return, now that the subject of the* skandhas *is disposed of, to the question of the consciousness which
survives death. This is the point which interests most people.
Do we possess more knowledge in Devachan than we do in
earth-life?*

THEO.—In one sense we can acquire more knowledge—
that is, we can develop further any faculty which we loved
and strove after during life, provided it is concerned with
abstract and ideal things, such as music, painting, poetry,
etc., since Devachan is merely an idealized and subjective
continuation of earth-life.

INQ.—*But if in Devachan the spirit is free from matter,
why should it not possess all knowledge?*

THEO.—Because, as I told you, the Ego is, so to say, wedded to the memory of its last incarnation. Thus, if you think over what I have said, and string all the facts together, you will realize that the devachanic state is not one of omniscience, but a transcendental continuation of the personal life just terminated. It is the rest of the soul from the toils of life.

INQ.—*But the scientific materialists assert that after the death of man nothing remains; that the human body simply disintegrates into its component elements; and that what we call soul is merely a temporary self-consciousness produced as a by-product of organic action, which will evaporate like steam. Is not theirs a strange state of mind?*

THEO.—Not at all strange, as far as I see. If they say that self-consciousness ceases with the body, then in their case they simply utter an unconscious prophecy; for once they are firmly convinced of what they assert, no conscious after-life is possible for them. For there *are* exceptions to every rule.

ON POST-MORTEM AND POSTNATAL CONSCIOUS-NESS.*

INQ.—*But if human self-consciousness survives death as a rule, why should there be exceptions?*

THEO.—In the fundamental principles of the spiritual world no exception is possible. But there are rules for those who see, and rules for those who prefer to remain blind.

INQ.—*Quite so, I understand. This is but an aberration of the blind man, who denies the existence of the sun because*

---

* A few portions of this chapter and of the preceding were published in *Lucifer* in the shape of a " Dialogue on the Mysteries of the After-life," in the January number, 1889. The article was unsigned, as if it were written by the editor, but it came from the pen of the author of the present volume.

he does not see it. But after death his spiritual eyes will certainly compel him to see. Is this what you mean ?

THEO.—He will not be compelled, nor will he see anything. Having persistently during life denied the continuance of existence after death, he will be unable to see it, because his spiritual capacity, having been stunted in life, cannot develop after death, and he will remain blind. By insisting that he *must* see it, you evidently mean one thing and I another. You speak of the spirit from the Spirit, or the flame from the Flame—of Âtmâ, in short—and you confuse it with the human soul, Manas. . . . You do not understand me; let me try to make it clear. The whole gist of your question is to know whether, in the case of a downright materialist, the complete loss of self-consciousness and self-perception after death is possible. Is it not so? I answer, it is possible. Believing firmly in our Esoteric Doctrine—which refers to the post-mortem period, or the interval between two lives or births, as merely a transitory state—I say that whether that post-mortem interval between two acts of the illusionary drama of life lasts one year or a million, it may, without any breach of the fundamental law, prove to be just the same state as that of a man in a dead faint.

INQ.—*But since you have just said that the fundamental law of the after-death state admits of no exceptions, how can this be ?*

THEO.—Nor do I say now that it does admit of an exception. But the spiritual law of continuity applies only to things which are truly real. To one who has read and understood *Mundaka Upanishad* and *Vedânta Sâra* all this becomes very clear. I will say more: it is sufficient only to understand what we mean by Buddhi and the duality of Manas to gain a clear perception why the materialist may fail to have a self-conscious survival after death. ¬Since

Manas, in its lower aspect, is the seat of the terrestrial mind, it can therefore give only that perception of the universe which is based on the evidence of that mind; it cannot give spiritual vision. It is said in the Eastern school that between Buddhi and Manas, the Ego, or Îshvara and Prajñâ,* there is in reality no more difference than between a forest and its trees, a lake and its waters, as the *Mundaka* teaches. One or a hundred trees dead from loss of vitality, or uprooted, are yet incapable of preventing the forest from being still a forest.

INQ.—*But, as I understand it, Buddhi represents in this simile the forest, and Manas-Taijasa † the trees. And if Buddhi is immortal, how can that which is similar to it—i.e., Manas-Taijasa—entirely lose its consciousness till the day of its new incarnation ? I cannot understand it.*

THEO.—You cannot because you will mix up an abstract representation of the whole with its casual changes of form. Remember that if it can be said of Buddhi-Manas that it is unconditionally immortal, the same cannot be said of the lower Manas, still less of Taijasa, which is merely an attribute. Neither of these—neither Manas nor Taijasa—can exist apart from Buddhi, the divine soul, because the first (Manas) is, in its lower aspect, a qualificative attribute of the terrestrial personality, and the second (Taijasa) is identical with the first, because it is the same Manas, only with the light of Buddhi reflected in it. In its turn, Buddhi would remain only an impersonal spirit without this element which it borrows from the human soul, which conditions

---

* Îshvara is the collective consciousness of the manifested deity, Brahmâ—i e., the collective consciousness of the Host of Dhyân Chohans of *The Secret Doctrine;* and Prajñâ is their individual wisdom.

† Taijasa means the radiant in consequence of its union with Buddhi—i e , Manas, the human soul, illuminated by the radiance of the divine soul. Therefore Manas-Taijasa may be described as radiant mind, the *human* reason lit by the light of the spirit; and Buddhi-Manas is the revelation of the divine plus human intellect and self-consciousness.

and makes of it, in this illusive universe, *as it were something separate* from the universal soul for the whole period of the cycle of incarnation. Say, rather, that Buddhi-Manas can neither die nor lose its united self-consciousness in eternity, nor the recollection of the previous incarnations in which the two—i.e., the spiritual and the human soul—had been closely linked together. But it is not so in the case of a materialist, whose human soul not only receives nothing from the divine soul, but even refuses to recognize its existence. You can hardly apply this axiom to the attributes and qualifications of the human soul, for it would be like saying that because your divine soul is immortal therefore the bloom on your cheek must also be immortal, whereas this bloom, like Taijasa, is simply a transitory phenomenon.

INQ.—*Do I understand you to say that we must not confuse in our minds the noumenon with the phenomenon, the cause with its effect?*

THEO.—I do say so, and repeat that, limited to Manas or the human soul alone, the radiance of Taijasa itself becomes a mere question of time, because both immortality and consciousness after death become, for the terrestrial personality of man, simply conditioned attributes, as they depend entirely on conditions and beliefs created by the human soul itself during the life of its body. Karma acts incessantly; we reap *in our after-life* only the fruit of that which we have ourselves sown in this.

INQ.—*But if my Ego can, after the destruction of my body, become plunged in a state of entire unconsciousness, then where can be the punishment for the sins of my past life?*

THEO.—Our philosophy teaches that karmic punishment reaches the Ego only in its next incarnation. After death it receives only the reward for the unmerited sufferings endured during its past incarnation.* The whole punishment after death, even for the materialist, consists, therefore, in the absence of any reward, and the utter loss of the consciousness of one's bliss and rest. Karma is the child of the terrestrial Ego, the fruit of the actions of the tree which is the objective personality visible to all, as much as the fruit of all the thoughts and even motives of the spiritual " I "; but Karma is also the tender mother who heals the wounds inflicted by her during the preceding life before she begins to torture the Ego by inflicting new wounds. If it may be said that there is not a mental or physical suffering in the life of a mortal which is not the direct fruit and consequence of some sin in a preceding existence, on the other hand, since the man does not preserve the slightest recollection of it in his actual life, feels himself not deserving of such punishment, and therefore thinks he suffers for no guilt of his own, he is thus sufficiently entitled to the fullest consolation, rest, and bliss in his post-mortem existence. Death ever comes to our spiritual selves as a deliverer and friend. For the materialist who, notwithstanding his materialism, was not a bad man, the interval between the two lives will be like the unbroken and placid sleep of a child—either entirely dreamless, or filled with pictures of which he will have no definite perception; while for the average mortal it will be a dream as vivid as life, and full of realistic bliss and visions.

INQ.—*Then the personal man must always go on suffering* blindly *the karmic penalties which the Ego has incurred?*

---

* Some Theosophists have taken exception to this phrase, but the words are those of Master, and the meaning attached to the word "unmerited" is that given above In the *Theosophical Siftings*, vol. i., No. 6, a phrase, criticized subsequently in *Lucifer*, was used which was intended to convey the same idea. In form, however, it was awkward and open to the criticism directed against it; but the essential idea was that men often suffer from the effects of the actions done by others, effects which thus do not strictly belong to their own Karma; and for these sufferings they of course deserve compensation.

THEO.—Not quite so. At the solemn moment of death every man, even when death is sudden, sees the whole of his past life marshaled before him in its minutest details. For one short instant the *personal* becomes one with the *individual* and all-knowing Ego. But this instant is enough to show him the whole chain of causes which have been at work during his life. He sees and now understands himself as he is, unadorned by flattery or self-deception. He reads his life, remaining as a spectator looking down into the arena he is quitting; he feels and knows the justice of all the suffering that has overtaken him.

INQ.—*Does this happen to every one ?*

THEO.—Without any exception. Very good and holy men see, we are taught, not only the life they are leaving, but even several preceding lives in which were produced the causes that made them what they were in the life just closing. They recognize the law of Karma in all its majesty and justice.

INQ.—*Is there anything corresponding to this before re-birth ?*

THEO.—There is. As the man at the moment of death has a retrospective insight into the life he has led, so, at the moment he is reborn onto earth, the Ego, awaking from the state of Devachan, has a prospective vision of the life which awaits him, and realizes all the causes that have led to it. He realizes them, and sees futurity, because it is between Devachan and rebirth that the Ego regains his full mânasic consciousness, and rebecomes for a short time the god he was, before, in compliance with karmic law, he first descended into matter and incarnated in the first man of flesh. The "golden thread" sees all its "pearls" and misses not one of them.

WHAT IS REALLY MEANT BY ANNIHILATION.

INQ.—*I have heard some Theosophists speak of a golden thread on which their lives were strung. What do they mean by this?*

THEO.—In the Hindû sacred books it is said that that which undergoes periodical incarnation is the *sûtrâtmâ*, which means literally the "thread soul." It is a synonym of the reincarnating Ego—Manas conjoined with Buddhi —which absorbs the mânasic recollections of all our preceding lives. It is so called because, like the pearls on a thread, so is the long series of human lives strung together on that one thread. In one of the Upanishads these recurrent rebirths are likened to the life of a mortal which oscillates periodically between sleep and waking.

INQ.—*This, I must say, does not seem very clear, and I will tell you why. For the man who awakes, another day commences, but he is the same in soul and body as he was the day before ; whereas at every incarnation a full change takes place not only of the external envelope, sex, and personality, but even of the mental and psychic capacities. The simile does not seem to me quite correct. The man who arises from sleep remembers quite clearly what he has done yesterday, the day before, and even months and years ago. But none of us has the slightest recollection of a preceding life or of any fact or event concerning it. I may forget in the morning what I have dreamed during the night; still I know that I have slept, and have the certainty that I lived during sleep ; but what recollection can I have of my past incarnation until the moment of death ? How do you reconcile this ?*

THEO.—Some people do recollect their past incarnations during life ; but these are Buddhas and Initiates. This is what the Yogîs call *samma sambuddha*, or the knowledge of the whole series of one's past incarnations.

INQ.—*But we ordinary mortals who have not reached* samma sambuddha, *how are we to understand this simile ?*

THEO.—By studying it and trying to understand more correctly the three kinds and characteristics of sleep. Sleep is a general and immutable law for man as for beast, but there are different kinds of sleep and still more different dreams and visions.

INQ.—*But this takes us to another subject. Let us return to the materialist who, though not denying dreams—for he could hardly do so—yet denies immortality in general and the survival of his own individuality.*

THEO.—And the materialist, without knowing it, is right. In one who has no inner perception of and faith in the immortality of his soul, that soul can never become Buddhi-Taijasa, but will remain simply Manas, and for Manas alone there is no immortality possible. In order to live a conscious life in the world to come, one has first of all to believe in that life during terrestrial existence. On these two aphorisms of the Secret Science all the philosophy as to post-mortem consciousness and the immortality of the soul is built. The Ego receives always according to its deserts. After the dissolution of the body there commences for it a period of full awakened consciousness, or a state of chaotic dreams, or an utterly dreamless sleep undistinguishable from annihilation; and these are the three kinds of sleep. If our physiologists find the cause of dreams and visions in an unconscious preparation for them during the waking hours, why cannot the same be admitted for the post-mortem dreams ? I repeat it: *death is sleep.* After death, before the spiritual eyes of the soul, begins a performance according to a program learned and very often unconsciously composed by ourselves: the practical carrying out of *correct* beliefs or of illusions which have been created by ourselves. The Methodist will be a Methodist, the Mussulman a Mussulman, at least for some time, in a perfect fools' paradise of each man's creation and making. These are the post-mortem fruits of the tree of life. Naturally our belief or unbelief in the fact of conscious immortality is unable to influence the unconditioned reality of the fact itself, once that it exists; but the belief or unbelief in that immortality as the property of independent or separate entities cannot fail to give color to that fact in its application to each of these entities. Now do you begin to understand it?

INQ.—*I think I do. The materialists, disbelieving in everything that cannot be proven to them by their five senses, or by scientific reasoning based exclusively on the data furnished by these senses, in spite of their inadequacy, and rejecting every spiritual manifestation, accept life as the only conscious existence. Therefore according to their beliefs so will it be unto them. They will lose their personal Ego, and will plunge into a dreamless sleep until a new awakening. Is it so?*

THEO.—Almost so. Remember the practically universal teaching of the two kinds of conscious existence—the terrestrial and the spiritual. The latter must be considered real from the very fact that it is inhabited by the eternal, changeless, and immortal Monad; whereas the incarnating Ego dresses itself up in new garments which are entirely different from those of its previous incarnations, and in which all except its spiritual prototype is doomed to a change so radical as to leave no trace behind.

INQ.—*How so? Can my conscious terrestrial "I" perish not only for a time, like the consciousness of the materialist, but so entirely as to leave no trace behind?*

THEO.—According to the teaching, it must so perish and in its entirety, all except the principle which, by uniting itself with the Monad, thereby becomes a purely spiritual and indestructible essence, one with it in the eternity.

But in the case of an out-and-out materialist, in whose personal "I" no Buddhi has ever reflected itself, how can that Buddhi carry away into the eternity one particle of that terrestrial personality? Your spiritual "I" is immortal; but from your present self it can carry away into eternity only that which has become worthy of immortality— namely, the simple aroma of the flower that has been mown down by death.

INQ.—*Well, and the flower, the terrestrial "I"?*

THEO.—The flower, as all past and future flowers which have blossomed and will have to blossom on the mother-bough—the *sûtrâtmâ*, all children of one root or Buddhi —will return to dust. Your present "I," as you yourself know, is not the body now sitting before me, nor yet is it what I would call Manas-Sûtrâtmâ, but Sûtrâtmâ-Buddhi.

INQ.—*But this does not explain to me at all why you call life after death immortal, infinite, and real, and the terrestrial life a simple phantom or illusion; since even that post-mortem life has limits, however much wider they may be than those of terrestrial life.*

THEO.—No doubt. The spiritual Ego of man moves in eternity like a pendulum between the hours of birth and death. But if these hours, marking the periods of life terrestrial and life spiritual, are limited in their duration, and if even the very number of such stages in eternity between sleep and awakening, illusion and reality, is also limited, on the other hand the spiritual pilgrim is eternal. And so the only reality in our conception is the hours of man's post-mortem life, when, disembodied—during the period of that pilgrimage which we call "the cycle of rebirths"— he stands face to face with truth, and not the mirages of his transitory earthly existences. Such intervals, however, their limitation notwithstanding, do not prevent the Ego, while ever perfecting itself, from following undeviatingly, though gradually and slowly, the path to its last transformation, when, having reached its goal, it becomes a divine being. These intervals and stages help toward this final result instead of hindering it; and without such limited intervals the divine Ego could never reach its ultimate goal. I have given you once already a familiar illustration by comparing the Ego, or the individuality, to an actor, and its numerous and various incarnations to the parts it plays. Will you call these parts or their costumes the individuality of the actor himself? Like that actor, the Ego is forced, during the cycle of necessity, which continues up to the very threshold of *paranirvâna*, to play many parts which may be unpleasant to it. But as the bee collects its honey from every flower, leaving the rest as food for the earthly worms, so does our spiritual individuality, whether we call it *sûtrâtmâ* or Ego. Collecting from every terrestrial personality into which Karma forces it to incarnate the nectar alone of the spiritual qualities and self-consciousness, it unites all these into one whole, and emerges from its chrysalis as the glorified Dhyân Chohan. So much the worse for those terrestrial personalities from which it could collect nothing. Such personalities assuredly cannot consciously outlive their terrestrial existence.

INQ.—*Thus, then, it seems that, for the terrestrial personality, immortality is still conditional. Is, then, immortality itself not unconditional?*

THEO.—Not at all. But immortality cannot touch the non-existent; for all that which exists as *sat*, or emanates from *sat*, immortality and eternity are absolute. Matter is the opposite pole of spirit, and yet the two are one. The essence of all this—i.e., spirit, force, and matter, or the three in one—is as endless as it is beginningless; but the form acquired by this triple unity during its incarnations, its externality, is certainly only the illusion of our personal conceptions. Therefore do we call Nirvâna and the universal life alone a reality, relegating the terrestrial life, its terrestrial personality included, and even its devachanic existence, to the phantom realm of illusion.

INQ.—*But why in such a case call sleep the reality, and waking the illusion ?*

THEO.—It is simply a comparison made to facilitate the grasping of the subject, and from the standpoint of terrestrial conceptions it is a very correct one.

INQ.—*And still I cannot understand, if the life to come is based on justice and merited retribution for all our terrestrial suffering, how in the case of materialists, many of whom are really honest and charitable men, there should remain of their personality nothing but the refuse of a faded flower.*

THEO.—Such a thing was never stated. No materialist, however unbelieving, can die forever in the fullness of his spiritual individuality. What was said is that consciousness can disappear either fully or partially in the case of a materialist, so that no conscious remains of his personality survive.

INQ.—*But surely this is annihilation ?*

THEO.—Certainly not. One can sleep a dead sleep and miss several stations during a long railway journey, without the slightest recollection or consciousness, and awake at another station and continue the journey past innumerable other halting-places till the end of the journey or the goal is reached. Three kinds of sleep were mentioned to you—the dreamless, the chaotic, and the one which is so real that dreams become full realities to the sleeper. If you believe in the latter, why can you not believe in the former? According to the after-life a man has believed in and expected, such is the life he will have. He who expected no

life to come will have an absolute blank, amounting to annihilation, in the interval between the two births. This is
just the carrying out of the program we spoke of—a program created by the materialists themselves. But there are
various kinds of materialists, as you say. A selfish, wicked
egoist, one who never shed a tear for any one but himself,
thus adding entire indifference to the whole world to his
unbelief, must, at the threshold of death, drop his personality forever. This personality having no tendrils of sympathy for the world around, and hence nothing to attach
it to *sûtrâtmâ*, it follows that with the last breath every
connection between the two is broken. There being no
Devachan for such a materialist, the *sûtrâtmâ* will reincar-
nate almost immediately. But those materialists who erred
in nothing but their disbelief will oversleep but one station.
And the time will come when such ex-materialists will perceive themselves in the eternity, and perhaps repent that
they lost even one day, one station, from the life eternal.

INQ.—*Still would it not be more correct to say that death
is birth into a new life, or a return once more into eternity?*

THEO.—You may if you like. Only remember that births
differ, and that there are births of still-born beings, which
are failures of nature. Moreover, with your fixed Western
ideas about material life, the words "living" and "being"
are quite inapplicable to the pure subjective state of post-
mortem existence. Save in a few philosophers who are not
read by the many, and who themselves are too confused to
present a distinct picture of it, your Western ideas of life
and death have become so narrow that on the one hand
they have led to crass materialism, and on the other to
the still more material conception of the other life which
the Spiritualists have formulated in their "summer-land."
There the souls of men eat, drink, marry, and live in a
paradise quite as sensual as that of Mohammed, and even

less philosophical.   Nor are the average conceptions of the
uneducated Christians any better; if possible, they are still
more material.   What between truncated angels, brass trum-
pets, golden harps, and material hell-fires, the Christian
heaven seems like a fairy scene at a Christmas pantomime.

It is because of these narrow conceptions that you find
such difficulty in understanding.   It is just because the life
of the disembodied soul, while possessing all the vividness
of reality, as in certain dreams, is devoid of every grossly
objective form of terrestrial life that the Eastern philosophers have compared it with visions of sleep.

DEFINITE WORDS FOR DEFINITE THINGS.

INQ.—*Do you not think that it is because there are no definite and fixed terms to indicate each "principle" in man, that
such a confusion of ideas arises in our minds with respect to
the respective functions of these principles?*

THEO.—I have thought of this myself.   The whole trouble
has arisen from our having begun with Sanskrit names in
our expositions of and discussion about the "principles,"
instead of immediately coining, for the use of Theosophists,
their equivalents in English.   We must try and remedy this
now.

INQ.—*You will do well, as it may avoid further confusion;
no two Theosophical writers, it seems to me, have hitherto
agreed to call the same principle by the same name.*

THEO.—The confusion is more apparent than real, however.   I have heard some of our Theosophists expressing
surprise, and criticizing several essays speaking of these
principles.   When examined, however, there was no worse
mistake in them than the use of the word "soul" to cover
the three principles, without specifying the distinctions.
The first and positively the clearest of our Theosophical

writers, Mr. A. P. Sinnett, has some comprehensive and admirably written passages on the "Higher Self."* Nevertheless his real idea has also been misconceived by some, owing to his using the word "soul" in a general sense. Yet here are a few passages which will show you how clear and comprehensive is all that he writes on the subject:

The human soul, once launched on the streams of evolution as a human individuality,† passes through alternate periods of physical and relatively spiritual existence. It passes from the one plane or stratum or condition of nature to the other under the guidance of its karmic affinities; living in incarnations the life which its Karma has preordained; modifying its progress within the limitations of circumstances; and—developing fresh Karma by its use or abuse of opportunities—it returns to spiritual existence (Devachan) after each physical life— through the intervening region of Kâmaloka—for rest and refreshment and for the gradual absorption into its essence, as so much cosmic progress, of the life's experience gained "on earth" or during physical existence. This view of the matter will, moreover, have suggested many collateral inferences to any one thinking over the subject; for instance, that the transfer of consciousness from the Kâmaloka to the devachanic stage of this progression would necessarily be gradual;‡ that, in truth, no hard-and-fast line separates the varieties of spiritual conditions; that even the spiritual and physical planes, as psychic faculties in living people show, are not so hopelessly walled off from one another as materialistic theories would suggest; that all states of nature are all around us simultaneously, and appeal to different perceptive faculties; and so on. . . . It is clear that during physical existence people who possess psychic faculties remain in connection with the planes of superphysical consciousness; and although most people may not be endowed with such faculties, we all—as the phenomena of sleep, even, and especially . . . those of somnambulism or mesmerism, show—are capable of entering into conditions of conscious-

---

* See *Transactions of the London Lodge of the Theosophical Society*, No. 7, October, 1885.

† The reincarnating Ego, or human soul, as he called it; the "causal body" with the Vedântins.

‡ The length of this "transfer" depends, however, on the degree of spirituality in the ex-personality of the disembodied Ego. For those whose lives were very spiritual this transfer, though gradual, is very rapid. The time becomes longer with the materialistically inclined.

ness that the five physical senses have nothing to do with. We—the souls within us—are not, as it were, altogether adrift in the ocean of matter. We clearly retain some surviving interest or rights in the shore from which, for a time, we have floated off. The process of incarnation, therefore, is not fully described when we speak of an *alternate* existence on the physical and spiritual planes, and thus picture the soul as a complete entity slipping entirely from the one state of existence to the other. The more correct definitions of the process would probably represent incarnation as taking place on this physical plane of nature by reason of an efflux emanating from the soul. The spiritual realm would all the while be the proper habitat of the soul, which would never entirely quit it; *and that non-materializable portion of the soul which abides permanently on the spiritual plane may fitly,* perhaps, be spoken of as the Higher Self.

This "Higher Self" is Âtmâ, and of course it is "non-materializable," as Mr. Sinnett says. Even more, it can never be objective under any circumstances, even to the highest spiritual perception. For Âtman, or the "Higher Self," is really Brahma, the Absolute, and indistinguishable from it. In hours of *samâdhi* the higher spiritual consciousness of the Initiate is entirely absorbed in the One Essence, which is Âtman, and therefore, being one with the whole, there can be nothing objective for it. Now some of our Theosophists have got into the habit of using the words "Self" and "Ego" as synonymous; of associating the term "Self" with only man's higher individual or even personal "Self" or Ego, whereas this term ought never to be applied except to the *One Universal Self*. Hence the confusion. When speaking of Manas, the "causal body," and connecting it with the Buddhic radiance, we may call it the "Higher Ego," never the "Higher Self." For even Buddhi, the spiritual soul, is not the *Self*, but the vehicle only of *Self*. All the other *selves*—such as the individual *self* and personal *self*—ought never to be spoken or written of without their qualifying and characteristic adjectives.

Thus in the above most excellent essay on the "Higher Self" the term is applied to the sixth principle or Buddhi

—of course in conjunction with Manas, as without such union there would be no *thinking* principle or element in the spiritual soul—and has in consequence given rise to just such misunderstandings. The statement that "a child does not acquire its *sixth* principle—or become a morally responsible being capable of generating Karma—until seven years old" proves what is meant therein by the term "Higher Self." Therefore the able author is quite justified in explaining that, after the "Higher Self" has passed into the human being and saturated the personality—in some of the finer organizations only—with its consciousness, "people with psychic faculties may indeed perceive this Higher Self through their finer senses from time to time." But so also are those who limit the term "Higher Self" to the Universal Divine Principle "justified" in misunderstanding him. For when, without being prepared for this shifting of metaphysical terms,* we read that while "fully manifesting on the physical plane . . . the Higher Self still remains a conscious spiritual Ego on the corresponding plane of nature," we are apt to see in the "Higher Self" of this sentence Âtmâ, and in the spiritual Ego Manas, or rather Buddhi-Manas, and forthwith to criticize the whole thing as incorrect.

To avoid henceforth such misapprehensions, I propose to translate the occult Eastern terms into their English equivalents, and offer these for future use.

The Higher Self is { Âtmâ, the inseparable ray of the Universal and One SELF. It is the God above, more than within, us. Happy the man who succeeds in saturating his *Inner Ego* with it !

---

* "Shifting of metaphysical terms" applies here only to the shifting of their translated equivalents from the Eastern expressions; for to this day there have never existed any such terms in English, every Theosophist having to coin his own terms to render his thought. It is high time, then, to settle on some definite nomenclature.

The Spiritual Divine Ego is { the spiritual soul or Buddhi, in close union with Manas, the mind-principle, without which the former is no Ego at all, but only the Âtmic Vehicle.

The Inner or *Higher Ego is* { Manas, the "fifth" principle, so called, independently of Buddhi. The mind-principle is only the *Spiritual Ego* when merged into one with Buddhi; no materialist being supposed to have in him *such* an Ego, however great his intellectual capacities. It is the permanent *individuality* or the reincarnating Ego.

The Lower or *Personal Ego is* { the physical man in conjunction with his *lower* self—i.e., animal instincts, passions, desires, etc. It is called the false *personality*, and consists of the lower Manas combined with Kâma Rûpa, and operating through the physical body and its phantom or double.

The remaining principle, Prâna, or life, is, strictly speaking, the radiating force or energy of Âtmâ—as the Universal Life and the One SELF—its lower, or rather (in its effects) more physical (because manifesting), aspect. Prâna, or life, permeates the whole being of the objective universe, and is called a principle only because it is an indispensable factor and the *deus ex machinâ* of the living man.

INQ.—*This division will answer better, I believe, as it is so much simplified in its combinations. The other is much too metaphysical.*

THEO.—If outsiders as well as Theosophists would agree to it, it would certainly make matters much more comprehensible.

X

ON THE NATURE OF OUR THINKING PRINCIPLE.

THE MYSTERY OF THE EGO.

INQ.—*In the quotation you brought forward a little while ago from the Buddhist Catechism I perceive a discrepancy which I should like to hear explained. It is there stated that the skandhas—memory included—change with every new incarnation. And yet it is asserted that the reflection of the past lives, which, we are told, are entirely made up of skandhas, "must survive." At the present moment I am not quite clear in my mind as to what it is precisely that survives, and I should like to have it explained. What is it? Is it only that "reflection," or those skandhas, or always that same Ego, the Manas?*

THEO.—I have just explained that the reincarnating principle, or that which we call the divine man, is indestructible throughout the life-cycle—indestructible as a thinking *entity*, and even as an ethereal form. The "reflection" is only the spiritualized *remembrance*, during the devachanic period, of the ex-personality—Mr. A or Mrs. B—with which the Ego identifies itself during that period. Since the devachanic period is but the continuation of the earth-life, so to say—the very acme and pith, in an unbroken series, of the few happy moments in that now past existence—the Ego has to identify itself with the personal consciousness of that earth-life if anything shall remain of it.

INQ.—*This means that the Ego, notwithstanding its divine nature, passes every such period between two incarnations in a state of mental obscuration or temporary insanity ?*

THEO.—You may regard it as you like. Believing that, outside the One Reality, nothing is more than a passing illusion—the whole universe included—we do not view it as insanity, but as a very natural sequence or development of the terrestrial life. What is life ? A bundle of the most varied experiences, of daily changing ideas, emotions, and opinions. In our youth we are often enthusiastically devoted to an ideal, to some hero or heroine whom we try to follow and revive ; a few years later, when the freshness of our youthful feelings has faded out and sobered down, we are the first to laugh at our fancies. And yet there was a day when we had so thoroughly identified our own personality with that of the ideal in our mind—especially if it was that of a living being—that it became entirely merged and lost in our ideal. Can it be said of a man of fifty that he is the same being that he was at twenty ? The inner man is the same ; the outward living personality is completely transformed and changed. Would you also call these changes in the human mental states insanity ?

INQ.—*How would* you *name them, and especially how would you explain the permanence of one and the evanescence of the other ?*

THEO.—We have our own doctrine ready, and to us it offers no difficulty. The clue lies in the double consciousness of our mind, and also in the dual nature of the mental principle. There is a spiritual consciousness—the mânasic mind illumined by the light of Buddhi—which subjectively perceives abstractions, and a sentient consciousness—the lower mânasic light—inseparable from our physical brain and senses. The latter consciousness is held in subjection by the brain and physical senses, and, being in its turn equally dependent on them, must of course fade out and finally die with the disappearance of the brain and physical senses. It is only the spiritual consciousness, whose root lies in eternity, which survives and lives forever, and may therefore be regarded as immortal. Everything else belongs to passing illusions.

INQ.—*What do you really understand by illusion in this case ?* .

THEO.—It is very well described in the above-mentioned essay on the " Higher Self," in which the author says:

The theory we are considering (the interchange of ideas between the Higher Ego and the lower self) harmonizes very well with the treatment of this world in which we live as a phenomenal world of illusion, the spiritual planes of Nature being, on the other hand, the noumenal world or plane of reality. That region of Nature in which, so to speak, the permanent soul is rooted is more real than that in which its transitory blossoms appear for a brief space to wither and fall to pieces, while the plant recovers energy for sending forth a fresh flower. Supposing flowers only were perceptible to ordinary senses, and their roots existed in a state of Nature intangible and invisible to us, philosophers in such a world who divined that there were such things as roots in another plane of existence would be apt to say of the flowers, " These are not the real plants; they are of no relative importance, merely illusive phenomena of the moment."

This is what I mean. It is not the world in which blossom the transitory and evanescent flowers of personal lives which is the real permanent world, but that one in which we find the root of consciousness, the root which is beyond illusion and dwells in the eternity.

INQ.—*What do you mean by the root dwelling in eternity ?*

THEO.—I mean by this root the thinking entity, the Ego which incarnates, whether we regard it as an angel, a spirit, or a force. Of that which falls under our sensuous perceptions only what grows directly from, or is attached to, this invisible root above can partake of its immortal life. Hence every noble thought, idea, and aspiration of the personality it informs, proceeding from and fed by this root, must become permanent. As to the physical consciousness, as it is a quality of the sentient but lower "principle" —Kâma Rûpa, or animal instinct, illuminated by the lower mânasic reflection, or the human soul—it must disappear. It is the higher consciousness which displays activity while the body is asleep or paralyzed, our memory registering but feebly and inaccurately—because automatically—such experiences, and often failing to be even slightly impressed by them.

INQ.—*But how is it that Manas, although you call it nous, a "God," is so weak during its incarnations as to be actually conquered and fettered by its body?*

THEO.—I might retort with a similar question, and ask, How is it that he whom you regard as "God of gods" and the One Living God is so weak as to allow evil (or the devil) to have the best of *him* as much as of all his creatures, both while in heaven, and also during the time he was incarnated on this earth? You are sure to reply again, This is a mystery, and we are forbidden to pry into the mysteries of God. But as we are not forbidden to do so by our religious philosophy, I answer that, unless a God descends as an *avatâra*, no divine principle can be otherwise than cramped and paralyzed by turbulent animal matter. Heterogeneity will always have the upper hand over homogeneity on this plane of illusions; and the nearer an essence is to its root-principle, primordial homogeneity, the more difficult it is for the latter to assert itself on earth.

Spiritual and divine powers lie dormant in every human being; and the wider the sweep of his spiritual vision the mightier will be the God within him. But few men can feel that God. As an average rule, deity is always bound and limited in our thought by earlier conceptions, ideas inculcated in us from childhood; therefore it is so difficult for you to understand our philosophy.

INQ.—*And is it this Ego of ours which is our God?*

THEO.—Not at all; "*a* God" is not the Universal Deity, but only a spark from the one ocean of Divine Fire. Our God *within* us, or "our Father in secret," is what we call the Higher Self, Âtmâ. Our incarnating Ego was a God in its origin, as were all the primeval emanations of the One Unknown Principle. But since its "fall into matter," having to incarnate throughout the cycle, in succession, from first to last, it is no longer a free and happy God, but a poor pilgrim on his way to regain that which he has lost. I can, answer you more fully by repeating what is said of the Inner Man in *Isis Unveiled* (ii., 593):

From the remotest antiquity *mankind* as a whole *have always been convinced of the existence of a personal spiritual entity within the personal physical man.* This inner entity was more or less divine, according to its proximity to the *crown*. . . . The closer the union, the more serene man's destiny, the less dangerous the external conditions. This belief is neither bigotry nor superstition, only an ever-present, instinctive feeling of the proximity of another spiritual and invisible world, which, though it be subjective to the senses of the outward man, is perfectly objective to the Inner Ego. Furthermore, they believed that *there are external and internal conditions which affect the determination of our will upon our actions.* They rejected fatalism, for fatalism implies a blind course of some still blinder power. But they believed in *destiny* (or Karma), which from birth to death every man is weaving thread by thread around himself, as a spider does his cobweb; and this destiny is guided either by that presence termed by some the guardian angel, or by our more intimate astral inner man, who is but too often the evil genius of the man of flesh (or the personality). Both these lead on . . . *man,* but one of them must prevail; and from the very beginning of the invisible affray the stern and implacable *law of compensation (and retribution)* steps in and takes its course, following faithfully the fluctuations (of the conflict). When the last strand is woven, and man is seemingly inwrapped in the network of his own doing, then he finds himself completely under the empire of this *self-made* destiny. It then either fixes him like the inert shell against the immovable rock, or like a feather carries him away in a whirlwind raised by his own actions.

Such is the destiny of the *man*—the true Ego, not the automaton, the *shell* that goes by that name. It is for this *man* to become the conqueror over matter.

THE COMPLEX NATURE OF MANAS.

INQ.—*But you wanted to tell me something of the essential nature of Manas, and of the relation in which the* skandhas *of physical man stand to it.*

THEO.—It is this nature, mysterious, protean, beyond any grasp, and almost shadowy in its correlations with the other principles, that is so difficult to realize, and still more difficult to explain. Manas is a principle, and yet it is an entity and individuality, or Ego. He is a God, and yet he is doomed to an endless cycle of incarnations, for each of which he is made responsible, and for each of which he has to suffer. All this seems as contradictory as it is puzzling; nevertheless, there are hundreds of people, even in America, who realize all this perfectly, for they comprehend the Ego not only in its integrity, but in its many aspects. But if I would make myself comprehensible, I must begin at the beginning and give you the genealogy of this Ego in a few lines.

INQ.—*Say on.*

THEO.—Try to imagine a spirit, a celestial being, whether we call it by one name or another, divine in its essential nature, yet not pure enough to be one with the ALL, and consequently having to purify its nature so that it may finally reach that goal. It can do so only by passing *individually* and *personally*—i.e., spiritually and physically— through every experience and feeling that exists in the manifold or differentiated universe. It has, therefore, after gaining experience in the lower kingdoms, and having ascended higher and still higher with every rung on the ladder of being, to pass through every experience on the human planes. In its very essence it is *thought*, and is therefore called in its plurality *mânasa-putras*, or "sons of the (universal) mind." This individualized thought is what we Theosophists call the real human Ego, the thinking entity imprisoned in a case of flesh and bones. This is surely a spiritual entity, not matter, and such entities are the incarnating Egos, informing the bundle of animal matter called mankind, who are called *mânasa-putras*, and are "minds." But once imprisoned or incarnate, their essence becomes dual; that is to say, the *rays* of the eternal Divine Mind, considered as individual entities, assume a twofold attribute: (*a*) their *essential*, inherent, characteristic, heaven-aspiring mind or higher Manas, and (*b*) the human quality of thinking, or animal cogitation, rationalized, owing to the superiority of the human brain, the kâma-tending or lower Manas. One gravitates toward Buddhi, the other tends downward to the seat of passions and animal desires. The latter have no room in Devachan, nor can they associate with the divine triad which ascends as *one* into mental bliss. Yet it is the Ego, the mânasic entity, which is held responsible for all the sins of the lower attributes, just as a parent is answerable for the transgressions of the child so long as the latter remains irresponsible.

INQ.—*Is this "child" the personality?*

THEO.—It is. But when it is stated that the personality dies with the body, that is not all. The body, which was only the objective symbol of Mr. A or Mrs. B, fades away with all the material *skandhas,* which are the visible expressions of it. But all that which during life constituted the *spiritual* bundle of experiences, the noblest aspirations, undying affections, and *unselfish* nature of Mr. A or Mrs. B, clings for the time of the devachanic period to the Ego, and the Ego is identified with the spiritual portion of the terrestrial entity, which has now passed away out of sight. The *actor* is so imbued with the rôle he has lately played that he dreams of it during the whole devachanic night, and this *vision* continues till the hour strikes for him to return to the stage of life to enact another part.

INQ.—*But how is it that this doctrine, which you say is as old as thinking men, has found no room, say, in Christian theology?*

THEO.—You are mistaken—it has; only theology has disfigured it out of all recognition, as it has many other doctrines. Theology calls the Ego the angel that God gives us, at the moment of our birth, *to take care of our soul.* Theological logic, instead of holding that " angel " responsible for the transgressions of the poor helpless "soul," makes the latter punishable for all the sins of both flesh and mind ! It is the soul, the immaterial "breath" of God and his alleged "creation," which, by some most amazing intellectual jugglery, is doomed to burn in a material hell without ever being consumed,* while the "angel" escapes scot-free, after folding his white pinions and wetting them with a few tears. Aye, these are our "ministering spirits," the "messengers of mercy" who are sent, Bishop Mant tells us—

> . . . to fulfil
> Good for salvation's heirs; for us they still
> Grieve when we sin, rejoice when we repent.

---

* Being of " an asbestos-like nature," according to the eloquent and fiery expression of a modern English Tertullian.

Yet it becomes evident that if all the bishops the world over were asked to define once for all what they mean by *soul* and its functions, they would be as unable to do so as to show us any shadow of logic in the orthodox belief !

THE DOCTRINE IS TAUGHT IN ST. JOHN'S GOSPEL.

INQ.—*To this the adherents of this belief might answer that, if even the orthodox dogma does promise the impenitent sinner and materialist a bad time of it in a rather too realistic inferno, it gives them, on the other hand, a chance for repentance to the last minute. Moreover, they do not teach annihilation, or loss of personality, which comes to the same thing.*

THEO.—If the church teaches nothing of the kind, on the other hand, Jesus does; and that is something to those, at least, who place Christ higher than Christianity.

INQ.—*Does Christ teach anything of the sort ?*

THEO.—He does; and every well-informed Occultist and even Kabalist will tell you so. Christ, or the Fourth Gospel at any rate, teaches reincarnation and also the annihilation of the personality, if you will only forget the dead letter and hold to the esoteric spirit. Remember verses 1 and 2 in chapter xv. of St. John. What does the parable speak about if not of the upper triad in man ? Âtmâ is the "husbandman," the spiritual Ego, or Buddhi (Christos), the "vine," while the animal and vital soul, the personality, is the "branch." "I am the *true* vine, and my Father is the husbandman. Every branch in me that beareth not fruit he taketh away. . . . As the branch cannot bear fruit of itself, except it abide in the vine; no more can ye, except ye abide in me. I am the vine, ye are the branches. . . . If a man abide not in me, he is cast forth as a branch, and is *withered*"—and cast into the fire and burned.

Now we explain it in this way : disbelieving in the hell-fires which theology discovers as underlying the threat to the "branches," we say that the "husbandman" means Âtmâ, the symbol for the infinite, impersonal principle,* while the "vine" stands for the spiritual soul, Christos, and each "branch" represents a new incarnation.

INQ.—*But what proofs have you to support such an arbitrary interpretation ?*

THEO.—Universal symbology is a warrant for its correctness and that it is not arbitrary.   Hermas says of "God" that he "planted the vineyard"—i.e., he created mankind. In the Kabalah it is shown that the Aged of the Aged, or the "Long Face," plants a "vineyard," typifying mankind, and a "vine," meaning life.   The Spirit of "King Messiah" is therefore shown as washing his garments in *the wine* from above, from the creation of the world.†   And King Messiah is the Ego purified by "washing his garments"—i.e., his personalities in rebirth—in the "wine from above," or Buddhi.   Adam, or A-dam, is "blood."   The life of the flesh is in the blood—*nephesh*, soul (Lev. xvii.).   And Adam Kadmon is the Only-Begotten.   Noah also plants a vineyard—the allegorical hotbed of future humanity.   As a consequence of the adoption of the same allegory, we find it reproduced in the *Codex Nazaræus*.   Seven vines—our seven races with their seven saviors or Buddhas—are procreated.   These seven vines spring from Jukabar Zivo, and Aebel Zivo waters them.‡   When the blessed will ascend among the creatures of Light, they shall see Javar Zivo, Lord of Life, and the First Vine.§   These kabalistic metaphors are thus naturally repeated in the Gospel according to St. John.

---

* During the Mysteries it is the hierophant, the "Father," who planted the "vine."   Every symbol has *seven* keys to it.   The discloser of the *plerôma* was always called "Father."   † *Zohar*, xl., 10.
‡ *Codex Nazaræus, Liber Adami Appellatus*—a Matth. Norberg, iii , 60, 61.
§ *Ibid* , ii., 281.

Let us not forget that—even according to those philosophies which ignore our septenary division—in the human system the Ego, or *thinking man*, is called the Logos, or the "Son" of soul and spirit. "Manas is the adopted son of King —— and Queen ——" (the esoteric equivalents for Âtmâ and Buddhi), says an occult work. He is the "man-god" of Plato, who crucifies himself in "space," or the duration of the life-cycle, for the redemption of matter. This he does by incarnating over and over again, thus leading mankind onward to perfection, and making thereby room for lower forms to develop into higher. Not for even one life does he cease progressing himself and also helping all physical Nature to progress; even the occasional, very rare event of his losing one of his personalities—in the case of the latter being entirely devoid of even a spark of spirituality—helps toward his individual progress.

INQ.—*But surely, if the* Ego *is held responsible for the transgressions of its personalities, it has to answer also for the loss, or rather the complete annihilation, of one of such.*

THEO.—Not at all, unless it has done nothing to avert this dire fate. But if, notwithstanding all its efforts, its voice, the *voice of conscience*, has been unable to penetrate through the wall of matter, then the obtuseness of the latter, which proceeds from the imperfect nature of the material, is classed with other failures of nature. The Ego is sufficiently punished by the loss of Devachan, and especially by having to incarnate almost immediately.

INQ.—*This doctrine of the possibility of losing one's soul— or personality, do you call it?—militates against the ideal theories of both Christians and Spiritualists, though Swedenborg adopts it to a certain extent in what he calls "spiritual death." Christians and Spiritualists will never accept it.*

THEO.—This can in no way alter a fact in Nature, if it be a fact, or prevent such a thing occasionally taking place.

The universe and everything in it, moral, mental, physical, psychic, or spiritual, is built on a perfect law of equilibrium and harmony. As said before in *Isis Unveiled*, the centripetal force could not manifest itself without the centrifugal in the harmonious revolutions of the spheres, and all forms and the progress of such forms are products of this dual force in Nature. Now the spirit, or Buddhi, is the centrifugal, and the soul, or Manas, the centripetal spiritual energy; and to produce one result they have to be in perfect union and harmony. Break or damage the centripetal motion of the earthly soul tending toward the center which attracts it; arrest its progress by clogging it with a heavier weight of matter than it can bear, or than is fit for the devachanic state, and the harmony of the whole will be destroyed. Personal life, or perhaps rather its ideal reflection, can only be continued if sustained by the twofold force; that is, by the close union of Buddhi and Manas in every rebirth or personal life. The least deviation from harmony damages it; and when it is destroyed beyond redemption the two forces separate at the moment of death. During a brief interval the *personal* form—called indifferently *kâma rûpa* and *mâyâvi rûpa*—the spiritual efflorescence of which, attaching itself to the Ego, follows it into Devachan and gives to the permanent *individuality* its *personal* coloring, for the time, so to speak, is carried off to remain in Kâmaloka and to be gradually annihilated. For it is after the death of the utterly depraved, the unspiritual, and the wicked beyond redemption that the critical and supreme moment arrives. If during life the ultimate and desperate effort of the Inner Self (Manas) to unite something of the personality with itself and the high glimmering ray of the divine Buddhi is thwarted; if this ray is allowed to be more and more shut out from the ever-thickening crust of the physical brain, the spiritual Ego or Manas, once freed from the body, remains severed entirely from the ethereal relic of the personality; and the latter, or Kâma Rûpa, following its earthly attractions, is drawn into and remains in Hades, which we call Kâmaloka. These are "the withered branches" mentioned by Jesus as being cut off from the "vine." Annihilation, however, is never instantaneous, and may require centuries sometimes for its accomplishment. But there the personality remains along with the *remnants* of other more fortunate personal Egos, and becomes with them a *shell* and an *elementary*. As said in *Isis Unveiled*, it is these two classes of "spirits," the shells and the elementaries, which are the leading "stars" on the great spiritual stage of "materializations." And, you may be sure of it, it is not they who incarnate; and therefore it is that so few of these "dear departed ones" know anything of reincarnation, and thereby mislead the Spiritualists.

, INQ.—*But does not the author of Isis Unveiled stand accused of having preached against reincarnation?*

THEO.—By those who have misunderstood what was said, yes. At the time that work was written reincarnation was not believed in by any Spiritualists, either English or American, and what is said there of reincarnation was directed against the French Spiritists, whose theory is as unphilosophical and absurd as the Eastern teaching is logical and self-evident in its truth. The reincarnationists of the Allan Kardec school believe in an arbitrary and immediate reincarnation. With them, the dead father can incarnate in his own unborn daughter, and so on. They have neither Devachan, Karma, nor any philosophical theory that would warrant or prove the necessity of consecutive rebirths. But how can the author of *Isis Unveiled* argue against *karmic* reincarnation, at long intervals varying between one thousand and fifteen hundred years, when it is the fundamental belief of both Buddhists and Hindûs?

INQ.—*Then you reject the theories of both the Spiritists and the Spiritualists in their entirety ?*

THEO.—Not in their entirety, but only with regard to their respective fundamental beliefs. Both rely on what their "spirits" tell them, and both disagree as much from each other as we Theosophists disagree from both. Truth is one; and when we hear the French spooks preaching reincarnation, and the English spooks denying and denouncing the doctrine, we say that either the French or the English "spirits" do not know what they are talking about. We believe, with the Spiritualists and the Spiritists, in the existence of "spirits," or invisible beings endowed with more or less intelligence. But while in our teachings their kinds and genera are legion, our opponents admit of no other than human disembodied "spirits," which, to our knowledge, are mostly kâmalokic *shells.*

INQ.— *You seem very bitter against "spirits." As you have given me your views and your reasons for disbelieving in the materialization of, and direct communication in séances with, the disembodied spirits, or the "spirits of the dead," would you mind enlightening me as to one more fact ? Why are some Theosophists never tired of saying how dangerous is intercourse with spirits, and mediumship ? Have they any particular reason for this ?*

THEO.—We must suppose so. I know *I* have. Owing to my familiarity for over half a century with these invisible but only too tangible and undeniable "influences," from the conscious elementals and semi-conscious shells down to the utterly senseless and nondescript spooks of all kinds, I claim a certain right to my views.

INQ.—*Can you give an instance or instances to show why these practices should be regarded as dangerous ?*

THEO.—This would require more time than I can give you. Every cause must be judged by the effects it produces. Go over the history of Spiritualism for the last fifty years, ever since its reappearance in this century in America, and judge for yourself whether it has done its votaries more good or harm. Pray understand me. I do not speak against real spiritualism, but against the modern movement which goes under that name, and the so-called philosophy invented to explain its phenomena.

INQ.—*Do you not believe in their phenomena at all?*

THEO.—It is because I believe in them with too good reason, and—save some cases of deliberate fraud—know them to be as true as that you and I live, that all my being revolts against them. Once more I speak only of physical, not mental or even psychic phenomena. Like attracts like. There are several high-minded, pure, good men and women, known to me personally, who have passed years of their lives under the direct guidance and even protection of high "spirits," whether disembodied or planetary. But *these* intelligences are not of the type of the "John Kings" and the "Ernests" who figure in séance-rooms. These intelligences guide and control mortals only in rare and exceptional cases to which they are attracted and magnetically drawn by the karmic past of the individual. It is not enough to sit "for development" in order to attract them. That only opens the door to a swarm of spooks, good, bad, and indifferent, to which the medium becomes a slave for life. It is against such promiscuous mediumship and intercourse with goblins that I raise my voice, not against spiritual Mysticism. The latter is ennobling and holy; the former is of just the same nature as the phenomena of two centuries ago, for which so many witches and wizards have been made to suffer. Read Glanvil and other authors on

the subject of witchcraft, and you will find recorded there
the parallels of most, if not all, of the physical phenomena
of nineteenth-century "Spiritualism."

INQ.—*Do you mean to suggest that it is all witchcraft and
nothing more?*

THEO.—I mean that, whether conscious or unconscious,
all this dealing with the dead is necromancy, and a most
dangerous practice. For ages before Moses such raising of
the dead was regarded by all the intelligent nations as sinful and cruel, inasmuch as it disturbs the rest of the souls
and interferes with their evolutionary development into
higher states. The collective wisdom of all past centuries
has ever been loud in denouncing such practices. Finally,
I say, what I have never ceased repeating orally and in print
for fifteen years: While some of the so-called "spirits"
do not know what they are talking about, repeating merely,
like poll-parrots, what they find in the mediums' and other
people's brains, others are most dangerous and can only
lead one to evil. These are two self-evident facts. Go
into spiritualistic circles of the Allan Kardec school, and
you find "spirits" asserting reincarnation and speaking
like Roman Catholics born. Turn to the "dear departed
ones" in England and America, and you will hear them
denying reincarnation through thick and thin, denouncing
those who teach it, and holding to Protestant views. Your
best, your most powerful mediums have all suffered in health
of body and mind. Think of the sad end of Charles Foster, who died in an asylum, a raving lunatic; of Slade, an
epileptic; of Eglinton—the best medium now in England
—subject to the same disease. Look back over the life of
D. D. Home, a man whose mind was steeped in gall and
bitterness, who never had a good word to say of any one
whom he suspected of possessing psychic powers, and who
slandered every other medium to the bitter end. This Cal-

vin of Spiritualism suffered for years from a terrible spinal disease, brought on by his intercourse with the "spirits," and died a perfect wreck. Think again of the sad fate of poor Washington Irving Bishop. I knew him in New York when he was fourteen, and he was undeniably a medium. It is true that the poor man stole a march on his "spirits" and baptized them "unconscious muscular action," to the great *gaudium* of all the corporations of highly learned and scientific fools, and to the replenishment of his own pocket. But *de mortuis nil nisi bonum;* his end was a sad one. He had strenuously concealed his epileptic fits—the first and strongest symptom of genuine mediumship—and who knows whether he was dead or in a trance when the post-mortem examination was performed? His relatives insist that he was alive, if we are to believe Reuter's telegrams. Finally, behold the veteran mediums, the founders and prime movers of modern Spiritualism—the Fox sisters. After more than forty years of intercourse, the "angels" have led them to become incurable sots, who are now denouncing, in public lectures, their own lifelong work and philosophy as a fraud. What kind of "spirits" must they be who prompted them, I ask you?

INQ.—*But is your inference a correct one?*

THEO.—What would you infer if the best pupils of a particular school of singing broke down from overstrained sore throats? That the method followed was a bad one? So I think the inference is equally fair with regard to Spiritualism when we see their best mediums fall a prey to such a fate. We can only say: Let those who are interested in the question judge the tree of Spiritualism by its fruits, and ponder over the lesson. We Theosophists have always regarded the Spiritualists as brothers having the same mystic tendency as ourselves; but they have always regarded us as enemies. We, being in possession of an older philosophy, have tried to help and warn them; but they have repaid us by reviling and traducing us and our motives in every possible way. Nevertheless the best English Spiritualists say just as we do, wherever they treat of their belief seriously. Hear " M.A. Oxon." confessing this truth:

Spiritualists are too much inclined to dwell exclusively on the intervention of external spirits in this world of ours, *and to ignore the powers of the incarnate* Spirit.*

Why vilify and abuse us, then, for saying precisely the same ? Henceforward we will have nothing more to do with Spiritualism. And now let us return to reincarnation.

---

* *Second Sight,* Introduction

XI.

ON THE MYSTERIES OF REINCARNATION.

PERIODICAL REBIRTHS.

INQ.—*You mean, then, that we have all lived on earth before in many past incarnations, and shall go on so living?*

THEO.—I do. The life-cycle, or rather the cycle of conscious life, begins with the separation of the mortal animal man into sexes, and will end with the close of the last generation of men in the seventh round and seventh race of mankind. Considering we are only in the fourth round and fifth race, its duration is more easily imagined than expressed.

INQ.—*And we keep on incarnating in new personalities all the time?*

THEO.—Most assuredly so; because this life-cycle or period of incarnation may be best compared to human life. As each such life is composed of days of activity separated by nights of sleep or of inaction, so in the incarnation-cycle an active life is followed by a devachanic rest.

INQ.—*And it is this succession of births that is generally defined as reincarnation?*

THEO.—Just so. It is only through these births that the perpetual progress of the countless millions of Egos toward

175

final perfection, and a final rest as long as was the period of activity, can be achieved.

INQ.—*And what is it that regulates the duration or special qualities of these incarnations?*

THEO.—Karma, the universal law of retributive justice.

INQ.—*Is it an intelligent law?*

THEO.—For the materialist, who calls the law of periodicity which regulates the marshaling of bodies, and all the other laws in Nature, blind forces and mechanical laws, no doubt Karma would be a law of chance and no more. For us no adjective or qualification could describe that which is impersonal and not an entity, but a universal operative law. If you question me about the causative intelligence in it, I must answer you, I do not know. But if you ask me to define its effects and tell you what these are in our belief, I may say that the experience of thousands of ages has shown us that they are absolute and unerring equity, wisdom, and intelligence. For Karma in its effects is an unfailing redresser of human injustice, and of all the failures of Nature; a stern adjuster of wrongs; a retributive law which rewards and punishes with equal impartiality. It is, in the strictest sense, "no respecter of persons," though, on the other hand, it can neither be propitiated nor turned aside by prayer. This is a belief common to Hindûs and Buddhists, who believe in Karma.

INQ.—*In this Christian dogmas contradict both, and I doubt whether any Christian will accept the teaching.*

THEO.—No; and Inman gave the reason for it many years ago. As he puts it:

The Christians will accept any nonsense, if promulgated by the church as a matter of faith; . . . the Buddhists hold that nothing which is contradicted by sound reason can be a true doctrine of Buddha.

The Buddhists do not believe in any pardon for their sins, except after an adequate and just punishment for each evil deed or thought in a future incarnation, and a proportionate compensation to the parties injured.

INQ.—*Where is it so stated?*

THEO.—In most of their sacred works. In the *Wheel of the Law* (p. 57) you may find the following Theosophical tenet:

Buddhists believe that every act, word, or thought has its consequence, which will appear sooner or later in the present or in the future state. Evil acts will produce evil consequences, good acts will produce good consequences: prosperity in this world or birth in heaven [Devachan] . . . in the future state.

INQ.—*Christians believe the same thing, do they not?*

THEO.—Oh no; they believe in the pardon and the remission of all sins. They are promised that if they only believe in the blood of Christ—an *innocent* victim!—in the blood offered by him for the expiation of the sins of the whole of mankind, it will atone for every mortal sin. And we believe neither in vicarious atonement, nor in the possibility of the remission of the smallest sin by any God—not even by a *personal* Absolute or Infinite, if such a thing could have any existence. What we believe in is strict and impartial justice. Our idea of the unknown Universal Deity, represented by Karma, is that it is a power which cannot fail, and can therefore have neither wrath nor mercy, but only absolute equity, which leaves every cause, great or small, to work out its inevitable effects. The saying of Jesus, "With what measure ye mete, it shall be measured to you again" (Matt. vii. 2), neither by expression nor implication points to any hope of future mercy or salvation by proxy. This is why, recognizing as we do in our philosophy the justice of this statement, we cannot recommend too strongly mercy, charity, and forgiveness of mutual offenses. "Resist not evil" and "render good for evil" are Buddhist precepts, and were first preached in view of the implacability of karmic law. For man to take the law into his own hands is in any case a sacrilegious presumption. Human law may use restrictive, not punitive measures; but a man who, believing in Karma, still revenges himself, still refuses to forgive every injury, whereby he would render good for evil, is a criminal, and only hurts himself. As Karma is sure to punish the man who has wronged another, by seeking to inflict an additional punishment on one's enemy, and, instead of leaving that punishment to the great Law, adding to it one's own mite, we only beget thereby a cause for the future reward of our enemy and a future punishment for ourself. The unfailing "regulator" in each incarnation affects the quality of its successor, and the sum of the merit or demerit in preceding incarnations determines the following rebirth.

INQ.—*Are we, then, to infer a man's past from his present?*

THEO.—Only so far as to believe that his present life is what it justly should be, to atone for the sins of the past life. Of course—seers and great Adepts excepted—we cannot, as average mortals, know what those sins were. From our paucity of data it is impossible for us to determine even what an old man's youth must have been; neither can we, for like reasons, draw final conclusions, merely from what we see in the life of some man, as to what his past life may have been.

WHAT IS KARMA?

INQ.—*But what is Karma?*

THEO.—As I have said, we consider it as the *ultimate law* of the universe, the source, origin, and fount of all other laws which exist throughout Nature. Karma is the unerring law which adjusts effect to cause, on the physical, mental, and spiritual planes of being. As no cause remains without its due effect from greatest to least, from a cosmic disturbance down to the movement of your hand, and as like produces like, Karma is that unseen and unknown law which *adjusts wisely, intelligently, and equitably* each effect to its cause, tracing the latter back to its producer. Though itself unknowable, its action is perceivable.

INQ.—*Then it is the " absolute," the " unknowable," again, and is not of much value as an explanation of the problems of life.*

THEO.—On the contrary. For though we do not know what Karma is *per se* and in its essence, we *do* know *how* it works, and we can define and describe its mode of action with accuracy. We only do *not* know its ultimate *cause*, just as modern philosophy universally admits that the *ultimate* cause of a thing is "unknowable."

INQ.—*And what has Theosophy to say in regard to the solution of the more practical needs of humanity? What is the explanation which it offers of the awful suffering and dire necessity prevalent among the so-called " lower classes" ?*

THEO.—To be pointed: according to our teaching, all these great social evils—the distinction of classes in society, and of the sexes in the affairs of life, the unequal distribution of capital and of labor—all are due to what we tersely but truly denominate Karma.

INQ.—*But surely all these evils which seem to fall upon the masses somewhat indiscriminately are not actual merited and individual Karma ?*

THEO.—No, they cannot be so strictly defined in their effects as to show that each individual environment, and the particular conditions of life in which each person finds himself, are nothing more than the retributive Karma which the individual has generated in a previous life. We must not lose sight of the fact that every atom is subject to the general law governing the whole body to which it belongs, and here we come upon the wider track of the karmic law. Do you not perceive that the aggregate of individual Karma becomes that of the nation to which those individuals belong, and, further, that the sum total of national Karma is that of the world? The evils that you speak of are not peculiar to the individual or even to the nation; they are more or less universal; and it is upon this broad line of human interdependence that the law of Karma finds its legitimate and equable issue.

INQ.—*Do I, then, understand that the law of Karma is not necessarily an individual law?*

THEO.—That is just what I mean. It is impossible that Karma could readjust the balance of power in the world's life and progress unless it had a broad and general line of action. It is held as a truth among Theosophists that the interdependence of humanity is the cause of what is called distributive Karma, and it is this law which affords the solution to the great question of collective suffering and its relief. It is an occult law, moreover, that no man can rise superior to his individual failings without lifting, be it ever so little, the whole body of which he is an integral part. In the same way no one can sin, nor suffer the effects of sin, alone. In reality there is no such thing as "separateness"; and the nearest approach to that selfish state which the laws of life permit is in the intent or motive.

INQ.—*And are there no means by which the distributive or national Karma might be concentrated or collected, so to speak, and brought to its natural and legitimate fulfilment without all this protracted suffering?*

THEO.—As a general rule, and within certain limits which define the age to which we belong, the law of Karma cannot be hastened or retarded in its fulfilment. But of this I am certain : the point of possibility in either of these directions has never yet been touched. Listen to the following recital of one phase of national suffering, and then ask yourself whether, admitting the working power of individual, relative, and distributive Karma, these evils are not capable of extensive modification and general relief. What I am about to read to you is from the pen of a national savior—one who, having overcome *self*, and being free to choose, has elected to serve humanity, in bearing at least as much as a woman's shoulders can possibly bear of national Karma. This is what she says:

Yes. Nature always does speak, don't you think? Only sometimes we make so much noise that we drown her voice. That is why it is so restful to go out of the town and nestle awhile in the Mother's arms. I am thinking of the evening on Hampstead Heath when we watched the sun go down; but oh, upon what suffering and misery that sun had set! A lady brought me yesterday a big hamper of wild-flowers. I thought some of my East End family had a better right to it than I, and so I took it down to a very poor school in Whitechapel this morning. You should have seen the pallid little faces brighten' Thence I went to pay for some dinners at a little cook-shop for some children. It was in a back street, narrow, full of jostling people; stench indescribable, from fish, meat, and other comestibles, all reeking in a sun that, in Whitechapel, festers instead of purifying. The cook-shop was the quintessence of all the smells. Indescribable meat-pies at 1*d.*, loathsome lumps of "food," and swarms of flies—a very altar of Beelzebub! All about, babies on the prowl for scraps, one, with the face of an angel, gathering up cherry-stones as a light and nutritious form of diet. I came westward with every nerve shuddering and jarred, wondering whether anything can be done with some parts of London save swallowing them up in an earthquake and starting their inhabitants afresh, after a plunge into some purifying Lethe, out of which not a memory might emerge! And then I thought of Hampstead Heath, and—pondered. If by any sacrifice one could win the power to save these people, the cost would not be worth counting; but, you see, *they* must be changed—and how can that be wrought? In the condition they now are, they would not profit by any environment in which they might be placed; and yet in their present surroundings they must continue to putrefy. It breaks my heart, this endless, hopeless misery, and the brutish degradation that is at once its outgrowth and its root. It is like the banian-tree; every branch roots itself and sends out new shoots.. What a difference between these feelings and the peaceful scene at Hampstead! And yet we who are the brothers and sisters of these poor creatures have only a right to use Hampstead Heaths to gain strength to save Whitechapels. [*Signed by a name too respected and too well known to be given to scoffers.*]

INQ.—*That is a sad but beautiful letter, and I think it presents with painful conspicuity the terrible workings of what you have called " relative " and " distributive" Karma. But alas ! there seems no immediate hope of any relief short of an earthquake, or some such general engulfment.*

THEO.—What right have we to think so while one half of humanity is in a position to effect an immediate relief of the privations which are suffered by their fellows ? When every individual has contributed to the general good what he can of money, of labor, and of ennobling thought, then, and only then, will the balance of national Karma be struck, and until then we have no right, nor any reasons, for saying that there is more life on the earth than Nature can support. It is reserved for the heroic souls, the saviors of our race and nation, to find out the cause of this unequal pressure of retributive Karma, and by a supreme effort to readjust the balance of power, and save the people from a moral engulfment a thousand times more disastrous and more permanently evil than the like physical catastrophe, in which you seem to see the only possible outlet for this accumulated misery.

INQ.—*Well, then, tell me generally how you describe this law of Karma.*

THEO.—We describe Karma as that law of readjustment which ever tends to restore disturbed equilibrium in the physical, and broken harmony in the moral world.

We say that Karma does not act in this or that particular way always, but that it always *does* act so as to restore harmony and preserve the balance of equilibrium, in virtue of which the universe exists.

INQ.—*Give me an illustration.*

THEO.—Later on I will give you a full illustration. Think now of a pond. A stone falls into the water and creates disturbing waves. These waves oscillate backward and forward till at last, owing to the operation of what physicists call the law of the dissipation of energy, they are brought to rest, and the water returns to its condition of calm tranquillity. Similarly *all* action, on every plane, produces disturbance in the balanced harmony of the universe, and the vibrations so produced will continue to roll backward and forward, if the area is limited, till equilibrium is restored. But since each such disturbance starts from some particular point, it is clear that equilibrium and harmony can only be restored by the reconverging *to that same point* of all the forces which were set in motion from it. And here you have proof that the consequences of a man's deeds, thoughts, etc., must all react upon *himself* with the same force with which they were set in motion.

INQ.—*But I see nothing of a moral character about this law. It looks to me like the simple physical law that action and reaction are equal and opposite.*

THEO.—I am not surprised to hear you say that. Americans have got so much into the ingrained habit of considering right and wrong, good and evil, as matters of an arbitrary code of law laid down either by men or imposed upon them by a personal God. We Theosophists, however, say that "good" and "harmony," and "evil" and "disharmony," are synonymous. Further, we maintain that all pain and suffering are results of want of harmony, and that the one terrible and only cause of the disturbance of harmony is *selfishness* in some form or other. Hence Karma gives back to every man the *actual consequences* of his own actions, without any regard to their moral character; but since he receives his due for *all*, it is obvious that he will be made to atone for all sufferings which he has caused, just as he will reap in joy and gladness the fruits of all the happiness and harmony he had helped to produce. I can do no better than quote for your benefit certain passages from books and articles written by those of our Theosophists who have a correct idea of Karma.

INQ.—*I wish you would, as your literature seems to be very sparing on this subject.*

THEO.—Because it is *the* most difficult of all our tenets. Some short time ago there appeared the following objection from a Christian pen:

Granting that the teaching in regard to Theosophy is correct, and that "man must be his own savior, must overcome self and conquer the evil that is in his dual nature, to obtain the emancipation of his soul"—what is man to do after he has been awakened and converted to a certain extent from evil or wickedness? How is he to get emancipation, or pardon, or the blotting out of the evil or wickedness he has already done?

To this Mr. J. H. Connelly replies very pertinently that no one can hope to "make the Theosophical engine run on the theological track." As he has it:

The possibility of shirking individual responsibility is not among the concepts of Theosophy. In this faith there is no such thing as pardoning, or "blotting out of evil or wickedness already done," otherwise than by the adequate punishment therefor of the wrong-doer and the restoration of the harmony in the universe that had been disturbed by his wrongful act. The evil has been his own, and while others must suffer its consequences, atonement can be made by nobody but himself.

The condition contemplated, . . . in which a man shall have been "awakened and converted to a certain extent from evil or wickedness," is that in which a man shall have realized that his deeds are evil and deserving of punishment. In that realization a sense of personal responsibility is inevitable, and just in proportion to the extent of his awakening or "converting" must be the sense of that awful responsibility. While it is strong upon him is the time when he is urged to accept the doctrine of vicarious atonement.

He is told that he must also repent; but nothing is easier than that. It is an amiable weakness of human nature that we are quite prone to regret the evil we have done when our attention is called and we have either suffered from it ourselves or enjoyed its fruits. Possibly close analysis of the feeling would show us that that which we regret is rather the necessity that seemed to require the evil as a means of attainment of our selfish ends than the evil itself.

Attractive as this prospect of casting our burden of sins " at the foot of the cross " may be to the ordinary mind, it does not commend itself to the Theosophic student. He does not apprehend why the sinner by attaining knowledge of his evil can thereby merit any pardon for, or the blotting out of, his past wickedness; or why repentance and future right living entitle him to a suspension in his favor of the universal law of relation between cause and effect. The results of his evil deeds continue to exist; the suffering caused to others by his wickedness is not blotted out. The Theosophical student takes the result of wickedness upon the innocent into his problem. He considers not only the guilty person, but his victims.

Evil is an infraction of the laws of harmony governing the universe, and the penalty thereof must fall upon the violator of that law himself. Christ uttered the warning, " Sin no more, lest a worse thing come unto thee," and St. Paul said, " Work out your own salvation;" " Whatsoever a man soweth, that shall he also reap." That, by the way, is a fine metaphoric rendering of the sentence of the Purânas, far antedating him—that " every man reaps the consequences of his own acts."

This is the principle of the law of Karma which is taught by Theosophy. Sinnett, in his *Esoteric Buddhism*, rendered Karma as " the law of ethical causation." " The law of retribution," as Madame Blavatsky translates its meaning, is better. It is the power which,

> Just, though mysterious, leads us on unerring,
> Through ways unmarked, from guilt to punishment.

But it is more. It rewards merit as unerringly and amply as it punishes demerit. It is the outcome of every act, of thought, word, and deed, and by it men mold themselves, their lives and happenings.

Eastern philosophy rejects the idea of a newly created soul for every baby born. It believes in a limited number of monads, evolving and growing more and more perfect through their assimilation of many successive personalities. Those personalities are the product of Karma, and it is by Karma and reincarnation that the human monad in time returns to its source—absolute deity.

E. D. Walker, in his *Reincarnation*, offers the following explanation:

Briefly, the doctrine of Karma is that we have made ourselves what we are by former actions, and are building our future eternity by present actions. There is no destiny but what we ourselves determine. There is no salvation or condemnation except what we ourselves bring about. . . . Because it offers no shelter for culpable actions and necessitates a sterling manliness, it is less welcome to weak natures than the easy religious tenets of vicarious atonement, intercession, forgiveness, and death-bed conversions. . . . In the domain of eternal justice the offense and the punishment are inseparably connected as the same event, because there is no real distinction between the action and its outcome. . . . It is Karma, or our old acts, that draws us back into earthly life. The spirit's abode changes according to its Karma, and this Karma forbids any long continuance in one condition, because *it* is always changing. So long as action is governed by material and selfish motives, just so long must the effect of that action be manifested in physical rebirths. Only the perfectly selfless man can elude the gravitation of material life. Few have attained this, but it is the goal of mankind.

And then the writer quotes from *The Secret Doctrine*:

Those who believe in Karma have to believe in destiny, which, from birth to death, every man is weaving, thread by thread, around himself, as a spider does his cobweb; and this destiny is guided either by the heavenly voice of the invisible prototype outside of us, or by our more intimate astral or inner man, who is but too often the evil genius of the embodied entity called man. Both these lead on the outward man, but one of them must prevail; and from the very beginning of the invisible affray the stern and implacable law of compensation steps in and takes its course, faithfully following the fluctuations. When the last strand is woven, and man is seemingly inwrapped in the network of his own doing, then he finds himself completely under the empire of this self-made destiny. . . .

An Occultist or a philosopher will not speak of the goodness or cruelty of Providence; but, identifying it with Karma-Nemesis, he will teach that, nevertheless, it guards the good and watches over them in this as in future lives; and that it punishes the evil-doer—aye, even to his seventh rebirth—so long, in short, as the effect of his having thrown into perturbation even the smallest atom in the infinite world of harmony has not been finally readjusted. For the only decree of Karma—an eternal and immutable decree—is absolute harmony in the world of matter as it is in the world of spirit. It is not, therefore, Karma that rewards or punishes, but it is we who reward or punish ourselves according to whether we work with, through, and along with Nature, abiding by the laws on which that harmony depends, or —break them.

Nor would the ways of Karma be inscrutable were men to work in union and harmony, instead of disunion and strife. For our ignorance of those ways—which one portion of mankind calls the ways of Providence, dark and intricate; while another sees in them the action of blind fatalism; and a third, simple chance, with neither gods nor devils to guide them—would surely disappear if we would but attribute all these to their correct cause. . . .

We stand bewildered before the mystery of our own making and the riddles of life that we will not solve, and then accuse the great Sphinx of devouring us. But verily there is not an accident of our lives, not a misshapen day or a misfortune, that could not be traced back to our own doings in this or in another life. . . .

The law of Karma is inextricably interwoven with that of reincarnation. . . . It is only this doctrine that can explain to us the mysterious problem of good and evil, and reconcile man to the terrible and apparent injustice of life. Nothing but such certainty can quiet our revolted sense of justice. For, when one unacquainted with the noble doctrine looks around him and observes the inequalities of birth and fortune, of intellect and capacities; when one sees honor paid to fools and profligates on whom fortune has heaped her favors by mere privilege of birth, and their nearest neighbor, with all his intellect and noble virtues—far more deserving in every way—perishing for want and for lack of sympathy; when one sees all this and has to turn away, helpless to relieve the undeserved suffering, one's ears ringing and heart aching with the cries of pain around him, that blessed knowledge of Karma alone prevents him from cursing life and men as well as their supposed creator. . . .

This law, whether conscious or unconscious, predestines nothing and no one. It exists from and in eternity truly, for it is eternity

itself; and as such, since no act can be coequal with eternity, it cannot
be said to act, for it is action itself. It is not the wave which drowns
the man, but the personal action of the wretch who goes deliberately
and places himself under the impersonal action of the laws that govern the ocean's motion. Karma creates nothing, nor does it design.
It is man who plants and creates causes, and karmic law adjusts the
effects, which adjustment is not an act, but universal harmony, tending
ever to resume its original position, like a bough, which, bent down
too forcibly, rebounds with corresponding vigor. If it happen to
dislocate the arm that tried to bend it out of its natural position, shall
we say it is the bough which broke our arm, or that our own folly has
brought us to grief? Karma has never sought to destroy intellectual
and individual liberty, like the God invented by the monotheists. It
has not involved its decrees in darkness purposely to perplex man, nor
shall it punish him who dares to scrutinize its mysteries. On the contrary, he who through study and meditation unveils its intricate paths,
and throws light on those dark ways, in the windings of which so
many men perish, owing to their ignorance of the labyrinth of life, is
working for the good of his fellow-men. Karma is an absolute and
eternal law in the world of manifestation; and as there can be only
one Absolute, as one eternal, ever-present Cause, believers in Karma
cannot be regarded as atheists or materialists, still less as fatalists;
for Karma is one with the Unknowable, of which it is an aspect, in
its effects in the phenomenal world.

Another able Theosophic writer, Mrs. P. Sinnett, in her
Purpose of Theosophy, says:

Every individual is making Karma either good or bad in each action
and thought of his daily round, and is at the same time working out in
this life the Karma brought about by the acts and desires of the last.
When we see people afflicted by congenital ailments it may be safely
assumed that these ailments are the inevitable results of causes started
by themselves in a previous birth. It may be argued that, as these
afflictions are hereditary, they can have nothing to do with a past incarnation; but it must be remembered that the Ego, the real man, the
individuality, has no spiritual origin in the parentage by which it is
reëmbodied, but it is drawn, by the affinities which its previous mode
of life attracted round it, into the current that carries it, when the time
comes for rebirth, to the home best fitted for the development of those
tendencies. . . . This doctrine of Karma, when properly understood,
is well calculated to guide and assist those who realize its truth to a

higher and better mode of life; for it must not be forgotten that not only our actions, but our thoughts also, are most assuredly followed by a crowd of circumstances that will influence for good or for evil our own future, and, what is still more important, the future of many of our fellow-creatures. If sins of omission and commission could in any case be only self-regarding, the effect on the sinner's Karma would be a matter of minor consequence. The effect that every thought and act through life carries with it for good or evil a corresponding influence on other members of the human family renders a strict sense of justice, morality, and unselfishness so necessary to future happiness or progress. A crime once committed, an evil thought sent out from the mind, are past recall—no amount of repentance can wipe out their results in the future. Repentance, if sincere, will deter a man from repeating errors; it cannot save him or others from the effects of those already produced, which will most unerringly overtake him either in this life or in the next rebirth.

Mr. J. H. Connelly proceeds:

The believers in a religion based upon such doctrine are willing it should be compared with one in which man's destiny for eternity is determined by the accidents of a single, brief, earthly existence, during which he is cheered by the promise that "as the tree falls, so shall it lie"; in which his brightest hope, when he wakes up to a knowledge of his wickedness, is the doctrine of vicarious atonement; and in which even that is handicapped, according to the Presbyterian Confession of Faith:

"By the decree of God, for the manifestation of his glory, some men and angels are predestinated unto everlasting life and others foreordained to everlasting death.

"These angels and men thus predestinated and foreordained are particularly and unchangeably designed; and their number is so certain and definite that it cannot be either increased or diminished. . . . As God hath appointed the elect unto glory, . . . neither are any other redeemed by Christ effectually called, justified, adopted, sanctified, and saved, but the elect only.

"The rest of mankind God was pleased, according to the unsearchable counsel of his own will, whereby he extendeth or withholdeth mercy as he pleaseth, for the glory of his sovereign power over his creatures, to pass by and to ordain them to dishonor and wrath for their sin, to the praise of his glorious justice."

This is what the able defender says. Nor can we do any better than wind up the subject as he does, by a quotation from a magnificent poem. As he says:

The exquisite beauty of Edwin Arnold's exposition of Karma in *The Light of Asia* tempts to its reproduction here, but it is too long for quotation in full. Here is a portion of it:

Karma—all that total of a soul
  Which is the things it did, the thoughts it had,
The " self " it wove with woof of viewless time
  Crossed on the warp invisible of acts.

  *   *   *   *   *   *

Before beginning and without an end,
  As space eternal and as surety sure,
Is fixed a Power divine which moves to good,
  Only its laws endure.

It will not be contemned of any one;
  Who thwarts it loses, and who serves it gains;
The hidden good it pays with peace and bliss,
  The hidden ill with pains.

It seeth everywhere and marketh all;
  Do right—it recompenseth! Do one wrong—
The equal retribution must be made,
  Though Dharma tarry long.

It knows not wrath nor pardon; utter-true,
  Its measures mete, its faultless balance weighs;
Times are as naught—to-morrow it will judge—
  Or after many days.

  *   *   *   *   *   *

Such is the law which moves to righteousness,
  Which none at last can turn aside or stay;
The heart of it is love, the end of it
  Is peace and consummation sweet. Obey.

And now I advise you to compare our Theosophic views upon Karma, the law of retribution, and say whether they are not both more philosophical and just than this cruel and idiotic dogma which makes of "God" a senseless fiend—

the tenet, namely, that the "elect only" will be saved, and the rest doomed to eternal perdition !

INQ.—*Yes, I see what you mean generally ; but I wish you could give some concrete example of the action of Karma.*

THEO.—That I cannot do. We can only feel sure, as I said before, that our present lives and circumstances are the direct results of our own deeds and thoughts in lives that are past. But we, who are not seers or Initiates, cannot know anything about the details of the working of the law of Karma.

INQ.—*Can any one, even an Adept or seer, follow out this karmic process of readjustment in detail ?*

THEO.—Certainly; "those who know" can do so by the exercise of powers which are latent even in all men.

WHO ARE THOSE WHO KNOW?

INQ.—*Does this hold equally of ourselves as of others ?*

THEO.—Equally. As just said, the same limited vision exists for all, save for those who have reached, in the present incarnation, the acme of spiritual vision and clairvoyance. We can only perceive that, if things ought to have been different with us, they would have been different; that we are what we have made ourselves, and have only what we have earned for ourselves.

INQ.—*I am afraid such a conception would only embitter us.*

THEO.—I believe it is precisely the reverse. It is disbelief in the just law of retribution that is more likely to awaken every combative feeling in man. A child, as much as a man, resents a punishment, or even a reproof, he believes to be unmerited, far more than he does a severer punishment, if he feels that it is merited. Belief in Karma is the highest motive for reconcilement to one's lot in this life, and the very strongest incentive toward effort to better the succeeding rebirth.   Both of these, indeed, would be destroyed if we supposed that our lot was the result of anything but strict *law*, or that destiny was in any other hands than our own.

INQ.—*You have just asserted that this system of reincarnation under karmic law commended itself to reason, justice, and the moral sense.   But, if so, is it not at some sacrifice of the gentler qualities of sympathy and pity, and thus a hardening of the finer instincts of human nature ?*

THEO.—Only apparently, not really.   No man can receive more or less than his deserts without a corresponding injustice or partiality to others; and a law which could be averted through compassion would bring about more misery than it saved, more irritation and curses than thanks. Remember, also, that we do not administer the law, if we do create causes for its effects; it administers itself; and again, that the most copious provision for the manifestation of *just* compassion and mercy is shown in the state of Devachan.

INQ.—*You speak of Adepts as being an exception to the rule of our general ignorance.   Do they really know more than we do of reincarnation and after-states ?*

THEO.—They do indeed.   By the training of faculties we all possess, but which they alone have developed to perfection, they have entered in spirit these various planes and states we have been discussing.   For long ages one generation of Adepts after another has studied the mysteries of being, of life, death, and rebirth, and all have taught in their turn some of the facts so learned.

INQ.—*And is the production of Adepts the aim of Theosophy ?*

THEO.—Theosophy considers humanity as an emanation from divinity on its return-path thereto. At an advanced point upon the path adeptship is reached by those who have devoted several incarnations to its achievement. For, remember well, no man has ever reached adeptship in the secret sciences in one life; but many incarnations are necessary for it after the formation of a conscious purpose and the beginning of the needful training. Many may be the men and women in the very midst of our Society who have begun this uphill work toward illumination several incarnations ago, and who yet, owing to the personal illusions of the present life, are either ignorant of the fact, or on the road to losing every chance, in this existence, of progressing any farther. They feel an irresistible attraction toward Occultism and the "higher life," and yet are too personal and self-opinionated, too much in love with the deceptive allurements of mundane life and the world's ephemeral pleasures, to give them up, and so lose their chance in their present birth. But, for ordinary men, for the practical duties of daily life, such a far-off result is inappropriate as an aim and quite ineffective as a motive.

INQ.—*What, then, may be their object or distinct purpose in joining the Theosophical Society?*

THEO.—Many are interested in our doctrines, and feel instinctively that they are truer than those of any dogmatic religion. Others have formed a fixed resolve to attain the highest ideal of man's duty.

THE DIFFERENCE BETWEEN FAITH AND KNOW-LEDGE, OR BLIND AND REASONED FAITH.

INQ.—*You say that they accept and believe in the doctrines of Theosophy. But as they do not belong to those Adepts you have just mentioned, then they must accept your teachings on*

" *blind faith.*"   *In what does this differ from that of conventional religions ?*

THEO.—As it differs on almost all the other points, so it differs on this one. What you call "faith," and that which is "blind faith," in reality, with regard to the dogmas of the Christian religions, becomes with us *knowledge*, the logical sequence of things we *know*, about *facts* in Nature. Your doctrines are based upon interpretation, therefore upon the *second-hand* testimony of seers; ours upon the unvarying and invariable testimony of seers. The ordinary Christian theology, for instance, holds that man is a creature of God, of three component parts—body, soul, and spirit— all essential to his integrity, and all, either in the gross form of physical earthly existence or in the etherealized form of post-resurrection experience, needed to so constitute him forever, each man having thus a permanent existence separate from other men and from the divine. Theosophy, on the other hand, holds that, man being an emanation from the unknown yet ever-present and infinite Divine Essence, his body and everything else is impermanent, hence an illusion; spirit alone in him being the one enduring substance, and even that losing its separated individuality at the moment of its complete reunion with the Universal Spirit.

INQ.—*If we lose even our individuality, then it becomes simply annihilation.*

THEO.—I say it does not, since I speak of *separate*, not of universal individuality. This individuality becomes as a part transformed into the whole; the "dewdrop" is not evaporated, but becomes the sea. Is physical man annihilated when from a fetus he becomes an old man? What kind of satanic pride must be ours if we place our infinitesimally small consciousness and individuality higher than the universal and infinite consciousness !

INQ.—*It follows, then, that there is, de facto, no man, but all is spirit?*

THEO.—You are mistaken. It follows that the union of spirit with matter is but temporary; or, to put it more clearly, since spirit and matter are one, being the two opposite poles of the universal manifested substance, spirit loses its right to the name so long as the smallest particle and atom of its manifesting substance still clings to any form, the result of differentiation. To believe otherwise is "blind faith."

INQ.—*Thus it is on knowledge, not on faith, that you assert that the permanent principle, the spirit, simply makes a transit through matter?*

THEO.—I would put it otherwise and say: We assert that the appearance of the permanent and *one* principle—spirit —*as matter* is transient, and therefore no better than an illusion.

INQ.—*Very well; and this given out on knowledge, not faith?*

THEO.—Just so. But as I see very well what you are driving at, I may just as well tell you that we hold faith such as you advocate to be a mental disease, and real faith—i.e., the *pistis* of the Greeks—as "belief based on knowledge," whether supplied by the evidence of physical or spiritual senses.

INQ.—*What do you mean?*

THEO.—If it is the difference between the two that you ,want to know, I mean that between *faith on authority* and *faith on one's spiritual intuition* there is a very great difference.

INQ.—*What is it?*

THEO.—One is human credulity and superstition, the other human belief and intuition. As Professor Alexander Wilder says in his Introduction to the *Eleusinian Mysteries:*

It is ignorance which leads to profanation. Men ridicule what they do not properly understand. . . . The undercurrent of this world is set toward one goal; and inside of human credulity . . . is a power almost infinite, a holy faith capable of apprehending the supremest truths of all existence.

Those who limit that "credulity" to human authoritative dogmas alone will never fathom that power, nor even perceive it in their natures.   It is stuck fast to the external plane, and is unable to bring forth into play the essence that rules it; for to do this they have to claim their right of private judgment, and this they never *dare* to do.

INQ.—*And is it this " intuition" which forces you to reject God as a personal Father, ruler, and governor of the universe?*

THEO.—Precisely. We believe in an ever-unknowable Principle; for only blind aberration can make one maintain that the universe, thinking man, and all the marvels contained even in the world of matter, could have grown without some *intelligent powers* to bring about the extraordinarily wise arrangement of all its parts. Nature may err, and often does, in its details and the external manifestations of its materials, never in its inner causes and results. Ancient pagans held far more philosophical views on this question than modern philosophers, whether agnostics, materialists, or Christians; and no pagan writer has ever yet advanced the proposition that cruelty and mercy are not finite feelings, and can therefore be made the attributes of an *infinite* God.   Their gods, therefore, were all finite. The Siamese author of the *Wheel of the Law* expresses the same idea about your personal God as ourselves; he says (p. 25):

A Buddhist might believe in the existence of a God sublime above all human qualities and attributes—a perfect God, above love and hatred and jealousy, calmly resting in a quietude that nothing could disturb; and of such a God he would speak no disparagement, not from a desire to please him or fear to offend him, but from natural veneration. But he cannot understand a God with the attributes and qualities of men; a God who loves and hates and shows anger; a Deity who, whether described as by Christian missionaries or by Mahometans or Brahmins * or Jews, falls below his standard of even an ordinary good man.

INQ.—*Faith for faith, is not the faith of the Christian who believes, in his human helplessness and humility, that there is a merciful Father in heaven who will protect him from temptation, help him in life, and forgive him his transgressions, better than the cold and proud, almost fatalistic, faith of the Buddhists, Vedântins, and Theosophists ?*

THEO.—Persist in calling our belief "faith" if you will. But once we are again on this ever-recurring question, I ask in my turn: Faith for faith, is not the one based on strict logic and reason better than the one which is based simply on human authority or—hero-worship ? Our "faith" has all the logical force of the arithmetical truism that two and two will produce four. Your faith is like the logic of some emotional women, of whom Tourgenyeff said that for them two and two were generally five, and a tallow candle into the bargain. Yours is a faith, moreover, which clashes not only with every conceivable view of justice and logic, but which, if analyzed, leads man to his moral perdition, checks the progress of mankind, and positively making of might right, transforms every second man into a Cain to his brother Abel.

HAS GOD THE RIGHT TO FORGIVE?

INQ.—*To what do you allude?*

THEO.—To the doctrine of "atonement." I allude to that dangerous dogma in which you believe, and which teaches

---

* Sectarian Brâhmans ar here meant. The Parabrahman of the Vedântins is the Deity we accept and believe in.

us that no matter how enormous our crimes against the laws of God and of man, we have but to believe in the self-sacrifice of Jesus for the salvation of mankind, and his blood will wash out every stain.   It is now twenty years that I have preached against it, and I may now draw your attention to a paragraph from *Isis Unveiled,* written in 1875. This is what Christianity teaches, and what we combat:

God's mercy is boundless and unfathomable. It is impossible to conceive of a human sin so damnable that the price paid in advance for the redemption of the sinner would not wipe it out if a thousandfold worse. And, furthermore, it is never too late to repent. Though the offender wait until the last minute of the last hour of the last day of his mortal life before his blanched lips utter the confession of faith, he may go to Paradise; the dying thief did so, and so may all others as vile. These are the assumptions of the church and of the clergy; assumptions banged at the heads of your countrymen by England's favorite preachers, right in the " light of the nineteenth century "— this most paradoxical age of all!

Now, to what does it lead?

INQ.—*Does it not make the Christian happier than the Buddhist or Brâhman?*

THEO.—No; not the educated man, at any rate, since the majority of these have long since virtually lost all belief in this cruel dogma.   But it leads those who still believe in it more easily *to the threshold of every conceivable crime* than any other I know of.   Let me quote to you from *Isis Unveiled* once more (ii., 542, 543):

If we step outside the little circle of creed and consider the universe as a whole balanced by the exquisite adjustment of parts, how all sound logic, how the faintest glimmering sense of justice, revolts against this vicarious atonement! If the criminal sinned only against himself, and wronged no one but himself; if by sincere repentance he could cause the obliteration of past events, not only from the memory of man, but also from that imperishable record which no deity—not even the Supremest of the Supreme—can cause to disappear, then this dogma might not be incomprehensible. But to maintain that one may wrong his fellow-man, kill, disturb the equilibrium of society and the natural order of things, and then—through cowardice, hope, or compulsion matters not—be forgiven by believing that the spilling of one blood washes out the other blood spilled—this is preposterous! Can the *results* of a crime be obliterated even though the crime itself should be pardoned? The effects of a cause are never limited to the boundaries of the cause, nor can the results of crime be confined to the offender and his victim. Every good as well as evil action has its effects, as palpably as the stone flung into calm water. The simile is trite, but it is the best ever conceived, so let us use it. The eddying circles are greater and swifter as the disturbing object is greater or smaller; but the smallest pebble—nay, the tiniest speck—makes its ripples. And this disturbance is not alone visible and on the surface. Below, unseen, in every direction—outward and downward—drop pushes drop until the sides and bottom are touched by the force. More, the air above the water is agitated, and this disturbance passes, as the physicists tell us, from stratum to stratum out into space for ever and ever; an impulse has been given to matter, and that is never lost, can never be recalled! . . .

So with crime and so with its opposite. The action may be instantaneous, the effects are eternal. When, after the stone is once flung into the pond, we can recall it to the hand, roll back the ripples, obliterate the force expended, restore the etheric waves to their previous state of non-being, and wipe out every trace of the act of throwing the missile, so that Time's record shall not show that it ever happened, then, *then* we may patiently hear Christians argue for the efficacy of this atonement.

and—cease to believe in karmic law. As it now stands, we call upon the whole world to decide which of our two doctrines is the most appreciative of deific justice, and which is more reasonable, even on simple human evidence and logic.

Inq.— *Yet millions believe in the Christian dogma and are happy.*

Theo.—Pure sentimentalism overpowering their thinking faculties, which no true philanthropist or altruist will ever accept. It is not even a dream of selfishness, but a nightmare of the human intellect. Look where it leads to, and tell me the name of that pagan country where crimes are more easily committed or more numerous than in Christian lands.   Look at the long and ghastly annual records of crimes committed in European countries; and behold Protestant and biblical America.   There *conversions* effected in prisons are more numerous than those made by public *revivals* and preaching.

See how the ledger-balance of Christian justice (!) stands.   Red-handed murderers, urged on by the demons of lust, revenge, cupidity, fanaticism, or mere brutal thirst for blood, who kill their victims, in most cases, without giving them time to repent or call on Jesus. These, perhaps, died sinful, and, of course—consistently with theological logic—met the reward of their greater or lesser offenses.   But the murderer, overtaken by human justice, is imprisoned, wept over by sentimentalists, prayed with and at, pronounces the charmed words of conversion, and goes to the scaffold a redeemed child of Jesus!   Except for the murder he would not have been prayed with, redeemed, pardoned.   Clearly this man did well to murder, for thus he gained eternal happiness!   And how about the victim, and his or her family, relatives, dependents, social relations; has justice no recompense for them? Must they suffer in this world and the next, while he who wronged them sits beside the "holy thief" of Calvary and is forever blessed? On this question the clergy keep a prudent silence.*

And now you know why Theosophists—whose fundamental belief and hope is justice for all, in heaven as on earth, and in Karma—reject this dogma.

INQ.—*The ultimate destiny of man, then, is not a heaven presided over by God, but the gradual transformation of matter into its primordial element, spirit?*

THEO.—It is to that final goal to which all tends in Nature.

INQ.—*Do not some of you regard this association or "fall of spirit into matter" as evil, and rebirth as a sorrow?*

---

* *Isis Unveiled, ibid.*

THEO.—Some do, and therefore strive to shorten their period of probation on earth. It is not, however, an unmixed evil, since it insures the experience upon which we mount to knowledge and wisdom. I mean that experience which *teaches* that the needs of our spiritual nature can never be met by other than spiritual happiness. As long as we are in the body we are subjected to pain, suffering, and all the disappointing incidents occurring during life. Therefore, and to palliate this, we finally acquire knowledge which alone can afford us relief and hope of a better future.

XII.

WHAT IS PRACTICAL THEOSOPHY?

DUTY.

INQ.—*Why, then, the need for rebirths, since all alike fail to secure a permanent peace ?*

THEO.—Because the final goal cannot be reached in any way but through life-experiences, and because the bulk of these consists in pain and suffering. It is only through the latter that we can learn. Joys and pleasures teach us nothing; they are evanescent, and can only in the long run bring satiety. Moreover, our constant failure to find any permanent satisfaction in life which would meet the wants of our higher nature shows us plainly that those wants can be met only on their own plane—to wit, the spiritual.

INQ.—*Is the natural result of this a desire to quit life by one means or another ?*

THEO.—If you mean by such desire " suicide," then I say, most decidedly not. Such a result can never be a " natural " one, but is ever due to a morbid brain-disease, or to most decided and strong materialistic views. It is the worst of crimes, and dire in its results. But if by desire you mean simply aspiration to reach spiritual existence, and not a wish to quit the earth, then I would call it a very

202

natural desire indeed. Otherwise voluntary death would be an abandonment of our present post and of the duties incumbent on us, as well as an attempt to shirk karmic responsibilities, and thus involve the creation of new Karma.

INQ.—*But if actions on the material plane are unsatisfying, why should duties, which are such actions, be imperative ?*

THEO.—First of all, because our philosophy teaches us that the object of doing our duties to all men first and to ourselves last is not the attainment of personal happiness, but of the happiness of others ; the fulfilment of right for the sake of right, not for what it may bring us. Happiness, or rather contentment, may indeed follow the performance of duty, but is not and must not be the motive for it.

INQ.—*What do you understand precisely by "duty" in Theosophy ? It cannot be the Christian duties preached by Jesus and his apostles, since you recognize neither.*

THEO.—You are once more mistaken. What you call "Christian" duties were inculcated by every great moral and religious reformer ages before the Christian era. All that was great, generous, heroic, was, in days of old, not only talked about and preached from pulpits as in our own time, but *acted upon*, sometimes by whole nations. The history of the Buddhist reform is full of the most noble and most heroically unselfish acts. "Be ye all of one mind, having compassion one of another; love as brethren, be pitiful, be courteous: not rendering evil for evil, or railing for railing: but contrariwise blessing," was practically carried out by the followers of Buddha several centuries before Peter. The ethics of Christianity are grand, no doubt; but, as undoubtedly, they are not new, and have originated as "pagan" duties.

INQ.—*And how would you define these duties, or "duty" in general, as you understand the term ?*

THEO.—Duty is that which is *due* to humanity—to our fellow-men, neighbors, family—and especially that which we owe to all those who are poorer and more helpless than we are ourselves. This is a debt which, if left unpaid during life, leaves us spiritually insolvent and moral bankrupts in our next incarnation. Theosophy is the quintessence of duty.

INQ.—*So is Christianity when rightly understood and carried out.*

THEO.—No doubt it is; but then, were it not a *lip-religion* in practice, Theosophy would have little to do amid Christians. Unfortunately it is but such lip-ethics. Those who practise their duty toward all, and for duty's own sake, are few; and fewer still are those who perform that duty, remaining content with the satisfaction of their own secret consciousness. It is

> The public voice
> Of praise, that honors virtue and rewards it,

which is ever uppermost in the minds of the "world-renowned" philanthropists. Modern ethics are beautiful to read about and hear discussed; but what are words unless converted into actions? Finally, if you ask me how we understand Theosophical duty practically and in view of Karma, I may answer you that our duty is to drink to the last drop, without a murmur, whatever contents the cup of life may have in store for us, to pluck the roses of life only for the fragrance they may shed on others, and to be ourselves content but with the thorns, if that fragrance cannot be enjoyed without depriving some one else of it.

INQ.—*All this is very vague. What do you do more than Christians do?*

THEO.—It is not what we members of the Theosophical Society do—though some of us try our best—but how much farther Theosophy leads to good than modern Christianity does. I say *action*—enforced action—instead of mere intention and talk. A man may be what he likes —the most worldly, selfish, and hard-hearted of men, even a deep-dyed rascal—and it will not prevent him from calling himself a Christian, or others from so regarding him. But no Theosophist has the right to this name unless he is thoroughly imbued with the correctness of Carlyle's truism, "The end of man is an *action* and not a *thought*, though it were the noblest," and unless he sets and models his daily life upon this truth. The profession of a truth is not yet the enactment of it; and the more beautiful and grand it sounds, the more loudly virtue or duty is talked about instead of being acted upon, the more forcibly it will always remind one of the Dead Sea fruit. *Cant* is the most loathsome of all vices, and cant is the most prominent feature of the greatest Protestant country of this century—England.

Inq.—*What do you consider as due to humanity at large?*

Theo.—Full recognition of equal rights and privileges for all, without distinction of race, color, social position, or birth.

Inq.—*When would you consider such due not given?*

Theo.—When there is the slightest invasion of another's right, be that other a man or a nation; when there is any failure to show him the same justice, kindness, consideration, or mercy which we desire for ourselves. The whole present system of politics is built on the oblivion of such rights and the most fierce assertion of national selfishness. The French say, "Like master, like man;" they ought to add, "Like national policy, like citizen."

Inq.—*Do you take any part in politics?*

Theo.—As a society we carefully avoid them, for the reasons given below. To seek to achieve political reforms before we have effected a reform in human nature is like putting new wine into old bottles. Make men feel and recognize in their innermost hearts what is their real, true duty to all men, and every old abuse of power, every iniquitous law in the national policy based on human, social, or political selfishness, will disappear of itself. Foolish is the gardener who tries to weed his flower-bed of poisonous plants by cutting them off from the surface of the soil, instead of tearing them out by the roots. No lasting political reform can be ever achieved with the same selfish men at the head of affairs as of old.

THE RELATIONS OF THE THEOSOPHICAL SOCIETY TO POLITICAL REFORMS.

INQ.—*The Theosophical Society is not, then, a political organization ?*

THEO.—Certainly not. It is international in the highest sense, in that its members comprise men and women of all races, creeds, and forms of thought, who work together for one object—the improvement of humanity ; but as a society it takes absolutely no part in any national or party politics.

INQ.—*Why is this ?*

THEO.—For the very reasons I have mentioned. Moreover, political action must necessarily vary with the circumstances of the time and with the idiosyncrasies of individuals. While, from the very nature of their position as Theosophists, the members of the Theosophical Society are agreed on the principles of Theosophy, or they would not belong to the Society at all, it does not thereby follow that they agree on every other subject. As a society they can only act together in matters which are common to all —that is, in Theosophy itself ; as individuals, each is left perfectly free to follow out his or her particular line of political thought and action, so long as this does not conflict with Theosophical principles or hurt the Theosophical Society.

INQ.—*But surely the Theosophical Society does not stand altogether aloof from the social questions which are now so fast coming to the front?*

THEO.—The very principles of the Theosophical Society are a proof that it does not—or, rather, that most of its members do not—so stand aloof. If humanity can only be developed mentally and spiritually by the enforcement, first of all, of the soundest and most scientific physiological laws, it is the bounden duty of all who strive for this development to do their utmost to see that those laws shall be generally carried out. All Theosophists are only too sadly aware that, in Occidental countries especially, the social condition of large masses of the people renders it impossible for either their bodies or their spirits to be properly trained, so that the development of both is thereby arrested. As this training and development is one of the express objects of Theosophy, the Theosophical Society is in thorough sympathy and harmony with all true efforts in this direction.

INQ.—*But what do you mean by " true efforts" ? Each social reformer has his own panacea, and each believes his to be the one and only thing which can improve and save humanity.*

·THEO.—Perfectly true; and this is the real reason why so little satisfactory social work is accomplished. In most of these panaceas there is no really guiding principle, and there is certainly no one principle which connects them all. Valuable time and energy are thus wasted; for men, instead of coöperating, strive one against the other, often, it is to be feared, for the sake of fame and reward rather than for the great cause which they profess to have at heart, and which should be supreme in their lives.

INQ.—*How, then, should Theosophical principles be applied so that social coöperation may be promoted and true efforts for social amelioration be carried on ?*

THEO.—Let me briefly remind you what these principles are: Universal Unity and Causation; Human Solidarity; the Law of Karma; Reincarnation. These are the four links of the golden chain which should bind humanity into one family, one Universal Brotherhood.

INQ.—*How ?*

THEO.—In the present state of society, especially in so-called civilized countries, we are continually brought face to face with the fact that large numbers of people are suffering from misery, poverty, and disease. Their physical condition is wretched, and their mental and spiritual faculties are often almost dormant. On the other hand, many persons at the opposite end of the social scale are leading lives of careless indifference, material luxury, and selfish indulgence. Neither of these forms of existence is mere chance. Both are the effects of the conditions which surround those who are subject to them, and the neglect of social duty on the one side is most closely connected with the stunted and arrested development on the other. In sociology, as in all branches of true science, the law of universal causation holds good. But this causation necessarily implies, as its logical outcome, that human solidarity on which Theosophy so strongly insists. If the action of one reacts on the lives of all—and this is the true scientific idea— then it is only by all men becoming brothers and all women sisters, and by all practising in their daily lives true brotherhood and true sisterhood, that the real human solidarity which lies at the root of the elevation of the race can ever be attained. It is this action and interaction, this true brotherhood and sisterhood, in which each shall live for all and all for each, which is one of the fundamental Theosophical principles that every Theosophist should be bound not only to teach, but to carry out in his or her individual life.

INQ.—*All this is very well as a general principle, but how would you apply it in a concrete way?*

THEO.—Look for a moment at what you would call the concrete facts of human society. Contrast the lives not only of the masses of the people, but of many of those who are called the middle and upper classes, with what they might be under healthier and nobler conditions, where justice, kindness, and love were paramount, instead of the selfishness, indifference, and brutality which now too often seem to reign supreme. All good and evil things in humanity have their roots in human character, and this character is, and has been, conditioned by the endless chain of cause and effect. But this conditioning applies to the future as well as to the present and the past. Selfishness, indifference, and brutality can never be the normal state of the race; to believe so would be to despair of humanity, and that no Theosophist can do. Progress can be attained, and only attained, by the development of the nobler qualities. Now, true evolution teaches us that by altering the surroundings of the organism we can alter and improve the organism; and in the strictest sense this is true with regard to man. Every Theosophist, therefore, is bound to do his utmost to help on, by all the means in his power, every wise and well-considered social effort which has for its object the amelioration of the condition of the poor. Such efforts should be made with a view to their ultimate social emancipation, or the development of the sense of duty in those who now so often neglect it in nearly every relation of life.

INQ.—*Agreed.   But who is to decide whether social efforts are wise or unwise ?*

THEO.—No one person and no society can lay down a hard-and-fast rule in this respect.   Much must necessarily be left to the individual judgment.   One general test may, however, be given: Will the proposed action tend to promote that true brotherhood which it is the aim of Theosophy to bring about ?   No real Theosophist will have much difficulty in applying such a test; once he is satisfied of this, his duty will lie in the direction of forming public opinion. And this can be attained only by inculcating those higher and nobler conceptions of public and private duties which lie at the root of all spiritual and material improvement. In every conceivable case he himself must be a center of spiritual action, and from him and his own daily individual life must radiate those higher spiritual forces which alone can regenerate his fellow-men.

INQ.—*But why should he do this ?   Are not he and all, as you teach, conditioned by their Karma, and must not Karma necessarily work itself out on certain lines ?*

THEO.—It is this very law of Karma which gives strength to all that I have said.   The individual cannot separate himself from the race, nor the race from the individual.   The law of Karma applies equally to all, although all are not equally developed.   In helping on the development of others the Theosophist believes that he is not only helping them to fulfil their Karma, but that he is also, in the strictest sense, fulfilling his own.   It is the development of humanity, of which both he and they are integral parts, that he has always in view, and he knows that any failure on his part to respond to the highest within him retards not only himself, but all, in their progressive march.   By his actions he can make it either more difficult or more easy for humanity to attain the next higher plane of being.

INQ.—*How does this bear on the fourth of the principles you mentioned, viz., reincarnation?*

THEO.—The connection is most intimate. If our present lives depend upon the development of certain principles which are a growth from the germs left by a previous existence, the law holds good as regards the future. Once grasp the idea that universal causation is not merely present, but past, present, and future, and every action on our present plane falls naturally and easily into its true place, and is seen in its true relation to ourselves and to others. Every mean and selfish action sends us backward and not forward, while every noble thought and every unselfish deed are stepping-stones to the higher and more glorious planes of being. If this life were all, then in many respects it would indeed be poor and mean; but regarded as a preparation for the next sphere of existence, it may be used as the golden gate through which we may pass—not selfishly and alone, but in company with our fellows—to the palaces which lie beyond.

ON SELF-SACRIFICE.

INQ.—*Is equal justice to all and love to every creature the highest standard of Theosophy?*

THEO.—No; there is an even far higher one.

INQ.—*What can it be?*

THEO.—The giving to others *more* than to one's self—*self-sacrifice.* Such was the standard and abounding measure which marked so preëminently the greatest teachers and masters of humanity—such as Gautama Buddha in history, and Jesus of Nazareth in the Gospels. This trait alone was enough to secure them the perpetual reverence and gratitude of the generations of men that came after them. We say, however, that self-sacrifice has to be performed with discrimination; and such a self-abandonment, if made without justice, or blindly, regardless of subsequent results, may often prove not only to have been made in vain, but even to be harmful.   One of the fundamental rules of Theosophy is justice to one's self—viewed as a unit of collective humanity, not as a personal self—justice, not more, but not less, than to others; unless, indeed, by the sacrifice of the one Self we can benefit the many.

Inq.—*Could you make your idea clearer by giving an instance ?*

Theo.—There are many instances to illustrate it in history.   Self-sacrifice for the practical good of many or several people Theosophy holds far higher than self-abnegation for a sectarian idea, such as that of "saving the heathen from damnation," for instance.   In our opinion, Father Damien, the young man of thirty who offered his whole life in sacrifice for the benefit and alleviation of the sufferings of the lepers at Molokai; who, after living for eighteen years alone with them, finally caught the loathsome disease and died, has not died in vain.   He has given relief and relative happiness to thousands of miserable wretches.   He has brought to them consolation, mental and physical.   He threw a streak of light into the black and dreary night of an existence the hopelessness of which is unparalleled in the records of human suffering.   He was a true Theosophist, and his memory will live forever in our annals.   In our sight this poor Belgian priest stands immeasurably higher than, for instance, all those sincere but vainglorious fools, the missionaries who have sacrificed their lives in the South Sea Islands or China.   What good have they done?   They went in one case to those who were not yet ripe for any truth; and in the other to a nation whose systems of religious philosophy are as grand as any, if only the men who have them would live up to the standard of their Confucius

and other sages. They died victims of irresponsible canni-
bals and savages, and of popular fanaticism and hatred;
whereas, by going to the slums of Whitechapel, or some
other such locality of those that stagnate right under the
blazing sun of our civilization, full of Christian savages and
mental leprosy, they might have done real good, and preserved their lives for a better and worthier cause.

INQ.—*But the Christians do not think so.*

THEO.—Of course not, for they act on an erroneous belief. They think that by baptizing the body of an irresponsible savage they save his soul from damnation. One church
forgets her martyrs, the other beatifies and raises statues to
such men as Labre, who sacrificed his body for forty years
only to benefit the vermin which it bred. Had we the
means to do so, we would raise a statue to Father Damien,
the true, practical saint, and perpetuate his memory forever
as a living exemplar of Theosophical heroism and of Buddha-
and Christ-like mercy and self-sacrifice.

INQ.—*Then you regard self-sacrifice as a duty ?*

THEO.—We do; and explain it by showing that altruism
is an integral part of self-development. But we have to dis-
criminate. A man has no right to starve himself *to death*
that another man may have food, unless the life of that
man is obviously more useful to the many than is his own
life. But it is his duty to sacrifice his own comfort, and to
work for others, if they are unable to work for themselves.
It is his duty to give all that is wholly his own and can
benefit no one but himself if he selfishly keeps it from others.
Theosophy teaches self-abnegation, but does not teach rash
and useless self-sacrifice, nor does it justify fanaticism.

INQ.—*But how are we to reach such an elevated status ?*

THEO.—By the enlightened application of our precepts
to practice; by the use of our higher reason, spiritual intui-

tion, and moral sense; and by following the dictates of what we call "the still small voice" of our conscience, which is that of our Ego, and speaks louder in us than the earthquakes and the thunders of Jehovah, wherein "the Lord is not."

INQ.—*If such are our duties to humanity at large, what do you understand by our duties to our immediate surroundings?*

THEO.—Just the same, plus those that arise from special obligations with regard to family ties.

INQ.—*Then it is not true, as it is said, that no sooner does a man enter into the Theosophical Society than he begins to be gradually severed from his wife, children, and family duties?*

THEO.—It is a groundless calumny, like so many others. The first of the Theosophical duties is to do one's duty by all men, and especially by those to whom one's *specific* responsibilities are due, because one has either voluntarily undertaken them—such as marriage ties—or because one's destiny has allied one to them—such as those we owe to parents or next of kin.

INQ.—*And what may be the duty of a Theosophist to himself?*

THEO.—To control and conquer, through the Higher Self, the lower self; to purify himself inwardly and morally; to fear no one, and naught, save the tribunal of his own conscience; never to do a thing by halves—i.e., if he thinks it the right thing to do, let him do it openly and boldly; and if wrong, never touch it at all. It is the duty of a Theosophist to lighten his burden by thinking of the wise aphorism of Epictetus, who says:

Be not diverted from your duty by any idle reflection the silly world may make upon you, for their censures are not in your power, and consequently should not be any part of your concern.

INQ.—*But suppose a member of your Society should plead inability to practise altruism to other people on the ground that*

" charity begins at home"; urging that he is too busy, or too poor, to benefit mankind or even any of its units ; what are your rules in such a case ?

THEO.—No man, on any pretext whatever, has a right to say that he can do nothing for others. " By doing the proper duty in the proper place, a man may make the world his debtor," says an English writer. A cup of cold water given in time to a thirsty wayfarer is a nobler duty, and of more worth, than a dozen dinners given away, out of season, to men who can afford to pay for them. No man who has not got it in him will ever become a Theosophist; but he may remain a member of our Society all the same. We have no rules by which we can force any man to become a practical Theosophist if he does not desire to be one.

INQ.—*Then why does he enter the Society at all ?*

THEO.—That is best known to him who does so. For, here again, we have no right to prejudge a person, not even if the voice of a whole community should be against him, and I may tell you why. In our day *vox populi*—so far as regards the voice of the educated, at any rate—is no longer *vox Dei*, but ever that of prejudice, of selfish motives, and often simply of unpopularity. Our duty is to sow seeds broadcast for the future, and see they are good; not to stop to inquire *why* we should do so, and how and wherefore we are obliged to lose our time, since those who will reap the harvest in days to come will never be ourselves.

ON CHARITY.

INQ.—*How do you Theosophists regard the Christian duty of charity ?*

THEO.—What charity do you mean—charity of mind, or practical charity on the physical plane ?

INQ.—*I mean practical charity, as your idea of universal brotherhood would include, of course, charity of mind.*

THEO.—Then you have in your mind the practical carrying out of the commandments given by Jesus in the Sermon on the Mount ?

INQ.—*Precisely so.*

THEO.—Then why call them "Christian"? For, although their Saviour preached and practised them, the last thing the Christians of to-day think of is to carry them out in their lives.

INQ.—*And yet many are those who pass their lives in dispensing charity.*

THEO.—Yes, out of the surplus of their great fortunes. But point out to me that Christian, among the most philanthropic, who would give the shivering and starving thief who steals his coat his cloak also, or offer his right cheek to him who smites him on the left, and never think of resenting it.

INQ.—*Ah ! but you must remember that these precepts have not to be taken literally. Times and circumstances have changed since Christ's day. Moreover, he spoke in parables.*

THEO.—Then why do not your churches teach that the doctrine of damnation and hell-fire is to be understood as a parable too ? Why do some of your most popular preachers, while virtually allowing these parables to be understood as you take them, insist on the literal meaning of the fires of hell and the physical tortures of an "asbestos-like" soul ? If one is a parable, then the other is. If hell-fire is a literal truth, then Christ's commandments in the Sermon on the Mount have to be obeyed to the very letter. And I tell you that many who do not believe in the divinity of Christ—like Count Leo Tolstoï and more than one

Theosophist—do carry out these noble and universal precepts literally; and many more good men and women would do so were they not more than certain that such a walk in life would very probably land them in a lunatic asylum—so Christian are your laws !

INQ.—*But surely every one knows that millions and millions are spent annually on private and public charities ?*

THEO.—Oh yes; and half of it sticks to the hands it passes through before getting to the needy, while a good portion of the remainder gets into the hands of professional beggars, who are too lazy to work, thus doing no good whatever to those who are really in misery and suffering. Have you not heard that the first result of the great outflow of charity toward the East End of London was to raise the rents in Whitechapel some twenty percent. ?

INQ.—*What would you do, then ?*

THEO.—Act individually and not collectively; follow the Northern Buddhist precepts:

Never put food into the mouth of the hungry by the hand of another.
Never let the shadow of thy neighbor [a third person] come between thyself and the object of thy bounty.
Never give to the sun time to dry a tear before thou hast wiped it.
Never give money to the needy, or food to the priest, who begs at thy door, *through thy servants*, lest thy money should diminish gratitude, and thy food turn to gall.

INQ.—*But how can this be applied practically ?*

THEO.—The Theosophical idea of charity means *personal* exertion for others; *personal* mercy and kindness; *personal* interest in the welfare of those who suffer; *personal* sympathy, forethought, and assistance in their troubles or needs. Theosophists do not believe in giving money through other people's hands or organizations. We believe in giving to the money a thousandfold greater power and effectiveness by our personal contact and sympathy with those who need it. We believe in relieving the starvation of the soul, as much, if not more than, the emptiness of the stomach; for gratitude does more good to the man who feels it than to him for whom it is felt. Where is the gratitude which your "millions of pounds" should have called forth, or the good feelings provoked by them? Is it shown in the hatred of the East End poor for the rich, in the growth of the party of anarchy and disorder, or by those thousands of unfortunate working-girls, victims to the "sweating" system, driven daily to eke out a living by going on the streets? Do your helpless old men and women thank you for the workhouses; or your poor for the poisonously unhealthy dwellings in which they are allowed to breed new generations of diseased, scrofulous, and rickety children, only to put money into the pockets of the insatiable Shylocks who own houses? Therefore it is that every sovereign of all those "millions" contributed by good and would-be charitable people falls like a burning curse instead of a blessing on the poor whom it should relieve. We call this *generating national Karma*, and terrible will be its results on the day of reckoning.

THEOSOPHY FOR THE MASSES.

INQ.—*And you think that Theosophy would, by stepping in, help to remove these evils, under the practical and adverse conditions of our modern life?*

THEO.—Had we more money, and had not most of the Theosophists to work for their daily bread, I firmly believe we could.

INQ.—*How? Do you expect that your doctrines could ever take hold of the uneducated masses, when they are so abstruse and difficult that well-educated people can hardly understand them ?*

THEO.—You forget one thing: that your much-boasted modern education is precisely that which makes it difficult for you to understand Theosophy. Your mind is so full of intellectual subtleties and preconceptions that your natural intuition and perception of truth cannot act. It does not require metaphysics or education to make a man understand the broad truths of Karma and reincarnation. Look at the millions of poor and uneducated Buddhists and Hindûs, to whom Karma and reincarnation are solid realities, simply because their minds have never been cramped and distorted by being forced into an unnatural groove. They have never had the innate human sense of justice perverted in them by being told to believe that their sins would be for-given because another man had been put to death for their sakes. And the Buddhists, note well, live up to their beliefs without a murmur against Karma or what they regard as a just punishment; whereas the Christian populace neither lives up to its moral ideal, nor accepts its lot contentedly. Hence murmuring and dissatisfaction, and the intensity of the struggle for existence in Western lands.

INQ.—*But this contentedness, which you praise so much, would do away with all motive for exertion and bring progress to a standstill.*

THEO.—And we Theosophists say that your vaunted progress and civilization are no better than a host of will-o'-the-wisps flickering over a marsh which exhales a poisonous and deadly miasma. This because we see selfish-ness, crime, immorality, and all the evils imaginable, pounc-ing upon unfortunate mankind from this Pandora's box which you call an age of progress, and increasing *pari passu* with the growth of your material civilization. At such a price, better the inertia and inactivity of Buddhist countries, which have resulted only as a consequence of ages of political slavery.

INQ.—*Then are all these metaphysics and mysticism with which you occupy yourself so much of no importance ?*

THEO.—To the masses, who need only practical guidance and support, they are not of much consequence; but for the educated, the natural leaders of the masses, those whose modes of thought and action will sooner or later be adopted by these masses, they are of the greatest importance. It is only by means of the philosophy that an intelligent and educated man can avoid the intellectual suicide of believing on blind faith; and it is only by assimilating the strict continuity and logical coherence of the Eastern, if not esoteric, doctrines that he can realize their truth. Conviction breeds enthusiasm, and "enthusiasm," says Bulwer Lytton, "is the genius of sincerity, and truth accomplishes no victories without it;" while Emerson most truly remarks that "every great and commanding movement in the annals of the world is the triumph of enthusiasm." And what is more calculated to produce such a feeling than a philosophy so grand, so consistent, so logical, and so all-embracing as our Eastern doctrines ?

INQ.—*And yet its enemies are very numerous, and every day Theosophy acquires new opponents.*

THEO.—And this is precisely what proves its intrinsic excellence and value. People hate only the things they fear, and no one goes out of his way to overthrow that which neither threatens nor rises beyond mediocrity.

INQ.—*Do you hope to impart this enthusiasm one day to the masses ?*

THEO.—Why not?—since history tells us that the masses adopted Buddhism with enthusiasm, while, as said before, the practical effect upon them of this philosophy of ethics is still shown by the smallness of the percentage of crime among Buddhist populations as compared with every other religion. The chief point is to uproot that most fertile source of all crime and immorality—the belief that it is possible for men to escape the consequences of their own actions. Once teach them that greatest of all laws, Karma and reincarnation, and besides feeling in themselves the true dignity of human nature, they will turn from evil and eschew it as they would a physical danger.

HOW MEMBERS CAN HELP THE SOCIETY.

INQ.—*How do you expect the Fellows of your Society to help in the work?*

THEO.—First, by studying and comprehending the Theosophical doctrines, so that they may teach others, especially the young people. Secondly, by taking every opportunity of talking to others and explaining to them what Theosophy is and what it is not; by removing misconceptions and spreading an interest in the subject. Thirdly, by assisting in circulating our literature by buying books when they have the means, by lending and giving them, and by inducing their friends to do so. Fourthly, by defending the Society from the unjust aspersions cast upon it by every legitimate device in their power. Fifthly, and most important of all, by the example of their own lives.

INQ.—*But all this literature, to the spread of which you attach so much importance, does not seem to me of much practical use in helping mankind. This is not practical charity.*

THEO.—We think otherwise. We hold that a good book which gives people food for thought, which strengthens and clears their minds, and enables them to grasp truths which they have dimly felt, but could not formulate—we hold that such a book does a real, substantial good. As to what you call practical deeds of charity, to benefit the bodies of our fellow-men, we do what little we can; but, as I have already told you, most of us are poor, while the Society itself has not even the money to pay a staff of workers. All of us who toil for it give our labor gratis, and in most cases money as well. The few who have the means of doing what are usually called charitable actions follow the Buddhist precepts and do their work themselves—not by proxy or by subscribing publicly to charitable funds. What the Theosophist has to do above all is to forget his personality.

WHAT A THEOSOPHIST OUGHT NOT TO DO.

INQ.—*Have you any prohibitory laws or clauses for Theosophists in your Society?*

THEO.—Many; but alas! none of them are enforced. They express the ideal of our organization; but the practical application of such things we are compelled to leave to the discretion of the Fellows themselves. Unfortunately, the state of men's minds in the present century is such that, unless we allow these clauses to remain, so to speak, obsolete, no man or woman would dare to risk joining the Theosophical Society. This is precisely why I feel forced to lay such a stress on the difference between true Theosophy and its hard-struggling and well-intentioned but still unworthy vehicle, the Theosophical Society.

INQ.—*May I be told what are these perilous reefs in the open sea of Theosophy?*

THEO.—Well may you call them reefs, as more than one otherwise sincere and well-meaning Fellow of the Theosophical Society has had his Theosophical canoe shattered into splinters on them! And yet to avoid certain things seems the easiest thing in the world to do. For instance, here is a series of such negatives, screening positive Theosophical duties:

No Theosophist should be silent when he hears evil reports or slanders spread about the Society or innocent persons, whether they be his colleagues or outsiders.

Inq.—*But suppose what one hears is the truth, or may be true without one knowing it ?*

Theo.—Then you must demand good proofs of the assertion, and hear both sides impartially, before you permit the accusation to go uncontradicted. You have no right to believe in evil until you get undeniable proof of the correctness of the statement.

Inq.—*And what should you do then ?*

Theo.—Pity and forbearance, charity and long-suffering, ought to be always there to prompt us to excuse our sinning brethren, and to pass the gentlest sentence possible upon those who err. A Theosophist ought never to forget what is due to the shortcomings and infirmities of human nature.

Inq.—*Ought he to forgive entirely in such cases ?*

Theo.—In every case, especially he who is sinned against.

Inq.—*But if by so doing he risks injuring or allows others to be injured, what ought he to do then ?*

Theo.—His duty—that which his conscience and higher nature suggest to him; but only after mature deliberation. Justice consists in doing no injury to any living being; but justice commands us also never to allow injury to be done to the many, or even to one innocent person, by allowing the guilty one to go unchecked.

Inq.—*What are the other negative clauses ?*

Theo.—No Theosophist ought to be contented with an idle or frivolous life, doing no real good to himself and still

less to others. He should work for the benefit of the few
who need his help, if he is unable to toil for humanity, and
thus work for the advancement of the Theosophical cause.

INQ.—*This demands an exceptional nature, and would come
rather hard upon some persons.*

THEO.—Then they had better remain outside of the
Theosophical Society, instead of sailing under false colors.
No one is asked to give more than he can afford, whether
in devotion, time, work, or money.

INQ.—*What comes next ?*

THEO.—No working member should set too great value
on his personal progress or proficiency in Theosophic stud-
ies; but must be prepared, rather, to do as much altruistic
work as lies in his power. He should not leave the whole
of the heavy burden and responsibility of the Theosophical
movement on the shoulders of the few devoted workers.
Each member ought to feel it his duty to take what share he
can in the common work, and help it by every means in his
power.

INQ.—*This is but just.   What comes next ?*

THEO.—No Theosophist should place his personal vanity
or feelings above those of his Society as a body. He who
sacrifices the latter, or other people's reputations, on the
altar of his personal vanity, worldly benefit, or pride, ought
not to be allowed to remain a member.   One cancerous
limb diseases the whole body.

INQ.—*Is it the duty of every member to teach others and
preach Theosophy ?*

THEO.—It is indeed.   No Fellow has a right to remain
idle on the excuse that he knows too little to teach.   For
he may always be sure that he will find others who know
still less than himself.   And also it is not until a man be-

gins to try to teach others that he discovers his own ignorance and tries to remove it.   But this is a minor clause.

INQ.—*What do you consider, then, to be the chief of these
negative Theosophical duties ?*

THEO.—To be ever prepared to recognize and confess
one's faults; to rather sin through exaggerated praise than
through too little appreciation of one's neighbor's efforts;
never to backbite or slander another person; always to say
openly and direct to his face anything you have against him;
never to make yourself the echo of anything you may hear
against another, nor harbor revenge against those who
happen to injure you.

INQ.—*But it is often dangerous to tell people the truth to
their faces. Do you not think so ?   I know of one of your
members who was bitterly offended, left the Society, and became its greatest enemy, only because he was told some unpleasant truths to his face, and was blamed for them.*

THEO.—Of such we have had many.   No member,
whether prominent or insignificant, has ever left us without
becoming our bitter enemy.

INQ.—*How do you account for it ?*

THEO.—It is simply this: having been, in most cases,
intensely devoted to the Society at first, and having lavished
upon it the most exaggerated praises, the only possible excuse such a backslider can make for his subsequent behavior and past short-sightedness is *to pose as an innocent
and deceived victim,* thus casting the blame from his own
shoulders on to those of the Society in general, and its
leaders especially. . Such persons remind one of the old
fable about the man with a distorted face, who broke his
looking-glass in the belief that it reflected his countenance
crookedly.

INQ.—*But what makes these people turn against the Society ?*

THEO.—Wounded vanity in some form or other, almost in every case. Generally because their dicta and advice are not taken as final and authoritative, or else because they are of those who would rather reign in hell than serve in heaven. Because, in short, they cannot bear to stand second to anybody in anything. So, for instance, one member—a true " Sir Oracle "—criticized and almost defamed every member in the Theosophical Society to outsiders as much as to Theosophists, under the pretext that they were all " untheosophical," blaming them precisely for what he was himself doing all the time. Finally he left the Society, giving as his reason a profound conviction that we were all (the founders especially) frauds ! Another one, after intriguing in every possible way to be placed at the head of a large section of the Society, finding that the members would not have him, turned against the founders of the Theosophical Society and became their bitterest enemy, denouncing one of them whenever he could, simply because the latter could not, and would not, force him upon the members. This was simply a case of an outrageous wounded vanity. Still another wanted to, and virtually did, practise black magic—i.e., undue personal psychological influence—on certain Fellows, while pretending devotion and every Theosophical virtue. When this was put a stop to, the member broke with Theosophy, and now slanders and lies against the same hapless leaders in the most virulent manner, endeavoring to break up the Society by blackening the reputation of those whom that worthy person was unable to deceive.

INQ.—*What would you do with such characters ?*

THEO.—Leave them to their Karma. Because one person does evil that is no reason for others to do so.

INQ.—*But, to return to slander, where is the line of demar-cation between backbiting and just criticism to be drawn? Is it not one's duty to warn one's friends and neighbors against those whom one knows to be dangerous associates?*

THEO.—If by allowing them to go on unchecked other persons may be thereby injured, it is certainly our duty to obviate the danger by warning them privately. But, true or false, no accusation against another person should ever be spread abroad. If true, and the fault hurts no one but the sinner, then leave him to his Karma. If false, then you will have avoided adding to the injustice in the world. Therefore keep silent about such things with every one not directly concerned. But if your discretion and silence are likely to hurt or endanger others, then I add, Speak the truth at all costs, and say with Annesley, "Consult duty, not events." There are cases when one is forced to ex-claim, "Perish discretion rather than allow it to interfere with duty!"

INQ.—*Methinks, if you carry out these maxims, you are likely to reap a nice crop of troubles!*

THEO.—And so we do. We have to admit that we are now open to the same taunt as the early Christians were. "See how these Theosophists love one another!" may now be said of us without a shadow of injustice.

INQ.—*Admitting yourself that there is at least as much, if not more, backbiting, slandering, and quarreling in the Theo-sophical Society as in the Christian churches, let alone scien-tific societies, what kind of brotherhood is this, may I ask?*

THEO.—A very poor specimen indeed as at present, and, until carefully sifted and reorganized, no better than all others. Remember, however, that human nature is the same in the Theosophical Society as out of it. Its mem-bers are no saints; they are at best sinners trying to do better, and liable to fall back owing to personal weakness. Add to this that our "brotherhood" is no recognized or established body, and stands, so to speak, outside of the pale of jurisdiction. Besides which, it is in a chaotic condition, and more unjustly unpopular than any other body. What wonder, then, that those members who fail to carry out its ideal should, after leaving the Society, turn for sympathetic protection to our enemies, and pour all their gall and bitterness into their too willing ears! Knowing that they will find support, sympathy, and ready credence for every accusation, however absurd, that it may please them to launch against the Theosophical Society, they hasten to do so, and vent their wrath on the innocent looking-glass which reflected too faithfully their faces. People never forgive those whom they have wronged. The sense of kindness received, and repaid by them with ingratitude, drives them into a madness of self-justification before the world and their own consciences. The former is but too ready to believe in anything said against a society it hates. The latter—but I will say no more, fearing I have already said too much.

INQ.—*Your position does not seem to me a very enviable one.*

THEO.—It is not. But do you not think that there must be something very noble, very exalted, very true, behind the Society and its philosophy, when the leaders and the founders of the movement still continue to work for it with all their strength? They sacrifice to it all comfort, all worldly prosperity and success, even to their good name and reputation—aye, even to their honor—to receive in return incessant and ceaseless obloquy, relentless persecution, untiring slander, constant ingratitude, and misunderstanding of their best efforts—blows and buffets from all sides—when by simply dropping their work they would find themselves immediately released from every responsibility, shielded from every further attack.

INQ.—*I confess such a perseverance seems to me very astounding, and I wondered why you did all this.*

THEO.—Believe me, for no self-gratification ; only in the hope of training a few individuals to carry on our work for humanity with its original program when the founders are dead and gone. They have already found a few such noble and devoted souls to replace them. The coming generations, thanks to these few, will find the path to peace a little less thorny, and the way a little widened, and thus all this suffering will have produced good results, and their self-sacrifice will not have been in vain. At present the main, fundamental object of the Society is to sow germs in the hearts of men which may in time sprout, and, under more propitious circumstances, lead to a healthy reform conducive of more happiness to the masses than they have hitherto enjoyed.

XIII.

ON THE MISCONCEPTIONS ABOUT THE THEO-
SOPHICAL SOCIETY.

THEOSOPHY AND ASCETICISM.

INQ.—*I have heard people say that your rules required all members to be vegetarians, celibates, and rigid ascetics ; but you have not told me anything of the sort yet.   Can you tell me the truth once for all about this ?*

THEO.—The truth is that our rules require nothing of the kind.   The Theosophical Society does not even expect, far less require, of any of its members that they should be ascetics in any way, except—if you call *that* asceticism— that they should try and benefit other people and be unselfish in their own lives.

INQ.—*But still many of your members are strict vegetarians, and openly avow their intention of remaining unmarried. This, too, is most often the case with those who take a prominent part in connection with the work of your Society.*

THEO.—That is only natural, because most of our really earnest workers are members of the inner section of the Society, about which I told you before.

INQ.—*Oh, then you do require ascetic practices in that inner section ?*

230

THEO.—No, we do not require or enjoin them even there. But I see that I had better give you an explanation of our views on the subject of asceticism in general, and then you will understand about vegetarianism and so on.

INQ.—*Please proceed.*

THEO.—As I have already told you, most people who become really earnest students of Theosophy and active workers in our Society wish to do more than study theoretically the truths we teach. They wish to *know* the truth by their own direct personal experience, and to study Occultism with the object of acquiring the wisdom and power which they feel they need in order to help others effectually and judiciously, instead of blindly and at haphazard. Therefore, sooner or later, they join the inner section.

INQ.—*But you said that "ascetic practices" are not obligatory even in that inner section.*

THEO.—No more they are; but the first thing which the members learn there is a true conception of the relation of the body, or physical sheath, to the inner, the true man. The relation and mutual interaction between these two aspects of human nature are explained and demonstrated to them, so that they soon become imbued with the supreme importance of the inner man over the outer case or body. They are taught that blind, unintelligent asceticism is mere folly; that such conduct as that of St. Labre, of which I spoke before, or that of the Indian fakirs and jungle ascetics, who cut, burn, and macerate their bodies in the most cruel and horrible manner, is simply self-torture for selfish ends—i.e., to develop will-power—but is perfectly useless for the purpose of assisting true spiritual or Theosophic development.

INQ.—*I see you regard only moral asceticism as necessary. It is as a means to an end, that end being the perfect equilib-*

rium of the inner *nature of man, and the attainment of complete mastery over the body, with all its passions and desires.*

THEO.—Just so.　But these means must be used intelligently and wisely, not blindly and foolishly; like an athlete who is training and preparing for a great contest, not like the miser who starves himself into illness that he may gratify his passion for gold.

INQ.—*I understand now your general idea ; but let us see how you apply it in practice.　How about vegetarianism, for instance ?*

THEO.—One of the great German scientists has shown that every kind of animal tissue, however you may cook it, still retains certain marked characteristics of the animal to which it belonged, and these characteristics can be recognized.　Apart from that, also, every one knows by the taste what meat he is eating.　We go a step farther, and prove that when the flesh of animals is assimilated by man as food, it imparts to him, physiologically, some of the characteristics of the animal it came from.　Moreover, occult science teaches and proves this to its students by ocular demonstration, showing also that this "coarsening" or "animalizing" effect on man is greatest from the flesh of the larger animals, less for birds, still less for fish and other cold-blooded animals, and least of all when he eats only vegetables.

INQ.—*Then would it be better not to eat at all ?*

THEO.—If he could live without eating, of course it would.　But as the matter stands, he must eat to live, and so we advise really earnest students to eat such food as will least clog and weight their brains and bodies, and will have the smallest effect in hampering and retarding the development of their intuition, their inner faculties and powers.

INQ.—*Then you do not adopt all the arguments which vege-tarians in general are in the habit of using?*

THEO.—Certainly not. Some of their arguments are very weak, and often based on assumptions which are quite false. But, on the other hand, many of the things they say are quite true. For instance, we believe that much disease, and especially the great predisposition to disease which is becoming so marked a feature in our time, is very largely due to the eating of meat, and especially of tinned meats. But it would take too long to go thoroughly into this question of vegetarianism on its merits; so please pass on to something else.

INQ.—*One question more: What are your members of the inner section to do with regard to their food when they are ill?*

THEO.—Follow the best practical advice they can get, of course. Do you not grasp yet that we never impose any hard-and-fast obligations in this respect? Remember once for all that in all such questions we take a rational, and never a fanatical, view of things. If from illness or long habit a man cannot go without meat, why, by all means, let him eat it. It is no crime; it will only retard his progress a little; for after all is said and done, the purely bodily actions and functions are of far less importance than what a man *thinks* and *feels;* what desires he encourages in his mind, and allows to take root and grow there.

INQ.—*Then with regard to the use of wine and spirits: I suppose you do not advise people to drink them?*

THEO.—They are worse for a man's moral and spiritual growth than meat, for alcohol in all its forms has a direct, marked, and very deleterious influence on his psychic con-dition. Wine and spirit drinking is only less destructive to the development of the inner powers than the habitual use of hashish, opium, and similar drugs.

THEOSOPHY AND MARRIAGE.

INQ.—*Now to another question : Must a man marry or remain a celibate ?*

THEO.—It depends on the kind of man you mean. If you refer to one who intends to live in the world; one who, even though a good, earnest Theosophist, and an ardent worker for our cause, still has ties and wishes which bind him to the world; who, in short, does not feel that he has done forever with what men call life, and that he desires one thing and one thing only—to know the truth and to be able to help others—then for such a one I say there is no reason why he should not marry, if he likes to take the risks of that lottery where there are so many more blanks than prizes. Surely you cannot believe us so absurd and fanatical as to preach against marriage altogether ? On the contrary, save in a few exceptional cases of practical Occultism, marriage is the only remedy against immorality.

INQ.—*But why cannot one acquire this knowledge and power when living a married life ?*

THEO.—My dear sir, I cannot go into physiological questions with you; but I can give you an obvious and, I think, a sufficient answer, which will explain to you the moral reasons we give for it. Can a man serve two masters ? No! Then it is equally impossible for him to divide his attention between the pursuit of Occultism and a wife. If he tries to, he will assuredly fail in doing either properly; and, let me remind you, practical Occultism is far too serious and dangerous a study for a man to take up unless he is in the most deadly earnest, and ready to sacrifice *all—himself first of all—*to gain his end. But this does not apply to the members of our inner section. I am only referring to those who are determined to tread that path of discipleship which leads to the highest goal. Most, if not all, of those who join our inner section are only beginners, preparing themselves in this life to enter in reality upon that path in lives to come.

THEOSOPHY AND EDUCATION.

INQ.—*One of your strongest arguments for the inadequacy of the existing forms of religion in the West, as also to some extent the materialistic philosophy which is now so popular, but which you seem to consider as an abomination of desolation, is the large amount of misery and wretchedness which undeniably exists, especially in our great cities. But surely you must recognize how much has been and is being done to remedy this state of things by the spread of education and the diffusion of intelligence.*

THEO.—The future generations will hardly thank you for such a "diffusion of intelligence," nor will your present education do much good to the poor starving masses.

INQ.—*Ah! but you must give us time. It is only a few years since we began to educate the people.*

THEO.—And what, pray, has your Christian religion been doing ever since the fifteenth century, once you acknowledge that the education of the masses has not been attempted till now—the very work, if ever there could be one, which a Christian—i.e., a Christ-following—church and people ought to perform?

INQ.—*Well, you may be right; but now—*

THEO.—Just let us consider this question of education from a broad standpoint, and I will prove to you that you are doing harm, not good, with many of your boasted improvements. The schools for the poorer children, though far less useful than they ought to be, are good in contrast with the vile surroundings to which they are doomed by your modern society. The *infusion* of a little practical Theosophy would help a hundred times more in life the poor suffering masses than all this diffusion of useless intelligence.

Inq.—*But really*—

Theo.—Let me finish, please. You have opened a subject on which we Theosophists feel deeply, and I must have my say. I quite agree that there is a great advantage to a small child bred in the slums, having the gutter for playground, and living amid continued coarseness of gesture and word, in being placed daily in a bright, clean school-room hung with pictures, and often gay with flowers. There it is taught to be clean, gentle, orderly; there it learns to sing and to play; has toys that awaken its intelligence; learns to use its fingers deftly; is spoken to with a smile instead of a frown; is gently rebuked or coaxed instead of cursed. All this humanizes the children, arouses their brains, and renders them susceptible to intellectual and moral influences. The schools are not all they might be and ought to be; but compared with the homes they are paradises; and they are slowly reacting on the homes. But while this is true of many of the board-schools, your system deserves the worst one can say of it.

Inq.—*So be it; go on.*

Theo.—What is the real object of modern education? Is it to cultivate and develop the mind in the right direction; to teach the disinherited and hapless people to carry with fortitude the burden of life allotted them by Karma; to strengthen their will; to inculcate in them the love of one's neighbor and the feeling of mutual interdependence and brotherhood; and thus to train and form the character for practical life? Not a bit of it. And yet these are undeniably the objects of all true education. No one denies it; all your educationalists admit it, and talk very big indeed on the subject. But what is the practical result of their action? Every young man and boy—nay, every one of the younger generation of schoolmasters—will answer, "The object of modern education is to pass examinations"—a system not to develop right emulation, but to generate and breed jealousy, envy, hatred almost, in young people for one another, and thus train them for a life of ferocious selfishness and struggle for honors and emoluments instead of kindly feeling.

INQ.—*I must admit you are right there.*

THEO.—And what are these examinations—the terror of modern boyhood and youth? They are simply a method of classification by which the results of your school-teaching are tabulated. In other words, they form the practical application of the modern science method to the *genus homo, qua* intellection. Now science teaches that intellect is a result of the mechanical interaction of the brain-stuff; therefore it is only logical that modern education should be almost entirely mechanical—a sort of automatic machine for the fabrication of intellect by the ton. Very little experience of examinations is enough to show that the education they produce is simply a training of the physical memory, and, sooner or later, all your schools will sink to this level. As to any real, sound cultivation of the thinking and reasoning power, it is simply impossible while everything has to be judged by the results as tested by competitive examinations. Again, school training is of the very greatest importance in forming character, especially in its moral bearing. Now, from first to last, your modern system is based on the so-called scientific revelations—the "struggle for existence" and the "survival of the fittest." All through his early life every man has these driven into

him by practical example and experience, as well as by
direct teaching, till it is impossible to eradicate from his
mind the idea that "self"—the lower, personal, animal self
—is the end-all and be-all of life. Here you get the great
source of all the after-misery, crime, and heartless selfishness, which you admit as much as I do. Selfishness, as
said over and over again, is the curse of humanity, and
the prolific parent of all the evils and crimes in this life;
and it is your schools which are the hotbeds of such selfishness.

INQ.—*That is all very fine as generalities, but I should like
a few facts, and to learn also how this can be remedied.*

THEO.—Very well, I will try and satisfy you. There are
three great divisions of scholastic establishments—board,
middle-class, and public schools, running up the scale from
the most grossly commercial to the idealistic classical, with
many permutations and combinations. The practical commercial begets the modern side, and the ancient and orthodox classical reflects its heavy respectability even as far as
the school-board pupil-teacher's establishments. Here we
plainly see the scientific and material commercial supplant-
ing the effete orthodox and classical. Neither is the reason
very far to seek. The objects of this branch of education
are, then, pounds, shillings, and pence, the *summum bonum*
of the nineteenth century. Thus the energies generated by
the brain-molecules of its adherents are all concentrated on
one point, and are therefore, to some extent, an organized
army of educated and speculative intellects of the minority
of men, trained against the hosts of the ignorant, simple-
minded masses doomed to be vampirized, lived and sat
upon by their intellectually stronger brethren. Such training is not only untheosophical; it is simply unchristian.
Result: the direct outcome of this branch of education is an
overflooding of the market with money-making machines,

with heartless, selfish men—animals—who have been most carefully trained to prey on their fellows and take advantage of the ignorance of their weaker brethren !

INQ.—*Well, but you cannot assert that of our great public schools, at any rate.*

THEO.—Not exactly, it is true. But though the *form* is different, the animating spirit is the same—untheosophical and unchristian, whether Eton and Harrow turn out scientists or divines and theologians.

INQ.—*Surely you do not mean to call Eton and Harrow "commercial"?*

THEO.—No. Of course the classical system is above all things *respectable*, and in the present day is productive of some good. It still remains the favorite at our great public schools, where not only an intellectual, but also a social education is obtainable. It is therefore of prime importance that the dull boys of aristocratic and wealthy parents should go to such schools to meet the rest of the young life of the "blood" and money classes. But, unfortunately, there is a huge competition even for entrance; for the moneyed classes are increasing, and poor but clever boys seek to enter the public schools by the rich scholarships, both at the schools themselves and from them to the universities.

INQ.—*According to this view, the wealthier "dullards" have to work even harder than their poorer fellows.*

THEO.—It is so. But, strange to say, the faithful of the cult of the "survival of the fittest" do not practise their creed; for their whole exertion is to make the naturally unfit supplant the fit. Thus, by bribes of large sums of money, they allure the best teachers from their natural pupils to mechanicalize their naturally unfit progeny into professions which they uselessly overcrowd.

INQ.—*And you attribute all this to what?*

THEO.—All this is owing to the perniciousness of a system which turns out goods to order, irrespective of the natural proclivities and talents of the youth. The poor little candidate for this progressive paradise of learning comes almost straight from the nursery to the treadmill of a preparatory school for sons of gentlemen. Here he is immediately seized upon by the workmen of the materio-intellectual factory, and crammed with Latin, French, and Greek accidence, dates and tables, so that if he have any natural genius it is rapidly squeezed out of him by the rollers of what Carlyle has so well called "dead vocables."

INQ.—*But surely he is taught something besides "dead vocables," and much of that which may lead him direct to Theosophy, if not entirely into the Theosophical Society?*

THEO.—Not much. For of history he will attain only sufficient knowledge of his own particular nation to fit him with a steel armor of prejudice against all other peoples, and be steeped in the foul cesspools of chronicled national hate and bloodthirstiness; and surely you would not call that—Theosophy?

INQ.—*What are your further objections?*

THEO.—Added to this is a smattering of selected, so called, biblical facts, from the study of which all intellect is eliminated. It is simply a memory lesson, the *why* of the teacher being a *why* of circumstances and not of reason.

INQ.—*Yes; but I have heard you congratulate yourself at the ever-increasing number of agnostics and atheists in our day, so that it appears that even people trained in the system you abuse so heartily* do *learn to think and reason for themselves.*

THEO.—Yes; but it is rather owing to a healthy reaction from that system than due to it. We immeasurably prefer agnostics, and even rank atheists, in our Society to bigots of whatever religion. An agnostic's mind is ever opened to the truth; whereas the latter blinds the bigot like the sun does an owl. The best—i.e., the most truth-loving, philanthropic, and honest—of our Fellows were, and are, agnostics and atheists, in the sense of disbelievers in a *personal* God. But there are no free-thinking boys and girls, and generally early training will leave its mark behind in the shape of a cramped and distorted mind. A proper and sane system of education should produce the most vigorous and liberal mind, strictly trained in logical and accurate thought, and not in blind faith. How can you ever expect good results while you pervert the reasoning faculty of your children by bidding them believe in the miracles of the Bible on Sunday, while for the six other days of the week you teach them that such things are scientifically impossible ?

INQ.—*What would you have, then ?*

THEO.—If we had money we would found schools which would turn out something else than reading and writing candidates for starvation. Children should above all be taught self-reliance, love for all men, altruism, mutual charity, and, more than anything else, to think and reason for themselves. We would reduce the purely mechanical work of the memory to an absolute minimum, and devote the time to the development and training of the inner senses, faculties, and latent capacities. We would endeavor to deal with each child as a unit, and to educate it so as to produce the most harmonious and equal unfoldment of its powers, in order that its special aptitudes should find their full natural development. We would aim at creating *free* men and women—free intellectually, free morally; unprejudiced in all respects, and, above all things, *unselfish*. And we believe that much, if not all, of this could be obtained by proper and truly Theosophical education.

WHY, THEN, IS THERE SO MUCH PREJUDICE AGAINST THE THEOSOPHICAL SOCIETY?

INQ.—*If Theosophy is even half of what you say, why should there exist such a terrible ill feeling against it? This is even more of a problem than anything else.*

THEO.—It is; but you must bear in mind how many powerful adversaries we have aroused ever since the formation of our Society. As I just said, if the Theosophical movement were one of those numerous modern crazes, as harmless at the end as they are evanescent, it would be simply laughed at—as it is now by those who still do not understand its real purport—and left severely alone. But it is nothing of the kind. Intrinsically, Theosophy is the most serious movement of this age, and one, moreover, which threatens the very life of most of the time-honored humbugs, prejudices, and social evils of the day—those evils which fatten and make happy the upper ten and their imitators and sycophants, the wealthy dozens of the middle classes, while they positively crush and starve out of existence the millions of the poor. Think of this, and you will easily understand the reason of such a relentless persecution by those others who, more observing and perspicacious, do see the true nature of Theosophy, and therefore dread it.

INQ.—*Do you mean to tell me that it is because a few have understood what Theosophy leads to, that they try to crush the movement? But if Theosophy leads only to good, surely you cannot be prepared to utter such a terrible accusation of perfidious heartlessness and treachery even against those few?*

THEO.—I am so prepared, on the contrary. I do not call the enemies we have had to battle with during the first nine or ten years of the Society's existence either powerful or dangerous, but only those who have arisen against us in the last three or four years. And these neither speak, write, nor preach against Theosophy, but work in silence and behind the backs of the foolish puppets who act as their visible marionettes. Yet, if invisible to most of the members of our Society, they are well known to the true founders and the protectors of our Society. But they must remain, for certain reasons, unnamed at present.

INQ.—*And are they known to many of you, or to yourself alone?*

THEO.—I never said that *I* knew them; I may or may not know them; but I know *of* them, and this is sufficient; and I defy them to do their worst. They may achieve great mischief and throw confusion into our ranks, especially among the faint-hearted and those who can judge only by appearances. They will not crush the Society, do what they may. Apart from these truly dangerous enemies —dangerous, however, only to those Theosophists who are unworthy of the name, and whose place is rather outside than within the Theosophical Society—the number of our opponents is more than considerable.

INQ.—*I have heard many Theosophists speak of a "power behind the Society," and of certain " Mahâtmâs," mentioned also in Mr. Sinnett's works, that are said to have founded the Society, to watch over and protect it.*

THEO.—You may laugh, but it is so.

XIV.

THE THEOSOPHICAL "MAHÂTMÂS."

ARE THEY "SPIRITS OF LIGHT" OR "GOBLINS DAMN'D"?

INQ.—*Who are, then, those whom you call your "Masters"? Some say they are "spirits," or some other kind of supernatural beings, while others call them "myths."*

THEO.—They are neither. I once heard one outsider say to another that they were a sort of "male mermaids," whatever such a creature may be. But if you listen to what people say you will never have a true conception of them. In the first place, they are *living men,* born as we are born, and doomed to die like every other mortal.

INQ.—*Yes, but it is rumored that some of them are a thousand years old. Is this true?*

THEO.—As true as the miraculous growth of hair on the head of Meredith's Shagpat. Truly, like the "Identical," no Theosophical shaving has hitherto been able to crop it. The more we deny them, the more we try to set people right, the more absurd do the inventions become. I have heard of Methuselah being nine hundred and sixty-nine years old; but, not being forced to believe in it, have laughed at the statement, for which I was forthwith regarded by many as a blasphemous heretic.

INQ.—*Seriously, though, do they outlive the ordinary age of men ?*

THEO.—What do you call the ordinary age ? I remember reading in the *Lancet* of a Mexican who was almost one hundred and ninety years old; but I have never heard of mortal man, layman or Adept, who could live even half the years allotted to Methuselah. Some Adepts do exceed, by a good deal, what you would call the ordinary age; yet there is nothing miraculous in it, and very few of them care to live very long.

INQ.—*But what does the word "Mahâtmâ" really mean ?*

THEO.—Simply " great soul "—great through moral elevation and intellectual attainment.· If the title of "great" is given to a drunken soldier like Alexander, why should we not call those " great " who have achieved far greater conquests in Nature's secrets than Alexander ever did on the field of battle ? Besides, the term is an Indian and a very old word.

INQ.—*And why do you call them " Masters"?*

THEO.—We call them " Masters " because they are our teachers, and because from them we have derived all the Theosophical truths, however inadequately some of us may have expressed, and others understood, them. They are men of great learning and still greater holiness of life, whom we term Initiates. They are not ascetics in the ordinary sense, though they certainly remain apart from the turmoil and strife of your Western world.

INQ.—*But is it not selfish thus to isolate themselves ?*

THEO.—Where is the selfishness ? Does not the fate of the Theosophical Society sufficiently prove that the world is neither ready to recognize them nor to profit by their teaching ? Of what use would Professor Clerk Maxwell have been to instruct a class of little boys in their multiplication table ?　Besides, they isolate themselves only from the West.　In their own country they go about as publicly as other people do.

INQ.—*Do you not ascribe to them supernatural powers ?*

THEO.—We believe in nothing supernatural, as I have told you already.　Had Edison lived and invented his phonograph two hundred years ago he would most probably have been burned along with it, and the whole attributed to the devil.　The powers which they exercise are simply the development of potencies lying latent in every man and woman, and the existence of which even official science begins to recognize.

INQ.—*Is it true that these men* inspire *some of your writers, and that many, if not all, of your Theosophical works were written under their dictation ?*

THEO.—Some of them have done so.　There are passages entirely dictated by them verbatim; but in most cases they only inspire the ideas, and leave the literary form to the writers.

INQ.—*But this in itself is miraculous ; is, in fact, a* miracle. *How can they do it ?*

THEO.—My dear sir, you are laboring under a great mistake, and it is science itself that will refute your arguments at no distant day.　Why should it be a "miracle," as you call it ?　A miracle is supposed to mean some operation which is supernatural, whereas there is really nothing above or beyond Nature and Nature's laws.　Among the many forms of the "miracle" which have come under modern scientific recognition there is hypnotism; and one phase of its power is known as "suggestion," a form of thought-transference, which has been successfully used in combating particular physical diseases, etc.　The time is not far distant when the world of science will be forced to acknowledge that there exists as much interaction between one mind and another, no matter at what distance, as between one body and another in closest contact. When two minds are sympathetically related, and the instruments through which they function are tuned to respond magnetically and electrically to one another, there is nothing which will prevent the transmission of thoughts from one to the other at will; for since the mind is not of such a tangible nature that distance can divide it from the subject of its contemplation, it follows that the only difference that can exist between two minds is a difference of *state*. So if this latter hindrance is overcome, where is the "miracle" of thought-transference, at whatever distance ?

INQ.—*But you will admit that hypnotism does nothing so miraculous or wonderful as that ?*

THEO.—On the contrary, it is a well-established fact that a hypnotist can affect the brain of his subject so far as to produce an expression of his own thoughts, and even his words, through the organism of his subject; and although the phenomena attaching to this method of actual thought-transference are as yet few in number, no one, I presume, will undertake to say how far their action may extend in the future, when the laws that govern their production are more scientifically established. And so, if such results can be produced by the knowledge of the mere rudiments of hypnotism, what can prevent the Adept in psychic and spiritual powers from producing results which, with your present limited knowledge of these laws, you are inclined to call "miraculous" ?

INQ.—*Then why do not our physicians experiment and try if they could not do as much ?* *

---

* Such, for instance, as Professor Bernheim and Dr C Lloyd Tuckey, of England; Professors Beaunis and Liégeois, of Nancy; Delbœuf, of Liège; Burot and Bourru, of Rochefort; Fontain and Sigard, of Bordeaux; Forel, of Zürich; and Drs. Despine,

THEO.—Because, first of all, they are not Adepts, with a thorough understanding of the secrets and laws of psychic and spiritual realms, but materialists, afraid to step outside the narrow groove of matter; and secondly, because they *must fail* at present, and, indeed, until they are brought to acknowledge that such powers are attainable.

INQ.—*And could they be taught ?*

THEO.—Not unless they were first of all prepared, by having the materialistic dross they have accumulated in their brains swept away to the very last atom.

INQ.—*This is very interesting. Tell me, have the Adepts thus inspired or dictated to many of your Theosophists ?*

THEO.—No; on the contrary, to very few. Such operations require special conditions. An unscrupulous but skilled Adept of the " Black Brotherhood "—" Brothers of the Shadow," and Dugpas, we call them—has far less difficulties to labor under. For, having no laws of a spiritual nature to trammel his actions, such a Dugpa sorcerer will most unceremoniously obtain control over any mind, and subject it entirely to his evil powers. But our Masters will never do that. They have no right—if they would escape falling into " black magic "—to obtain entire mastery over any one's immortal Ego, and can therefore act only on the physical and psychic nature of the subject, leaving thereby the free will of the latter wholly undisturbed. Hence, unless a person has been brought into psychic relationship with the Masters, and is assisted by virtue of his full faith in and devotion to his teachers, the latter, whenever transmitting their thoughts to one with whom these conditions are not fulfilled, experience great difficulties in penetrating into the cloudy chaos of that person's sphere. But this is

of Marseilles; Van Renterghem and Van Eeden, of Amsterdam; Wetterstrand, of Stockholm, Schrenck-Notzing, of Leipzig; and many other physicians and writers of eminence.

no place to treat of a subject of this nature. Suffice it to say that if the power exists, then there are Intelligences (embodied or disembodied) which guide this power, and living, conscious instruments through whom it is transmitted and by whom it is received. We have only to beware of "*black* magic."

INQ.—*But what do you really mean by "black magic"?*

THEO.—Simply abuse of psychic powers, or of any secret of Nature; the fact of applying to selfish and sinful ends the powers of Occultism. A hypnotizer who, taking advantage of his powers of "suggestion," forced a subject to steal or murder would be called by us a "black magician." The famous "rejuvenating system" of Dr. Brown-Séquard, of Paris, through a loathsome animal injection into human blood—a discovery all the medical papers of Europe are now discussing—if true, is unconscious black magic.

INQ.—*But this is medieval belief in witchcraft and sorcery! Even the law itself has ceased to believe in such things.*

THEO.—So much the worse for the law, as it has been led, through such lack of discrimination, into committing more than one judiciary mistake and crime. It is the term alone that frightens you with its "superstitious" ring in it. Would not law punish an abuse of hypnotic powers, as I just mentioned? Nay, it has so punished it already in France and Germany; yet it would indignantly deny that it applied punishment to a crime of evident "sorcery." You cannot believe in the efficacy and reality of the powers of suggestion by physicians and mesmerizers or hypnotizers, and then refuse to believe in the same powers when used for evil motives. And if you do, then you believe in "sorcery"! You cannot believe in good and disbelieve in evil, accept genuine money and refuse to credit such a thing as false coin. Nothing can exist without its contrast; and no day, no light, no good, could have any representation as such in your consciousness were there no night, no darkness, no evil, to offset and contrast them.

Inq.—*Indeed, I have known men who, while thoroughly believing in that which you call great psychic or magic powers, laughed at the very mention of witchcraft and sorcery.*

Theo.—What does it prove? Simply that they are illogical. So much the worse for them, again. And we, knowing as we do of the existence of good and holy Adepts, believe as thoroughly in the existence of bad and unholy Adepts, or—Dugpas.

Inq.—*But if the Masters exist, why do they not come out before all men and refute once for all the many charges which are made against Madame Blavatsky and the Society?*

Theo.—What charges?

Inq.—*That they do not exist, and that she has invented them. Does not all this injure her reputation?*

Theo.—In what way can such an accusation injure her in reality? Did she ever make money on their presumed existence, or derive benefit or fame therefrom? I answer that she has gained only insults, abuse, and calumnies, which would have been very painful had she not learned long ago to remain perfectly indifferent to such false charges. For what does it amount to after all? Why, to an implied compliment, which, if the fools, her accusers, were not carried away by their blind hatred, they would have thought twice before uttering. To say that she has invented the Masters comes to this: that she must have invented every bit of philosophy that has ever been given out in Theosophical literature. She must be the author of the letters from which *Esoteric Buddhism* was written; the sole inventor of every tenet found in *The Secret Doctrine*, which, if the world were just, would be recognized as supplying many of the missing links of science, as will be discovered a hundred years hence. By saying what they do they are also giving her the credit of being far cleverer than the hundreds of men (many *very* clever and not a few scientific men) who believe in what she says—inasmuch as she must have fooled them all! If they speak the truth, then she must be several Mahâtmâs rolled into one, like a nest of Chinese boxes.

INQ.—*They say that from beginning to end they were a romance which Madame Blavatsky has woven from her own brain.*

THEO.—Well, she might have done many things less clever than this. At any rate, we have not the slightest objection to this theory. As she always says now, she almost prefers that people should not believe in the Masters. She declares openly that she would rather people should seriously think that the only "Mahâtmâ-land" is the gray matter of her brain, and that, in short, she has evolved them out of the depths of her own inner consciousness, than that their names and grand ideal should be so infamously desecrated as they are at present. At first she used to protest indignantly against any doubts as to their existence. Now she never goes out of her way to prove or disprove it. Let people think what they like.

INQ.—*But if you have such wise and good men to guide the Society, how is it that so many mistakes have been made?*

THEO.—The Masters do *not* guide the Society—not even the founders—and no one has ever asserted that they did; they only watch over and protect it. This is amply proved by the fact that no mistakes have been able to cripple it, and no scandals from within, nor the most damaging attacks from without, have been able to overthrow it. The

Masters look at the future, not at the present, and every mistake is so much more accumulated wisdom for days to come.   That other "Master" who sent out the man with the five talents did not tell him how to double them, nor did he prevent the foolish servant from burying his one tal- ent in the earth.   Each must acquire wisdom by his own experience and merits.   The Christian churches, who claim a far higher Master, the very Holy Ghost itself, have ever been, and are still, guilty not only of "mistakes," but of a series of bloody crimes throughout the ages.   Yet no Chris- tian would deny, for all that, his belief in *that* Master, I suppose, although his existence is far more hypothetical than that of the Mahâtmâs, as no one has ever seen the Holy Ghost and his guidance of the church; moreover, their own ecclesiastical history distinctly contradicts.   *Errare humanum est.*   Let us return to our subject.

THE ABUSE OF SACRED NAMES AND TERMS.

INQ.—*Then what I have heard, namely, that many of your Theosophical writers claim to have been inspired by these Masters, or to have seen and conversed with them, is not true ?*

THEO.—It may or it may not be true.   How can I tell? The burden of proof rests with them.   Some of them—a few, very few indeed—have either distinctly lied or were hallucinated when boasting of such inspiration; others were truly inspired by great Adepts.   The tree is known by its fruits; and as all Theosophists have to be judged by their deeds and not by what they write or say, so *all* Theosophical books must be accepted on their merits, and not according to any claim to authority which they may put forward.

INQ.—*But would Madame Blavatsky apply this to her own works—The Secret Doctrine, for instance ?*

THEO.—Certainly ; she says expressly in the preface that she gives out the doctrines that she has learned from the Masters, but claims no inspiration whatever for what she has lately written. As for our best Theosophists, they would also, in this case, far rather that the names of the Masters had never been mixed up with our books in any way. With few exceptions, most of such works are not only imperfect, but positively erroneous and misleading. Great are the desecrations to which the names of two of the Masters have been subjected. There is hardly a medium who has not claimed to have seen them. Every bogus swindling society, for commercial purposes, now claims to be guided and directed by " Masters," often supposed to be far higher than ours ! Many and heavy are the sins of those who have advanced these claims, prompted either by desire for lucre, vanity, or irresponsible mediumship. Many persons have been plundered of their money by such societies, which offer to sell the secrets of power, knowledge, and spiritual truth for worthless gold. Worst of all, the sacred names of Occultism and the holy keepers thereof have been dragged in this filthy mire, polluted by being associated with sordid motives and immoral practices, while thousands of men have been held back from the path of truth and light through the discredit and evil report which such shams, swindles, and frauds have brought upon the whole subject. I say again, every earnest Theosophist regrets to-day, from the bottom of his heart, that these sacred names and things have ever been mentioned before the public, and fervently wishes that they had been kept secret within a small circle of trusted and devoted friends.

CONCLUSION.

THE FUTURE OF THE THEOSOPHICAL SOCIETY.

INQ.—*Tell me, what do you expect for Theosophy in the future?*

THEO.—If you speak of THEOSOPHY, I answer that, as it has existed eternally throughout the endless cycles upon cycles of the past, so it will ever exist throughout the infinitudes of the future, because Theosophy is synonymous with EVERLASTING TRUTH.

INQ.—*Pardon me; I meant to ask you rather about the prospects of the Theosophical Society.*

THEO.—Its future will depend almost entirely upon the degree of selflessness, earnestness, devotion, and, last but not least, on the amount of knowledge and wisdom possessed by those members on whom it will fall to carry on the work and to direct the Society after the death of the founders.

INQ.—*I quite see the importance of their being selfless and devoted, but I do not quite grasp how their knowledge can be as vital a factor in the question as these other qualities. Surely the literature which already exists, and to which constant additions are still being made, ought to be sufficient.*

THEO.—I do not refer to technical knowledge of the esoteric doctrine, though that is most important; I spoke

254

rather of the great need which our successors in the guidance of the Society will have of unbiased and clear judgment. Every such attempt as the Theosophical Society has hitherto ended in failure, because, sooner or later, it has degenerated into a sect, set up hard-and-fast dogmas of its own, and so lost by imperceptible degrees that vitality which living truth alone can impart. You must remember that all our members have been bred and born in some creed or religion; that all are more or less of their generation, both physically and mentally; and consequently that their judgment is but too likely to be warped and unconsciously biased by some or all of these influences. If, then, they cannot be freed from such inherent bias, or at least taught to recognize it instantly and so avoid being led away by it, the result can only be that the Society will drift off on to some sand-bank of thought or another, and there remain, a stranded carcass, to molder and die.

INQ.—*But if this danger be averted?*

THEO.—Then the Society will live on into and through the twentieth century. It will gradually leaven and permeate the great mass of thinking and intelligent people with its large-minded and noble ideas of religion, duty, and philanthropy. Slowly but surely it will burst asunder the iron fetters of creeds and dogmas, of social and caste prejudices; it will break down racial and national antipathies and barriers, and will open the way to the practical realization of the Brotherhood of all men. Through its teaching, through the philosophy which it has rendered accessible and intelligible to the modern mind, the West will learn to understand and appreciate the East at its true value. Further, the development of the psychic powers and faculties, the premonitory symptoms of which are already visible in America, will proceed healthily and normally. Mankind will be saved from the terrible dangers, both mental and bodily, which are inevitable when that unfolding takes place, as it threatens to do, in a hotbed of selfishness and all evil passions. Man's mental and psychic growth will proceed in harmony with his moral improvement, while his material surroundings will reflect the peace and fraternal good will which will reign in his mind, instead of the discord and strife which are everywhere apparent around us to-day.

INQ.—*A truly delightful picture !   But tell me, do you really expect all this to be accomplished in one short century ?*

THEO.—Scarcely. But I must tell you that during the last quarter of every hundred years an attempt is made by those Masters of whom I have spoken to help on the spiritual progress of humanity in a marked and definite way. Toward the close of each century you will invariably find that an outpouring or upheaval of spirituality— or call it Mysticism, if you prefer—has taken place. Some one or more persons have appeared in the world as their agents, and a greater or less amount of occult knowledge and teaching has been given out. If you care to do so, you can trace these movements back, century by century, as far as our detailed historical records extend.

INQ.—*But how does this bear on the future of the Theosophical Society ?*

THEO.—If the present attempt, in the form of our Society, succeeds better than its predecessors have done, then it will be in existence as an organized, living, and healthy body when the time comes for the effort of the twentieth century. The general condition of men's minds and hearts will have been improved and purified by the spread of its teachings, and, as I have said, their prejudices and dogmatic illusions will have been, to some extent at least, removed. Not only so, but besides a large and accessible literature ready to men's hands, the next impulse will find a numerous and *united* body of people ready to welcome the new torch-bearer of Truth. He will find the minds of men prepared for his message, a language ready for him in which to clothe the new truths he brings, an organization awaiting his arrival, which will remove the merely mechanical, material obstacles and difficulties from his path. Think how much one to whom such an opportunity is given could accomplish. Measure it by comparison with what the Theosophical Society actually *has* achieved in the last fourteen years, without any of these advantages, and surrounded by hosts of hindrances which would not hamper the new leader. Consider all this, and then tell me whether I am too sanguine when I say that if the Theosophical Society survives and lives true to its mission, to its original impulses, through the next hundred years—tell me, I say, if I go too far in asserting that earth will be a heaven in the twenty-first century in comparison with what it is now !

GLOSSARY.

GLOSSARY

GLOSSARY.

A.

Absoluteness. When predicated of the Universal Principle, it denotes an abstraction, which is more correct and logical than to apply the adjective "absolute" to that which can have neither attributes nor limitations.

Adam Kadmon (*Heb.*). Archetypal Man, humanity. The "heavenly Man" not fallen into sin. Kabalists refer it to the ten Sephiroth on the plane of human perception. In the Kabalah Adam Kadmon is the manifested *logos* corresponding to our third *logos*, the unmanifested being the first paradigmic, ideal Man, and symbolizing the universe *in abscondito*, or in its "privation" in the Aristotelian sense. The first *logos* is the "light of the world," the second and the third its gradually deepening shadows.

Adept (*Lat. adeptus*). In Occultism, one who has reached the stage of initiation and become a Master in the science of Esoteric Philosophy.

Æther (*Gr.*). With the ancients, the divine luminiferous substance which pervades the whole universe; the "garment" of the supreme deity, Zeus or Jupiter. With the moderns, ether, for the meaning of which, in physics and chemistry, see Webster's or some other dictionary. In esotericism æther is the third principle of the cosmic septenary, matter (earth) being the lowest, and *âkâsha* the highest.

Agathon (*Gr.*). Plato's supreme deity—lit., the "Good." Our *âlaya* or the "soul of the world."

Agnostic. A word first used by Professor Huxley to indicate one who believes nothing which cannot be demonstrated by the senses.

Ahankâra (*Sans.*). The conception of "I," self-consciousness or self-identity; the "I," or egoistical and mâyâvic principle in man, due to our ignorance, which separates our "I" from the Universal One *Self.* Personality; egoism also.

Ain Suph (*Heb.*). The "boundless" or "limitless" Deity emanating and extending. Ain Suph is also written En Soph and Ain Soph; for no one, not even the rabbis, is quite sure of their vowels. In the religious metaphysics of the old Hebrew philosophers the One Principle was an abstraction like *Parabrahman*, though modern Kabalists have succeeded by mere dint of sophistry and paradoxes in making a "Supreme God" of it, and nothing higher. But with the early Chaldean Kabalists Ain Suph was "without form or being," with "no likeness with anything else." (Franck's *Die Kabbala*, p. 126.) That Ain Suph has never been considered as the "creator" is proved conclusively by the fact that such an orthodox Jew as Philo gives the name of "creator" to the *logos*, who stands next the "Limitless One" and is the "*second* God." "The *second* God is in its [Ain Suph's] wisdom," says Philo. Deity is *No-Thing;* it is nameless, and therefore called Ain Suph—the word *ain* meaning *nothing.* (See also Franck, *ibid.,* p. 153.)

Alchemy (in Arabic *Ul-Khemi*) is, as the name suggests, the chemistry of nature. Ul-Khemi or Al-Kimia, however, is really an Arabianized word, taken from the Greek χημεία, from χυμός, "juice," extracted from a plant.

Alchemy deals with the finer forces of Nature and the various conditions of matter in which they are found to operate. Seeking under the veil of language more or less artificial to convey to the uninitiated so much of the *mysterium magnum* as is safe in the hands of a selfish world, the Alchemist postulates as his first principle the existence of a certain *universal solvent* in the homogeneous substance from which the elements were evolved, which substance he calls pure gold, or *summum materiæ*. This solvent, also called *menstruum universale*, possesses the power of removing all the seeds of disease from the human body, of renewing youth and prolonging life. Such is the *lapis philosophorum* (philosopher's stone). Alchemy first penetrated into Europe through Geber, the great Arabian sage and philosopher, in the eighth century of our era; but it was known and practised long ages ago in China and Egypt. Numerous papyri on Alchemy, and other proofs that it was the favorite study of kings and priests, have been exhumed, and preserved under the generic name of Hermetic treatises. Alchemy is studied under three distinct aspects, which admit of many different interpretations, viz., the cosmic, the human, and the terrestrial.

These three methods were typified under the three alchemical properties—sulphur, mercury, and salt. Different writers have stated that there are three, seven, ten, and twelve processes, respectively; but they are all agreed there is but one object in Alchemy, which is to transmute gross metals into pure gold. But what that *gold* really is very few people understand correctly. No doubt there is such a thing in Nature as transmutation of the baser metal into the nobler; but this is only one aspect of Alchemy—the terrestrial or purely material, for we see the same process taking place in the bowels of the earth. Yet, besides and beyond this interpretation, there is in Alchemy a symbolical meaning, purely psychic and spiritual. While the

Kabalist-Alchemist seeks for the realization of the former, the Occultist-Alchemist, spurning the gold of the earth, gives all his attention to, and directs his efforts only toward, the transmutation of the baser *quaternary* into the divine upper *trinity* of man, which, when finally blended, are one. The spiritual, mental, psychic, and physical planes of human existence are in Alchemy compared to the four elements, fire, air, water, and earth, and are each capable of a three-fold constitution, i.e., fixed, unstable, and volatile. Little or nothing is known by the world concerning the origin of this archaic branch of philosophy; but it is certain that it antedates the construction of any known zodiac, and, as dealing with the personified forces of Nature, probably also any of the mythologies of the world. Nor is there any doubt that the true secrets of transmutation (on the physical plane) were known in days of old, and lost before the dawn of the so-called historical period. Modern chemistry owes its best fundamental discoveries to Alchemy; but regardless of the undeniable truism of the latter that there is but *one* element in the universe, chemistry placed metals in the class of elements, and is only now beginning to find out its gross mistake. Even some encyclopedists are forced to confess that if most of the accounts of transmutation are fraud or delusion, " yet some of them are accompanied by testimony *which renders them probable.* By means of the galvanic battery even the alkalis have been discovered to have a metallic basis. The possibility of obtaining metal from other substances which contain the ingredients composing it, of *changing one metal into another, . . .* must therefore be left undecided. Nor are all Alchemists to be considered impostors. Many have labored under the conviction of obtaining their object with indefatigable patience and purity of heart, which is soundly recommended by Alchemists as the principal requisite for the success of their labors."

Alexandrian Philosophers (or School). This famous school arose in Alexandria (Egypt), which was for long ages a seat of learning and philosophy. It was famous for its library, founded by Ptolemy Soter at the very beginning of his reign (Ptolemy died in 283 B.C.)—a library which once boasted seven hundred thousand rolls or volumes (Aulus Gellius); for its museum, the first real academy of sciences and arts; for its world-renowned scholars, such as Euclid, the father of scientific geometry, Apollonius of Perga, the author of the still extant work on Conic Sections, Nicomachus, the arithmetician; for astronomers, natural philosophers, anatomists such as Herophilus and Erasistratus, physicians, musicians, artists, etc. But it became still more famous for its Eclectic or New-Platonic school, founded by Ammonius Saccas in 173 A.D., whose disciples were Origen, Plotinus, and many other men now famous in history. The most celebrated schools of the Gnostics had their origin in Alexandria. Philo Judæus, Josephus, Iamblichus, Porphyry, Clement of Alexandria, Eratosthenes the astronomer, Hypatia the virgin philosopher, and numberless other stars of second magnitude, all belonged at various times to these great schools, and helped to make of Alexandria one of the most justly renowned seats of learning that the world has ever produced.

Altruism. From *alter*, other. A quality opposed to egoism. Actions tending to do good to others, regardless of self.

Ammonius Saccas. A great and good philosopher who lived in Alexandria between the second and third centuries of our era, the founder of the Neoplatonic school of the Philaletheians or "lovers of truth." He was of poor birth and born of Christian parents, but endowed with such prominent, almost divine goodness as to be called Theodidaktos, the "God-taught." He honored that which was good in Christianity, but broke with it and the churches at

an early age, being unable to find in it any superiority over
the old religions.

Analogeticists. The disciples of Ammonius Saccas,
so called because of their practice of interpreting all sacred
legends, myths, and mysteries by a principle of analogy
and correspondence, which rule is now found in the Kabalistic system, and preëminently so in the schools of Esoteric
Philosophy in the East. (See "The Twelve Signs of the
Zodiac," by T. Subba Row, in *Five Years of Theosophy*.)

Ânanda (*Sans.*). Bliss, joy, felicity, happiness. The
name of a favorite disciple of Gautama, the Lord Buddha.

Anaxagoras. A famous Ionian philosopher who lived
500 B.C., studied philosophy under Anaximenes of Miletus,
and settled, in the days of Pericles, at Athens. Socrates,
Euripides, Archelaus, and other distinguished men and
philosophers were among his disciples and pupils. He was
a most learned astronomer, and was one of the first to explain openly that which was taught secretly by Pythagoras,
viz., the movements of the planets, the eclipses of the sun
and moon, etc. It was he who taught the theory of chaos,
on the principle that "nothing comes from nothing" (*ex
nihilo nihil fit*); and of atoms as the underlying essence
and substance of all bodies, "of the same nature as the
bodies which they formed." These atoms, he taught, were
primarily put in motion by *nous* (universal intelligence, the
mahat of the Hindûs), which *nous* is an immaterial, eternal,
spiritual entity; by this combination the world was formed,
the material gross bodies sinking down, and the ethereal
atoms (or fiery ether) rising and spreading in the upper
celestial regions. Antedating modern science by over two
thousand years, he taught that the stars were of the same
material as our earth, and the sun a glowing mass; that
the moon was a dark, uninhabitable body, receiving its light
from the sun; and beyond the aforesaid science he con-
fessed himself thoroughly convinced that *the real existence*

of things perceived by our senses could not be demonstrably proved. He died in exile at Lampsacus, at the age of seventy-two.

Anima Mundi (*Lat.*). The "soul of the world," the same as the *âlaya* of the Northern Buddhists; the divine essence which pervades, permeates, animates, and informs all things, from the smallest atom of matter to man and god. It is in a sense "the seven-skinned Mother" of the stanzas in *The Secret Doctrine ;* the essence of seven planes of sentiency, consciousness, and differentiation, both moral and physical. In its highest aspect it is *nirvâna ;* in its lowest, the *astral light.* It was feminine with the Gnostics, the early Christians, and the Nazarenes; bisexual with other sects, who considered it only in its four lower planes, of igneous and ethereal nature in the objective world of forms, and divine and spiritual in its three higher planes. When it is said that every human soul was born by detaching itself from the *anima mundi*, it is meant, esoterically, that our higher Egos are of an essence identical with *it*, and that *mahat* is a radiation of the ever unknown universal Absolute.

Anoia (*Gr.*). "Want of understanding," "folly." The term applied by Plato and others to the lower Manas when too closely allied with Kâma, which is characterized by irrationality (*anoia*). The Greek *anoia* or *agnoia* is evidently a derivative of the Sanskrit *ajñâna* (phonetically, *agnyâna*), or ignorance, irrationality, and absence of knowledge.

Anthropomorphism. From the Greek *anthropos*, man. The act of endowing God or the gods with a human form and human attributes or qualities.

Anugitâ (*Sans.*). A Upanishad, using the term in a general sense. One of the philosophical treatises in the *Mahâbhârata*, the great Indian epic. A very occult treatise. It is translated in "The Sacred Books of the East" series.

Apollo Belvedere. Of all the ancient statues of Apollo
—the son of Jupiter and Latona, called Phœbus, Helios,
the Radiant, and the Sun—the best and most perfect is that
of this name, which is in the Belvedere Gallery in the Vati-
can at Rome. It is called the Pythian Apollo, as the god
is represented in the moment of his victory over the serpent
Python. The statue was found in the ruins of Antium in
1503.

Apollonius of Tyana. A wonderful philosopher born
in Cappadocia about the beginning of the first century; an
ardent Pythagorean, who studied the Phenician sciences
under Euthydemus, and Pythagorean philosophy and other
subjects under Euxenus of Heraclea. According to the
tenets of the Pythagorean school, he remained a vegetarian
the whole of his long life, ate only fruit and herbs, drank
no wine, wore vestments made only of plant-fibers, walked
barefooted, and let his hair grow to the full length, as all
the Initiates have done before and after him. He was initiated by the priests of the temple of Æsculapius (Asklepios)
at Ægæ, and learned many of the "miracles" for healing
the sick wrought by the god of medicine. Having prepared
himself for a higher initiation by a silence of five years, and
by travel—visiting Antioch, Ephesus, and Pamphylia, and
other parts—he repaired via Babylon to India, alone, all
his disciples having abandoned him, as they feared to go
to the "land of enchantments." A casual disciple, Damis,
whom he met on the way, accompanied him, however, on
his travels. At Babylon he was initiated by the Chaldees
and Magi, according to Damis, whose narrative was copied
by one named Philostratus one hundred years later. After
his return from India he showed himself a true Initiate in
that the pestilence, earthquakes, deaths of kings, and other
events which he prophesied, duly happened.

At Lesbos the priests of Orpheus became jealous of him
and refused to initiate him into their peculiar mysteries,

though they did so several years later. He preached to the
people of Athens and other states the purest and noblest
ethics, and the phenomena he produced were as wonderful
as they were numerous and well authenticated. "How is
it," inquires Justin Martyr, in dismay—"how is it that the
talismans (*telesmata*) of Apollonius have power?—for they
prevent, as *we see*, the fury of the waves, and the violence
of the winds, and the attacks of wild beasts; and *while
our Lord's miracles are preserved by tradition alone*, those of
Apollonius *are most numerous, and actually manifested in
present facts ?* " (*Quest.*, xxiv.) But an answer is easily
found to this in the fact that, after crossing the Hindu-
Koosh, Apollonius had been directed by a king to the
abode of the sages, whose abode it may be to this day, and
who taught him their unsurpassed knowledge. His dia-
logues with the Corinthian Menippus give us truly the esoteric catechism, and disclose (when understood) many an
important mystery of Nature. Apollonius was the friend,
correspondent, and guest of kings and queens, and no
wonderful or "magic" powers are better attested than his.
Toward the close of his long and wonderful life he opened
an esoteric school at Ephesus, and died at the ripe old age
of one hundred years.

Archangel. Highest, supreme angel. From the two
Greek words, *arch*, first, and *angelos*, messenger.

Arhat (*Sans.*). Also pronounced and written *aráhat,
arhan, rahat*, etc. The "worthy one"; a perfected *árya;*
one exempt from reincarnation, "deserving divine honors."
This was the name first given to the Jain, and subsequently
to the Buddhist holy men initiated into the esoteric mysteries. The Arhat is one who has entered the last and highest path, and is thus emancipated from rebirth.

Arians. The followers of Arius, a presbyter of the
church in Alexandria in the fourth century. One who,
holds that Christ is a created and human being, inferior to

God the Father, though a grand and noble man, a true Adept, versed in all the divine mysteries.

Aristobulus. An Alexandrian writer and an obscure philosopher. A Jew who tried to prove that Aristotle explained the esoteric thoughts of Moses.

Âryan. Lit., "the holy." Those who had mastered the "noble truths" (*ârya-satyâni*) and entered the "noble path" (*ârya-mârga*) to *nirvâna* or *moksha*, the great "fourfold" path. They were originally known as Rishis; but now the name has become the epithet of a race, and our Orientalists, depriving the Hindû Brâhmans of their birthright, have made Aryans of all Europeans. Since, in esotericism, the four paths or stages can only be entered through great spiritual development and "growth in holiness," they are called the *ârya-mârga*. The degrees of arhatship, called respectively *srotâpatti, sakridâgâmin, anâgâmin*, and *arhat*, or the four classes of Âryas, correspond to the four paths and truths.

Aspect. The form (*rûpa*) under which any principle in septenary man or Nature manifests is called an *aspect* of that principle in Theosophy.

Astral Body. The ethereal counterpart or double of any physical body—*doppelgänger*.

Astrology. The science which defines the action of celestial bodies upon mundane affairs, and claims to foretell future events from the positions of the stars. Its antiquity is such as to place it among the very earliest records of human learning. It remained for long ages a secret science in the East, and its final expression remains so to this day, its exoteric application only having been brought to any degree of perfection in the West during the lapse of time since Varâha Mihira wrote his book on Astrology, some fourteen hundred years ago. Claudius Ptolemy, the famous geographer and mathematician who founded the system of astronomy known under his name, wrote his

Tetrabiblos, which is still the basis of modern Astrology, A.D. 135. The science of horoscopy is studied now chiefly under four heads, viz.: (1) *Mundane,* in its application to meteorology, seismology, husbandry. (2) *State* or *Civic,* in regard to the future of nations, kings, and rulers. (3) *Horary,* in reference to the solving of doubts arising in the mind upon any subject. (4) *Genethliacal,* in connection with the future of individuals from birth unto death. The Egyptians and the Chaldees were among the most ancient votaries of Astrology, though their modes of reading the stars and the modern methods differ considerably. The former claimed that Belus, the Bel or Elu of the Chaldees, a scion of the Divine Dynasty, or the dynasty of the King-gods, had belonged to the land of Chemi, and had left it to found a colony from Egypt on the banks of the Euphrates, where a temple, ministered by priests in the service of the "lords of the stars," was built. As to the origin of the science, it is known, on the one hand, that Thebes claimed the honor of the invention of Astrology, whereas, on the other hand, all are agreed that it was the Chaldees who taught that science to the other nations. Now Thebes antedated considerably not only "Ur of the Chaldees," but also Nipur, where Bel was first worshiped—Sin, his son (the moon), being the presiding deity of Ur, the land of the nativity of Terah, the Sabean and astrolater, and of Abram, his son, the great astrologer of biblical tradition. All tends, therefore, to corroborate the Egyptian claim. If later on the name of astrologer fell into disrepute in Rome and elsewhere, it was owing to the frauds of those who wanted to make money of that which was part and parcel of the sacred science of the Mysteries, and who, ignorant of the latter, evolved a system based entirely on mathematics, instead of on transcendental metaphysics with the physical celestial bodies as its *upâdhi* or material basis. Yet, all persecutions notwithstanding, the number of adherents to Astrology among the most intellectual and scientific minds was always very great. If Cardan and Kepler were among its ardent supporters, then later votaries have nothing to blush for, even in its now imperfect and distorted form. As said in *Isis Unveiled* (i., 259): "Astrology is to exact astronomy what psychology is to exact physiology. In astrology and psychology one has to step beyond the visible world of matter and enter into the domain of transcendent spirit."

Athenagoras. A Platonic philosopher of Athens who wrote *An Apology for the Christians*, in A.D. 177, addressed to Marcus Aurelius, to prove that the accusations brought against them—viz., that they were incestuous and ate murdered children—were untrue.

Âtman, or Âtmâ (*Sans.*). The universal spirit, the divine monad, the seventh "principle," so called, in the *exoteric* septenary classification of man. The supreme soul.

Aura (*Gr.* and *Lat.*). A subtle, invisible essence or fluid that emanates from human, animal, and other bodies. It is a psychic effluvium partaking of both the mind and the body, as there is both an electrovital and at the same time an electromental aura; called in Theosophy the âkâshic or magnetic aura. In Roman Catholic martyrology, a saint.

Avatâra (*Sans.*). Divine incarnation. The descent of a god, or some exalted being who has progressed beyond the necessity for rebirth, into the body of a simple mortal. Krishna was an *avatâra* of Vishnu. The Dalai-Lama is regarded as an *avatâra* of Avalokiteshvara, and the Teschu-Lama as one of Tson-kha-pa, or Amitâbha. There are two kinds of *avatâras*, one born from woman and the other "parentless"—*anupâdaka.*

B.

Be-ness. A term coined by Theosophists to render more accurately the essential meaning of the untranslatable word *sat*. The latter word does not mean "being," for the term "being" presupposes a sentient consciousness of existence. But as the term *sat* is applied solely to the absolute principle, that universal, unknown, and ever unknowable principle which philosophical pantheism postulates, calling it the basic root of cosmos and cosmos itself, it could not be translated by the simple term "being." *Sat*, indeed, is not even, as translated by some Orientalists, the "incomprehensible entity"; for it is no more an entity than a non-entity, but both. It is, as said, absolute *be-ness*, not "being"; the one secondless, undivided, and indivisible all; the root of Nature both visible and invisible, objective and subjective, comprehensible and never to be fully comprehended.

Bhagavad-Gîtâ (*Sans.*). Lit., the "Lord's Song." A portion of the *Mahâbhârata*, the great epic poem of India. It contains a dialogue wherein Krishna—the "charioteer" —and Arjuna, his *chelâ*, have a discussion upon the highest spiritual philosophy. The work is preëminently occult or esoteric.

Black Magic. Sorcery, necromancy, or the raising of the dead and other selfish abuses of abnormal powers. This abuse may be unintentional; still it has to remain "black" magic whenever anything is produced phenomenally simply for one's own gratification.

Böhme, Jakob. A mystic and great philosopher, one of the most prominent Theosophists of the medieval ages. He was born about 1575 at Old Diedenberg, some two miles from Görlitz (Silesia), and died in 1624, at the age of nearly fifty. When a boy he was a common shepherd, and, after learning to read and write in a village school, became an apprentice to a poor shoemaker at Görlitz. He was a natural clairvoyant of the most wonderful power. With no education or acquaintance with science he wrote works which are now proved to be full of scientific truths; but these, as he himself says of what he wrote, he "saw as in a great deep in the eternal." He had "a thorough view of the universe, as in chaos," which yet opened itself in him, from time to time, "as in a young planet," he says. He was a thorough-born mystic, and evidently of a constitution which is most rare; one of those fine natures whose material envelope impedes in no way the direct, even if only occasional, intercommunication between the intellectual and spiritual Ego. It is this Ego which Jakob Böhme, as so many other untrained mystics, mistook for God. "Man must acknowledge," he writes, "that his knowledge is not his own, but from God, who manifests the *ideas* of wisdom to the soul of man *in what measure he pleases*." Had this great Theosophist been born three hundred years later he might have expressed it otherwise. He would have known that the "God" who spoke through his poor uncultured and untrained brain was his own divine Ego, the omniscient deity within himself, and that what that deity gave out was not "what measure he pleased," but in the measure of the capacities of the mortal and temporary dwelling It informed.

Book of the Keys. An ancient Kabalistic work. The original is no longer extant, though there may be spurious or disfigured copies or forgeries of it.

Brahma (*Sans.*). The student must distinguish between the neuter Brahma and the male "creator" of the Indian Pantheon, Brahmâ. The former Brahma or Brahman is the impersonal, supreme, and uncognizable soul of the universe, from the essence of which all emanates, and into which all returns; which is incorporeal, immaterial, unborn, eternal, beginningless, and endless. It is all-pervading, animating the highest god as well as the smallest mineral atom. Brahmâ, on the other hand, the male and the alleged "creator," exists in his manifestation periodically only, and passes into *pralaya*—i.e., disappears and is *annihilated*—as periodically.

Brahmâ's Day. A period of 4,320,000,000 years, during which Brahmâ, having emerged out of his Golden Egg (*hiranya-garbha*), creates and fashions the material world (for he is simply the fertilizing and creative force in Nature). After this period, the worlds being destroyed in turn by fire and water, he vanishes with objective Nature; and then comes

Brahmâ's Night. A period of equal duration, in which Brahmâ is said to be asleep. Upon awakening he recommences the process, and this goes on for an Age of Brahmâ, composed of alternate "Days" and "Nights," and lasting for 100 years of 3,110,400,000,000 solar years each. It requires fifteen figures to express the duration of such an age, after the expiration of which the *mahâpralaya* or Great Dissolution sets in, and lasts in its turn for the same space of fifteen figures.

Brahma-Vidyâ (*Sans.*). The knowledge or esoteric science about the true nature of the two Brahmas (Brahma and Brahmâ).

Buddha (*Sans.*). "The Enlightened." Generally known as the title of Gautama Buddha, the Prince of Kapilavastu, the founder of modern Buddhism. The highest degree of knowledge and holiness. To become a Buddha one has to break through the bondage of sense and personality; to acquire a complete perception of the real *Self*, and learn not to separate it from all the other selves; to learn by experience the utter unreality of all phenomena, foremost of all the visible cosmos; to attain a complete detachment from all that is evanescent and finite, and to live while yet on earth only in the immortal and everlasting.

Buddhi (*Sans.*). Universal soul or mind. *Mahâbuddhi* is a name of *mahat*; also the spiritual soul in man (the sixth principle, exoterically), the vehicle of Âtmâ (the seventh, according to the exoteric enumeration).

Buddhism is the religious philosophy taught by Gautama Buddha. It is now split into two distinct churches, the Southern and Northern. The former is said to be the purer, as having preserved more religiously the original teachings of the Lord Buddha. The Northern Buddhism is confined to Tibet, China, and Nepaul. But this distinction is incorrect. If the Southern Church is nearer, and has not, in fact, departed—except, perhaps, in trifling dogmas, due to the many councils held after the death of the Master—from the public or exoteric teachings of Shâkyamuni, the Northern Church is the outcome of Siddhârtha Buddha's esoteric teachings, which he confined to his elect Bhikshus and Arhats. Buddhism, in fact, cannot be justly judged in our age either by one or the other of its exoteric popular forms. Real Buddhism can be appreciated only by blending the philosophy of the Southern Church and the metaphysics of the Northern schools. If one seems too iconoclastic and stern, and the other too metaphysical and transcendental, even to being overcharged with the weeds of Indian exotericism—many of the gods of its Pantheon having been transplanted under new names into Tibetan soil—it is due to the popular expression of Buddhism in both churches. Correspondentially they stand in their relation to each other as Protestantism to Roman Catholicism. Both err by an excess of zeal and erroneous interpretations, though neither the Southern nor the Northern Buddhist clergy have ever departed from truth consciously; still less have they acted under the dictates of *priestocracy*, ambition, or an eye to personal gain and power, as the later churches have.

Buddhi-Taijasa (*Sans.*). A very mystic term, capable of several interpretations. In Occultism, however, and in relation to the human "principles" (exoterically), it is a term to express the state of our dual Manas, when, reunited during a man's life, it bathes in the radiance of Buddhi, the spiritual soul. For Taijasa means "the radiant"; and Manas, becoming radiant in consequence of its union with Buddhi, and being, so to speak, merged into it, is identified with the latter; the trinity has become one; and, as the element of Buddhi is the highest, it becomes Buddhi-Taijasa. In short, it is the human soul illuminated by the radiance of the divine soul, the human reason lit by the light of the spirit or divine SELF-consciousness.

C.

Caste. Originally the system of the four hereditary classes into which the Indian population was divided: Brâhman, Kshatriya, Vaishya, and Shûdra—(a) descendants of Brahmâ; (b) warrior; (c) mercantile; and (d) the lowest or agricultural class. From these four hundreds of divisions and minor castes have sprung.

Causal Body. This "body," which is in reality no body at all, either objective or subjective, but Buddhi, the spiritual soul, is so called because it is the direct cause of the *sushupti* state, leading to the *turîya* state, the highest state of *samâdhi*. It is called *kâranopâdhi*, "the basis of the cause," by the Târaka Râja Yogîs, which in the Vedânta system corresponds to both the *vijñânamaya* and *ânandamaya kosha* (the latter coming next to Âtmâ, and therefore being the vehicle of the universal spirit). Buddhi alone could not be called a "causal body," but becomes one in conjunction with Manas, the incarnating entity or Ego.

Chelâ (*Hindî*). A disciple. The pupil of a Guru or sage; the follower of some Adept or school of philosophy.

Chrestos (*Gr.*). The early Gnostic term for Christ. This technical term was used in the fifth century B.C. by Æschylus, Herodotus, and others. The *manteumata pythocresta*, or the "oracles delivered by a Pythian god" through a pythoness, are mentioned by the former (*Choeph.*, 901), and *pythocrestos* is derived from *chrao*. *Chresterion* is not only the "test of an oracle," but an offering to, or for, the oracle. *Chrestes* is one who explains oracles, a "prophet and soothsayer," and *Chresterios*, one who serves an oracle or a god. The earliest Christian writer, Justin Martyr, in his first *Apology*, calls his coreligionists *Chrestians*. "It is only through ignorance that men call themselves Christians, instead of Chrestians," says Lactantius (lib. iv., cap. vii.). The terms Christ and Christians, spelled originally **Chrest** and **Chrestians**, were borrowed from the temple vocabulary of the pagans. *Chrestos* meant, in that vocabulary, "a disciple on probation," a candidate for hierophantship; who, when he had attained it, through initiation, long trials, and suffering, and had been anointed (i.e., "rubbed with oil," as Initiates and even idols of the gods were, as the last touch of ritualistic observance), was changed into *Christos*—the "purified" in esoteric or mystery language. In mystic symbology, indeed, Christes or Christos meant that the "way," the "path," was already trodden and the goal reached; when the fruits of this arduous labor—uniting the *personality* of evanescent clay with the indestructible *individuality*—transformed it thereby into the immortal Ego. "At the end of the way stands the Christes," the Purifier; and, the union once accomplished, the Chrestos, the "man of sorrow," became Christos himself. Paul, the Initiate, knew this, and meant this precisely when he is made to say in bad translation, "I travail in birth again until Christ be formed in you" (Gal. iv. 19), the true rendering of which is, "until you form the Christos within yourselves." But the profane, who knew only that Chrestos was in some way connected with priest and prophet, and knew nothing about the hidden meaning of Christos, insisted, as did Lactantius and Justin Martyr, on being called Chrestians instead of Christians. Every good individual, therefore, may find Christ in his "inner man," as Paul expresses it (Eph. iii. 16, 17), whether he be Jew, Mussulman, Hindû, or Christian.

Christ. See "Chrestos."

Christian Scientist. A newly coined term for denoting the practitioners of a healing art by will. The name is a misnomer, since Buddhist or Jew, Hindû or materialist, can practise this new form of "Western Yoga" with equal success if he can only guide and control his will with sufficient firmness. The "Mental Scientists" are another rival school. These work by a universal denial of every disease and evil imaginable, and claim, syllogistically, that since universal spirit cannot be subject to the ailings of flesh, and since every atom is spirit and *in* spirit, and since, finally, they—the healers and the healed—are all absorbed in this spirit or deity, there is not, nor can there be, such a thing as disease. This prevents in no wise both Christian and Mental Scientists from succumbing to disease and nursing chronic ailments for years in their own bodies just like other ordinary mortals.

Clairaudience. The faculty—whether innate or acquired by occult training—of hearing things at whatever distance.

Clairvoyance. The faculty of seeing with the inner eye, or spiritual sight. As now used, it is a loose and flippant term, embracing under its meaning both a happy guess due to natural shrewdness or intuition, and also that faculty which was so remarkably exercised by Jakob Böhme and Swedenborg. Yet even these two great seers, since they could never rise superior to the general spirit of the Jewish Bible and sectarian teachings, have sadly confused what they saw, and fallen far short of true clairvoyance.

Clemens Alexandrinus. A church father and voluminous writer, who had been a Neoplatonist and a disciple of Ammonius Saccas. He was one of the few Christian philosophers between the second and third centuries of our era at Alexandria.

College of Rabbis. A college at Babylon, most famous during the early centuries of Christianity; but its glory was greatly darkened by the appearance in Alexandria of Hellenic teachers, such as Philo Judæus, Josephus, Aristobulus, and others. The former avenged themselves on their successful rivals by speaking of the Alexandrians as Theurgists and unclean prophets. But the Alexandrian believers in thaumaturgy were not regarded as sinners and impostors when orthodox Jews were at the head of such schools of "Hazim." These were colleges for teaching prophecy and occult sciences. Samuel was the chief of such a college at Ramah; Elisha at Jericho. Hillel had a regular academy for prophets and seers; and it is Hillel, a pupil of the Babylonian college, who was the founder of the sect of the Pharisees and the great orthodox rabbis.

Cycle (*Gr.*). From *kuklos.* The ancients divided time into endless cycles, wheels within wheels, all such periods being of various duration, and each marking the beginning or end of some event, either cosmic, mundane, physical, or metaphysical. There were cycles of only a few years, and cycles of immense duration. The great Orphic cycle, referring to the ethnological change of races, lasted one hundred and twenty thousand years, and that of Cassandrus one hundred and thirty-six thousand. The latter brought about a complete change in planetary influences and their correlations between men and gods—a fact entirely lost sight of by modern astrologers.

D.

Deist. One who admits the possibility of the existence of a God or gods, but claims to know nothing of either, and denies revelation. An agnostic of olden times.

Deva (*Sans.*). A god, a "resplendent" deity—*deva* (*deus*), from the root *div*, to shine. A Deva is a celestial being—whether good, bad, or indifferent—which inhabits the three "worlds" or the three planes above us. There are thirty-three groups or three hundred and thirty millions of them.

Devachan. The "dwelling of the gods." A state intermediate between two earth-lives, into which the Ego (Âtmâ-Buddhi-Manas, or the Trinity made one) enters after its separation from Kâma Rûpa and the disintegration of the lower principles, on the death of the body on earth.

Dhammapada (*Pâli*). A work containing various aphorisms from the Buddhist Scriptures.

Dhyân Chohans. Lit., the "lords of contemplation." The highest gods, answering to the Roman Catholic archangels. The divine intelligences charged with the supervision of cosmos.

Dhyâna (*Sans.*). One of the six *pâramitâs* or perfections. A state of abstraction which carries the ascetic practising it far above the region of sensuous perception and out of the world of matter. Lit., "contemplation." The six stages of *dhyâna* differ only in the degrees of abstraction of the personal Ego from sensuous life.

Double. The same as the astral body or *doppelgänger*.

E.

Ecstasis (*Gr.*). A psychospiritual state; a physical trance which induces clairvoyance, and a beatific state which brings on visions.

Ego (*Lat.*). "I"; the consciousness in man of the "I am I," or the feeling of "I-am-ship." Esoteric Philosophy teaches the existence of two Egos in man, the mortal or *personal*, and the higher, the divine or *impersonal;* calling the former "personality," and the latter "individuality."

Egoity. Egoity means "individuality"—never "personality," as it is the opposite of egoism or "selfishness," the characteristic *par excellence* of the latter.

Eidôlon (*Gr.*). The same as that which we term the human phantom, the astral form.

Elementals. Spirits of the elements. The creatures

evolved in the four kingdoms or elements—earth, air, fire, and water. They are called by the Kabalists gnomes (of the earth), sylphs (of the air), salamanders (of the fire), and undines (of the water). Except a few of the higher kinds and their rulers, they are rather the forces of Nature than ethereal men and women. These forces, as the servile agents of the occultist, may produce various effects; but if employed by "elementaries" (Kâma Rûpas)—in which case they enslave the mediums—they will deceive. All the lower invisible beings generated on the fifth, sixth, and seventh planes of our terrestrial atmosphere are called elementals—peris, devs, jinns, sylvans, satyrs, fauns, elves, dwarfs, trolls, norns, kobolds, brownies, nixies, goblins, pinkies, banshees, moss-people, white ladies, spooks, fairies, etc.

Eleusinia (*Gr.*). The Eleusinian Mysteries were the most famous and the most ancient of all the Greek Mysteries (with the exception of the Samothracian), and were performed near the hamlet of Eleusis, not far from Athens. Epiphanius traces them to the days of Iacchos (1800 B.C.). They were held in honor of Demeter, the great Ceres, and the Egyptian Isis; and the last act of the performance referred to a sacrificial victim of atonement and a resurrection, when the Initiate was admitted to the highest degree of Epopt. The festival of the Mysteries began in the month of Boëdromion (September), the time of grape-gathering, and lasted from the 15th to the 22d—seven days. The Hebrew Feast of Tabernacles—the feast of ingatherings—in the month of Ethanim (the seventh), also began on the 15th and ended on the 22d of that month. The name of the month (Ethanim) is derived, according to some, from *adonim, adonia, attenim, ethanim,* and was in honor of Adonai, or Adonis (Tham), whose death was lamented by the Hebrews in the groves of Bethlehem. The sacrifice of "bread and wine" was performed both in the Eleusinia and during the Feast of Tabernacles.

Emanation. This doctrine, in its metaphysical meaning, is opposed to evolution, yet one with it. Science teaches that, physiologically, evolution is a mode of generation in which the germ that develops the fetus preëxists already in the parent, the development and final form and characteristics of that germ being accomplished by Nature; and that (as in its cosmology) the process takes place *blindly*, through the correlation of the elements and their various compounds. Occultism teaches that this is only the *apparent* mode, the real process being *emanation*, guided by intelligent forces under an immutable law. Therefore, while the occultists and Theosophists believe thoroughly in the doctrine of evolution as given out by Kapila and Manu, they are "emanationists" rather than "evolutionists." The doctrine of emanation was at one time universal. It was taught by the Alexandrian as well as by the Indian philosophers, by the Egyptian, the Chaldæan and Hellenic hierophants, and also by the Hebrews (in their Kabalah, and even in Genesis). For it is only owing to deliberate mistranslation that the Hebrew word *asdt* was translated "angels" from the Septuagint, while it means "emanations," "eons," just as with the Gnostics. Indeed, in Deuteronomy (xxxiii. 2) the word *asdt* or *ashdt* is translated as "fiery law," while the correct rendering of the passage should be, "from his right went [not *a fiery law*, but] *a fire according to law*," viz., that the fire of one flame is imparted to and caught up by another —like as in a trail of inflammable substance. This is precisely emanation, as shown in *Isis Unveiled*. "In evolution, as it is now beginning to be understood, there is supposed to be in all matter an impulse to take on a higher form—a supposition clearly expressed by Manu and other Hindû philosophers of the highest antiquity. The philosopher's tree illustrates it in the case of the zinc solution. The controversy between the followers of this school and the emanationists may be briefly stated thus: the evolutionist stops all inquiry at the borders of 'the unknowable'; the emanationist believes that nothing can be evolved—or, as the word means, unwombed or born—except it has first been involved, thus indicating that life is from a spiritual potency above the whole."

Esoteric. Hidden, secret. From the Greek *esotericos*, inner, concealed.

Esoteric Bodhism. Secret wisdom or intelligence; from the Greek *esotericos*, inner, and the Sanskrit *bodhi*, knowledge, in contradistinction to *buddhi*, the *faculty* of knowledge or intelligence, and *buddhism*, the philosophy or law of *buddha*, the "Enlightened." Also written "Budhism," from *budha* (intelligence, wisdom), the son of Soma.

Eurasians. An abbreviation of "European-Asians." The mixed colored races, the children of the white fathers and the dark mothers of India, and *vice versa*.

Exoteric. Outward, public; the opposite of esoteric or hidden.

Extracosmic. Outside of cosmos or Nature. A nonsensical word invented to assert the existence of a *personal* god independent of or outside Nature *per se;* for as Nature, or the universe, is infinite and limitless, there can be nothing outside it. The term is coined in opposition to the pantheistic idea that the whole cosmos is animated or informed with the spirit of deity, Nature being but the garment, and matter the illusive shadows, of the real unseen Presence.

F.

Ferho (*Syriac ?*). The highest and greatest creative power with the Nazarene Gnostics.

Fire-Philosophers. The name given to the Hermetists and alchemists of the middle ages, and also to the Rosicrucians. The latter, the successors of Theurgists, regarded fire as the symbol of deity. It was the source not only of material atoms, but the container of the spiritual and psychic forces energizing them. Broadly analyzed, fire is a triple principle; esoterically, a septenary, as are all the rest of the elements. As man is composed of spirit, soul, and body, *plus* a fourfold aspect, so is fire. As in the works of Robert Flood (Robertus de Fluctibus), one of the famous Rosicrucians, fire contains, firstly, a visible flame (body); secondly, an invisible, astral fire (soul); and thirdly, spirit. The four aspects are (*a*) heat (life), (*b*) light (mind), (*c*) electricity (kâmic or molecular powers), and (*d*) the synthetic essences *beyond spirit*, or the radical cause of its existence and manifestation. For the Hermetist or Rosicrucian, when a flame is extinct on the objective plane, it has only passed from the seen world into the unseen, from the knowable into the unknowable.

G.

Gautama (*Sans.*). A proper name in India. It is that of the Prince of Kapilavastu, son of Suddhodana, the Shâkhya king of a small territory on the borders of Nepaul, born in the seventh century B.C., now called the "savior of the world." Gautama, or Gotama, was the sacerdotal name of the Shâkhya family. Born a simple mortal, he rose to Buddhahood through his own personal and unaided merit; a man—verily greater than any god !

Gebirol. Solomon ben-Yehudah, called in literature Avicebron. An Israelite by birth; a philosopher, poet, and Kabalist; a voluminous writer and a mystic. He was born in the eleventh century at Malaga (1021), educated at Saragossa, and died at Valencia in 1070, murdered by a Mohammedan. His fellow-religionists called him Salomon the Sephardi, or the Spaniard, and the Arabs, Abu Ayyub Suleiman ben-Ya'hya Ibn Djebirol, while the Scholastics named him Avicebron (see Myer's *Qabbalah*). Ibn Gebirol was certainly one of the greatest philosophers and scholars of his age. He wrote much in Arabic, and most of his manuscripts have been preserved. His greatest work appears to be the *Me'qor' Hayyim*—i.e., Fountain of Life—"one of the earliest exposures of the secrets of the speculative Kabalah," as his biographer informs us.

Gnôsis (*Gr.*). Lit., "knowledge." The technical term used by the schools of religious philosophy, both before and during the first centuries of so-called Christianity, to denote the object of their inquiry. This spiritual and sacred knowledge, the *gupta-vidyâ* of the Hindûs, could only be obtained by initiation into spiritual mysteries of which the ceremonial "Mysteries" were a type.

Gnostics (*Gr.*). The philosophers who formulated and taught the Gnôsis or knowledge. They flourished in the first three centuries of the Christian era. The following were eminent: Simon Magus, Valentinus, Basilides, Marcion, etc.

Golden Age. The ancients divided the life-cycle into the Golden, Silver, Bronze, and Iron Ages. The Golden was an age of primeval purity, simplicity, and general happiness.

Great Age. There are several "Great Ages" mentioned by the ancients. In India the Great Age embraced the whole *mahâmanvantara*, the "Age of Brahmâ," each "Day" of which represents the life-cycle of a "chain," i.e., it embraces a period of seven "rounds" (see *Esoteric Buddhism*, by A. P. Sinnett). Thus, while a "Day" and a "Night" represent, as *manvantara* and *pralaya*, 8,640,-000,000 years, an "Age" lasts through a period of 311,-040,000,000,000; after which the *pralaya* or dissolution of the universe becomes universal. With the Egyptians and Greeks the Great Age referred only to the Tropical or Sidereal Year, the duration of which is 25,868 solar years. Of the complete age—that of the gods—they said nothing, as it was a matter to be discussed and divulged only at the

Mysteries, and during the initiation ceremonies. The Great Age of the Chaldees was the same in figures as that of the Hindûs.

Guhya-Vidyâ (*Sans.*). The secret knowledge of mystic mantras.

Gupta-Vidyâ (*Sans.*). The same as *guhya-vidyâ.* Esoteric or secret science, knowledge.

Gyges. "The ring of Gyges" has become a familiar metaphor in European literature. Gyges was a Lydian, who, after murdering the King Candaules, married his widow. Plato tells us that Gyges, descending once into a chasm of the earth, discovered a brazen horse, within whose opened side was the skeleton of a man of gigantic stature, who had a brazen ring on his finger. This ring, when placed on his own finger, made him invisible.

H.

Hades (*Gr.*). *Aïdes* is the "invisible," the land of shadows; one of whose regions was Tartarus, a place of complete darkness, as was also the region of profound dreamless sleep in Amenti. Judging by the allegorical description of the punishments inflicted therein, the place was purely karmic. Neither Hades nor Amenti was the hell still preached by some retrograde priests and clergymen; and whether represented by the Elysian Fields or by Tartarus, it could only be reached by crossing the river to the "other shore." As well expressed in *Egyptian Belief* (Bonwick), the story of Charon, the ferryman of the Styx, is to be found not only in Homer, but in the poetry of many lands. The *River* must be crossed before gaining the Isles of the Blest. The Ritual of Egypt described a Charon and his boat long ages before Homer. He is Khu-en-ra, "the hawk-headed steersman."

Hallucinations. A state produced sometimes by physi-

ological disorders, sometimes by mediumship, and at others
by drunkenness.   But the cause that produces the visions
has to be sought deeper than physiology.   All such, particularly when produced through mediumship, are preceded
by a relaxation of the nervous system, invariably generating an abnormal magnetic condition which attracts to the
sufferer waves of astral light.   It is these latter that furnish
the various hallucinations, which, however, are not always,
as physicians would explain them, mere empty and unreal
dreams.   No one can see that which does not exist—i.e.,
which is not impressed—in or on the astral waves.   But a
seer may perceive objects and scenes, whether past, present,
or future, which have no relation whatever to himself; and
perceive, moreover, several things entirely disconnected from
each other at one and the same time, so as to produce the
most grotesque and absurd combinations.   Both drunkard
and seer, medium and Adept, see their respective visions in
the astral light; only while the drunkard, the madman, and
the untrained medium, or one in a brain-fever, see because
they cannot help it, and evoke jumbled visions, unconsciously to themselves without being able to control them,
the Adept and the trained seer have the choice and the control of such visions.   They know where to fix their gaze,
how to steady the scenes they wish to observe, and how
to see beyond the upper outward layers of the astral light.
With the former such glimpses into the *waves* are hallucinations; with the latter they become the faithful reproduction of what actually has been, is, or will be taking place.
The glimpses at random caught by the medium, and his
flickering visions in the deceptive light, are transformed
under the guiding will of the Adept and seer into steady
pictures, the truthful representation of that which he wills
to come within the focus of his perception.

   Hell. A term which the Anglo-Saxon race has evidently
derived from the name of the Scandinavian goddess *Hela,*

just as the word *Ad*, in Russian and other Slavonian tongues, expressing the same conception, is derived from the Greek *Hades ;* the only difference between the Scandinavian cold hell and the hot hell of the Christians being found in their respective temperatures. But the idea of these overheated regions is not original with the Europeans, many people having entertained the conception of an under-world climate; as well we may, if we localize our hell in the center of the earth. All exoteric religions—the creeds of the Brâhmans, Buddhists, Zoroastrians, Mohammedans, Jews, and the rest— make their hells hot and dark, though many are more attractive than frightful. The idea of a hot hell is an afterthought, the distortion of an astronomical allegory. With the Egyptians hell became a place of punishment by fire not earlier than the Seventeenth or Eighteenth Dynasty, when Typhon was transformed from a god into a devil. But at whatever time they implanted this dread superstition in the minds of the poor ignorant masses, the scheme of a burning hell and souls tormented therein is purely Egyptian. Ra (the Sun) became the Lord of the Furnace, in *Karr*, the hell of the Pharaohs, and the sinner was threatened with misery "in the heat of infernal fires." "A lion was there," says Dr. Birch, "and was called the roaring monster." Another describes the place as "the bottomless pit and lake of fire, into which the victims are thrown" (compare Revelation). The Hebrew word *gaïhinnom* (gehenna) had never really the significance given to it in Christian orthodoxy.

Hermas. An ancient Greek writer, of whose works only a few fragments now remain extant.

Hierogrammatists. The title given to those Egyptian priests who were intrusted with the writing and reading of the sacred and secret records. The "scribes of the secret records," literally. They were the instructors of the neophytes preparing for initiation.

Hierophant. From the Greek *hierophantes*, literally "he who explains sacred things "; a title belonging to the highest Adepts in the temples of antiquity, who were the teachers and expounders of the Mysteries, and the initiators into the final great Mysteries. The Hierophant stood for the demiurge, and explained to the postulants for initiation the various phenomena of creation that were produced for their tuition. " He was the sole expounder of the exoteric secrets and doctrines. It was forbidden even to pronounce his name before an uninitiated person. He sat in the East, and wore as symbol of authority a golden globe suspended from the neck. He was also called *mystagogus.*" (Mackenzie, *The Royal Masonic Cyclopedia.*)

Hillel. A great Babylonian rabbi of the century preceding the Christian era. He was the founder of the sect of the Pharisees, a learned and a saintly man.

Hináyâna (*Sans.*). The "small vehicle"; a scripture and a school of the Buddhists, contrasted with the *mahâyâna,* the "great vehicle." Both schools are mystical. Also, in exoteric superstition, the lowest form of transmigration.

Homogeneity. From the Greek words *homos,* the same, and *genos,* kind. That which is of the same nature throughout, undifferentiated, non-compound, as gold is *supposed* to be.

Hypnotism. A name given by Dr. Braid to the process by which one man of strong will-power plunges another of weaker mind into a kind of trance; once in such a state, the latter will do anything *suggested* to him by the hypnotizer. Unless produced for beneficial purposes, the Occultists would call it black magic or sorcery. It is the most dangerous of practices, morally and physically, as it interferes with the nerve-fluids.

I.

Iamblichus. A great Theosophist and an Initiate of the third century. He wrote a great deal about the various kinds of demons who appear through evocation, but spoke severely against such phenomena. His austerities, purity of life, and earnestness were great. He is credited with having been levitated ten cubits high from the ground, as are some modern Yogîs and mediums.

Illusion. In Occultism everything finite (such as the universe and all in it) is called " illusion " or *mâyâ*.

Individuality. One of the names given in Theosophy and Occultism to the human higher Ego. We make a distinction between the immortal and divine and the mortal human Ego which perishes. The latter, or " personality " (personal Ego), survives the dead body only for a time in Kâmalôka; the " individuality " prevails forever.

Initiate. From the Latin *initiatus*. The designation of any one who was received into and had revealed to him the mysteries and secrets of either Masonry or Occultism. In times of antiquity they were those who had been initiated into the arcane knowledge taught by the Hierophants of the Mysteries; and in our modern days those who have been initiated by the Adepts of mystic lore into the mysterious knowledge, which, notwithstanding the lapse of ages, has yet a few real votaries on earth.

Îshvara (*Sans.*). The " Lord," or the personal god, *divine spirit in man*. Literally, " sovereign " (independent) existence. A title given to Shiva and other gods in India. Shiva is also called Îshvaradeva, or Sovereign Deva.

J.

Javidan Khirad (*Pers.*). A work on moral precepts.

Jhâna (*Pâli*). The Sanskrit *jñâna*, knowledge, occult wisdom.

Josephus, Flavius. A historian of the first century; a Hellenized Jew who lived in Alexandria and died at Rome. He was credited by Eusebius with having written the sixteen

famous lines relating to Christ, which were most probably
interpolated by Eusebius himself, the greatest forger among
the church fathers. This passage, in which Josephus, although he was an ardent Jew and died in Judaism, is nevertheless made to acknowledge the *Messiahship* and divine
origin of Jesus, is now declared spurious both by most of
the Christian bishops (Lardner among others) and even by
Paley. (See his *Evidences of Christianity*.) It was for
centuries one of the weightiest proofs of the real existence
of Jesus, the Christ.

Jukabar Zivo. A Gnostic term. The "Lord of the
Eons" in the Nazarene system. He is the procreator
(emanator) of the seven "Holy Lives" (the seven primal
Dhyân Chohans or archangels, each representing one of
the cardinal virtues), and is himself called the third Life
(third Logos). In the *Codex Nazaræus* he is addressed as
the "Helm" and "Vine" of the food of life. Thus he is
identical with Christ (Christos), who says, "I am the true
vine, and my Father is the husbandman." (John xv. 1.)
It is well known that Christ is regarded in the Roman
Catholic Church as the "Chief of the Eons," as also is
Michael, "who is as God." Such also was the belief of
the Gnostics.

· K.

Kabalah (*Heb.*). "The hidden wisdom of the Hebrew
rabbis of the middle ages, derived from the older secret
doctrines concerning divine things and cosmogony, which
were combined into a theology after the time of the captiv-
ity of the Jews in Babylon." All the works that fall under
the esoteric category are termed Kabalistic.

Kâmaloka (*Sans.*). The *semi*-material plane, to us subjective and invisible, where the disembodied "personalities,"
the astral forms called Kâma Rûpa, remain until they fade

out from it by the complete exhaustion of the effects of the mental impulses that created these *eidolons* of the lower animal passions and desires. It is the Hades of the ancient Greeks and the Amenti of the Egyptians—the Land of Silent Shadows.

Kâma Rûpa (*Sans.*). Metaphysically and in our Esoteric Philosophy it is the subjective form created, through the mental and physical desires and thoughts in connection with things of matter, by all sentient beings; a form which survives the death of its body. After that death, three of the seven "principles" (or, let us say, planes of the senses and consciousness on which the human instincts and ideation act in turn), viz., the body, its astral prototype, and physical vitality, being of no further use, remain on earth; the three higher principles, grouped into one, merge into a state of Devachan, in which state the higher Ego will remain until the hour for a new reincarnation arrives, and the *eidolon* of the ex-personality is left alone in its new abode. Here the pale copy of the man that was vegetates for a period of time, the duration of which is variable according to the element of materiality which is left in it, and which is determined by the past life of the defunct. Bereft as it is of its higher mind, spirit, and physical senses, if left alone to its own senseless devices it will gradually fade out and disintegrate. But if forcibly drawn back into the terrestrial sphere, whether by the passionate desires and appeals of the surviving friends or by regular necromantic practices— one of the most pernicious of which is mediumship—the "spook" may prevail for a period greatly exceeding the span of the natural life of its body. Once the Kâma Rûpa has learned the way back to living human bodies, it becomes a vampire feeding on the vitality of those who are so anxious for its company. In India these *eidolons* are called *pisâchas*, and are much dreaded.

Kapilavastu (*Sans.*). The birthplace of the Lord Buddha, called the "yellow dwelling," the capital of the monarch who was the father of Gautama Buddha.

Kardec, Allan. The adopted name of the founder of the French Spiritists, whose real name was Rivaille. It was he who gathered and published the trance utterances of certain mediums, and afterward made a "philosophy" of them, between the years 1855 and 1870.

Karma (*Sans.*). Physically, Action; metaphysically, the Law of Retribution; the Law of Cause and Effect, or Ethical Causation. It is Nemesis only in the sense of bad Karma. It is the eleventh *nidâna* in the concatenation of causes and effects in orthodox Buddhism; yet it is the power that controls all things, the resultant of moral action, the metaphysical *samskâra*, or the moral effect of an act committed for the attainment of something which gratifies a personal desire. There is the Karma of merit and the Karma of demerit. Karma neither punishes nor rewards; it is simply the *one universal law* which guides unerringly, and, so to say, blindly, all other laws productive of certain effects along the grooves of their respective causations. When Buddhism teaches that "Karma is that moral kernel (of any being) which alone survives death and continues in transmigration" or reincarnation, it simply means that there remains naught after each personality but the causes produced by it, causes which are undying, i.e., which cannot be eliminated from the universe until replaced by their legitimate effects, and, so to speak, wiped out by them. And such causes, unless compensated with adequate effects during the life of the person who produced them, will follow the reincarnated Ego and reach it in its subsequent incarnations, until a full harmony between effects and causes is fully reëstablished. No "personality"—a mere bundle of material atoms and instinctual and mental characteristics— can, of course, continue as such in the world of pure spirit. Only that which is immortal in its very nature and divine in its essence—namely, the Ego—can exist forever. And as it is that Ego which chooses the personality it will inform after each Devachan, and which receives through these personalities the effects of the karmic causes produced, it is therefore the Ego, that *Self*—which is the "moral kernel" referred to, and in fact embodied Karma itself—"which alone survives death."

Kether (*Heb.*). "The Crown, the highest of the ten Sephiroth; the first of the supernal triad. It corresponds to the Macroprosopos, Vast Countenance, or Arikh Anpin, which differentiates into Chokmah and Binah."

Krishna (*Sans.*). The most celebrated *avatâra* of Vishnu, the "savior" of the Hindûs, and the most popular god. He is the eighth *avatâra*, the son of Devaki and nephew of Kansha, the Indian Herod, who, while seeking for him among the shepherds and cowherds who concealed him, slew thousands of their newly born babes. The story of Krishna's conception, birth, and childhood is the exact prototype of the New Testament story. The missionaries, of course, try to show that the Hindûs stole the story of the nativity from the early Christians who came to India.

Kshetrajña, or Kshetrajñeshvara (*Sans.*). Embodied spirit in Occultism, the conscious Ego in its highest manifestations; the reincarnating principle, or the "Lord" in us.

Kumâra (*Sans.*). A virgin boy or young celibate. The first *kumâras* are the seven sons of Brahmâ, born out of the limbs of the god in the so-called *ninth* "creation." It is stated that the name was given to them owing to their formal refusal to "procreate" their species, and thus they "remained Yogîs" according to the legend.

L.

Labre, St. A Roman saint solemnly beatified a few years ago. His great holiness consisted in sitting at one

of the gates of Rome night and day for forty years, and remaining unwashed through the whole of that time, the result
of which was that he was eaten by vermin to his bones.

Lao-Tze (*Chin.*). A great sage, saint, and philosopher,
who was the contemporary of Confucius.

Law of Retribution. See " Karma."

Linga Sharîra (*Sans.*). "Astral body," i.e., the aërial
symbol of the body. This term designates the *doppelgänger*,
or the "astral body" of man or animal. It is the *eidolon*
of the Greeks, the vital and *prototypal* body, the reflection
of the man of flesh. It is born before man, and dies or
fades out with the disappearance of the last atom of the
body.

Logos (*Gr.*). The *manifested* deity with every nation
and people; the outward expression or the effect of the
cause which is ever concealed. Thus speech is the *logos* of
thought; hence, in its metaphysical sense, it is aptly translated by the terms " Verbum " and " Word."

Long Face. A Kabalistic term; Arikh Anpin in Hebrew,
or "Long Face"; in Greek, Macroprosopos, as contrasted
with "Short Face," or Zeir Anpin, the Microprosopos. One
relates to deity, the other to man, the "little image of the
great form."

Longinus, Dionysius Cassius. A famous critic and
philosopher, born in the very beginning of the third century
(about A.D. 213). He was a great traveler, and attended
at Alexandria the lectures of Ammonius Saccas, the founder
of Neoplatonism, but was rather a critic than a follower.
Porphyry (the Jew Malek or Malchus) was his pupil before
he became the disciple of Plotinus. It is said of him that
he was a living library and a walking museum. Toward
the end of his life he became the instructor in Greek literature of Zenobia, queen of Palmyra. She repaid his services
by accusing him before the Emperor Aurelian of having
advised her to rebel against the latter, a crime for which

Longinus, with several others, was put to death by the emperor in 273.

M.

Macrocosm. The "great universe" or cosmos.

Magic. The "great" science. According to Deveria and other Orientalists, "magic was considered as a sacred science inseparable from religion" by the oldest and most civilized and learned nations. The Egyptians, for instance, were a most sincerely religious nation, as were, and are still, the Hindûs. "Magic consists of, and is acquired by, the worship of the gods," says Plato. Could, then, a nation which, owing to the irrefragable evidence of inscriptions and papyri, is proved to have firmly believed in magic for thousands of years have been deceived for so long a time? And is it likely that generations upon generations of a learned and pious hierarchy, many among whom led lives of self-martyrdom, holiness, and asceticism, would have gone on deceiving themselves and the people (or even only the latter) for the pleasure of perpetuating belief in "miracles"? Fanatics, we are told, will do anything to enforce belief in their gods or idols. To this we reply: In such cases Brâhmans and Egyptian *rekhget-amens* or Hierophants would not have popularized the belief *in the power of man to command the services of the gods by magic practices ;* which gods are in truth but the occult powers or potencies of Nature, personified by the learned priests themselves, who reverenced in them only the attributes of the one unknown and nameless principle. As Proclus, the Platonist, ably puts it: "Ancient priests, when they considered that there is a certain alliance and sympathy in natural things to each other, and in things manifest to occult powers, and discovered that all things subsist in all, *fabricated a sacred science from this mutual sympathy and similarity,* . . . and applied for occult purposes both celestial and terrene natures, by means

of which, through a certain similitude, they deduced divine
natures into this inferior abode." Magic is the science of
communicating with and directing supernal supramundane
potencies, as well as commanding those of lower spheres; a
practical knowledge of the hidden mysteries of Nature, which
are known only to the few, because they are so difficult to
acquire without falling into sin against the law. Ancient
and medieval mystics divided magic into three classes—
Theurgia, Goetia, and Natural Magic. "Theurgia has long
since been appropriated as the peculiar sphere of the Theosophists and metaphysicians," says Kenneth Mackenzie.
"Goetia is black magic, and 'natural' or white magic has
risen with healing in its wings to the proud position of an
exact and progressive study." The remarks added by our
late learned brother are remarkable: "The realistic desires
of modern times have contributed to bring magic into disrepute and ridicule. . . . Faith (in one's own self) is an
essential element in magic, and existed long before other
ideas which presume its preëxistence. It is said that it
takes a wise man to make a fool; and a man's idea must
be exalted almost to madness—i.e., his brain susceptibilities
must be increased far beyond the low, miserable status of
modern civilization—before he can become a true magician,
for a pursuit of this science implies a certain amount of isolation and an abnegation of self." A very great isolation,
certainly, the achievement of which constitutes a wonderful
phenomenon, a miracle in itself. Withal, magic is not something *supernatural*. As explained by Iamblichus: "They,
through the sacerdotal theurgy, announce that they are
able to ascend to *more elevated and universal essences*, and
to those that are established above fate, viz., to god and
the demiurgus; neither employing matter, nor assuming any
other things besides, except the observation of a sensible
time." Already some are beginning to recognize the existence of subtle powers and influences in Nature, in which

they have hitherto known naught. But, as Dr. Carter Blake truly remarks, "the nineteenth century is not that which has observed the genesis of new, nor the completion of old, methods of thought;" to which Mr. Bonwick adds that "if the ancients knew but little of our mode of investigation into the secrets of Nature, we know still less of their mode of research."

Magic, Black. Sorcery, abuse of powers.

Magic, Ceremonial. Magic, according to Kabalistic rites, worked out, as alleged by the Rosicrucians and other mystics, by invoking powers spiritually higher than man, and commanding elementals who are far lower than himself on the scale of being.

Magic, White. "Beneficent magic," so called, is divine magic, devoid of selfishness, love of power, of ambition or lucre, and bent only on doing good to the world in general and one's neighbor in particular. The smallest attempt to use one's abnormal powers for the gratification of self makes of these powers sorcery or black magic.

Mahâmanvantara (*Sans.*). The great interludes between the *Manus*, the period of universal activity. *Manvantara* here implies simply a period of activity, as opposed to *pralaya* or rest, without reference to the length of the cycle.

Mahat (*Sans.*). Lit., the "great" one. The first principle of universal intelligence and consciousness. In the Paurânic philosophy, the first product of root-nature or *pradhâna* (the same as *mûlaprakriti*); the producer of *manas*, the thinking principle, and of *ahankâra*, egotism, or the feeling of "I am I" in the lower Manas.

Mahâtmâ (*Sans.*). Lit., "great soul." An Adept of the highest order. An exalted being, who, having attained to the mastery over his lower principles, is therefore living unimpeded by the "man of flesh." Mahâtmâs are in possession of knowledge and power commensurate with the

·stage they have reached in their spiritual evolution. Called in Pâli Arahats or Rahats.

·**Mahâyâna** (*Sans.*). A school of Buddhistic philosophy; lit., the "great vehicle." A mystical system founded by Nâgârjuna. Its books were written in the second·century B.C.

Manas (*Sans.*). Lit., "mind." The mental faculty which makes of a man an intelligent and moral being, and distinguishes him from the mere animal; a synonym of *mahat.* Esoterically, however, it means, when unqualified, the higher Ego, or the sentient reincarnating principle in man. When qualified, it is called by Theosophists Buddhi-Manas, or the spiritual soul, in contradistinction to its human reflection, Kâma-Manas.

Mânasa-putra (*Sans.*). Lit., "the sons of mind" or mind-born sons; a name given to our higher Egos before they incarnated in mankind. In the *exoteric,* though allegorical and symbolical Purânas (the ancient mythological writings of Hindûs), it is the title given to the mind-born sons of Brahmâ, the *kumâras.*

Manas-sûtrâtmâ (*Sans.*). Two words meaning "mind" (*manas*) and "thread-soul" (*sûtrâtmâ*). It is, as said, the synonym of our Ego, or that which reincarnates. It is a technical term of Vedântic philosophy.

Manas-Taijasa (*Sans.*). Lit., the "radiant" Manas; ·a state of the higher Ego which only high metaphysicians are able to realize and comprehend. The same as "Buddhi-Taijasa," which see.

Mantras (*Sans.*). Verses from the Vedic works, used as incantations and charms. By *mantras* are meant all those portions of the Vedas which are distinct from the Brâhmanas, or their interpretation.

Manu (*Sans.*). The great Indian legislator. The name comes from the Sanskrit root *man,* to think, Man really standing only for Svâyambhuva, the first of the Manus, who started from Svayambhû, the Self-existent, who is hence the Logos and the progenitor of mankind. Manu is the first legislator—almost a divine being.

Manvantara (*Sans.*). A period of manifestation, as opposed to *pralaya*, dissolution or rest; the term is applied to various cycles, especially to a Day of Brahmâ, 4,320,-000,000 solar years, and to the reign of one Manu, 306,-720,000. Lit., *Manu-antara*, between Manus. (See *Secret Doctrine*, ii., 68 *et seq.*)

Master. A translation from the Sanskrit *guru*, "spiritual teacher," and adopted by the Theosophists to designate the Adepts, from whom they hold their teachings.

Materialist. Not necessarily only one who believes in neither God nor soul; but also any person who materializes the purely spiritual; such as believers in an anthropomorphic deity, in a soul capable of burning in hell-fire, and a hell and paradise as localities instead of states of consciousness. American "Substantialists," a Christian sect, are materialists, as also the so-called Spiritualists.

Materializations. In Spiritualism the word signifies the objective appearance of the so-called "spirits of the dead," who reclothe themselves occasionally in matter; i.e., they form for themselves, out of the materials at hand, found in the atmosphere and the emanations of those present, a temporary body bearing the human likeness of the defunct, as he appeared when alive. Theosophists accept the phenomena of "materialization," but they reject the theory that it is produced by "spirits," i.e., the immortal principles of disembodied persons. Theosophists hold that when the phenomena are genuine—which is a fact of rarer occurrence than is generally believed—they are produced by the *larvæ*, the *eidolons*, or kâmalokic "ghosts" of the dead personalities. (See "Kâmaloka" and "Kâma Rûpa.") As Kâmaloka is on the earth-plane and differs from its degree of materiality only in the degree of its plane of consciousness, for which reason it is concealed from our normal sight, the occasional apparition of such shells is as natural as that of electric balls and other atmospheric phenomena. Electricity as a fluid, or atomic matter (for Occultists hold with Maxwell that it is atomic), is ever, though invisibly, present in the air. This fluid can also manifest under various shapes, but only when certain conditions are present to "materialize" it, when it passes from its own on to our plane and makes itself objective. Similarly with the *eidolons* of the dead. They are present around us, but, being on another plane, do not see us any more than we see them. But whenever the strong desires of living men and the conditions furnished by the abnormal constitutions of mediums are combined together, these *eidolons* are drawn—nay, *pulled* —down from their plane on to ours and made objective. This is necromancy; it does no good to the dead, and great harm to the living, in addition to the fact that it interferes with a law of Nature. The occasional materialization of the "astral bodies" or doubles of living persons is quite another matter. These "astrals" are often mistaken for the apparitions of the dead, since, chameleon-like, our own "elementaries," along with those of the disembodied and cosmic elementals, will often assume the appearance of those images which are strongest in our thoughts. In short, at the so-called "materialization séances" it is those present and the medium who *create* the peculiar "apparition." Independent apparitions belong to another kind of psychic phenomena.

　Mâyâ (*Sans.*). Illusion; the cosmic power which renders phenomenal existence and the perceptions thereof possible. In Hindû philosophy that alone which is changeless and eternal is called *reality;* all that which is subject to change through decay and differentiation, and which has, therefore, a beginning and an end, is regarded as *mâyâ,* illusion.

Mediumship. A word now accepted to indicate that abnormal psychophysiological state which leads a person to take the .fancies of his imagination, his hallucinations, real or artificial, for realities. No entirely healthy person on the physiological and psychic planes can ever be a medium. That which mediums see, hear, and sense is "real," but *untrue;* it is either gathered from the astral plane, so deceptive in its vibrations and suggestions, or from pure hallucinations, which have no actual existence but for him who perceives them. "Mediumship" is a kind of vulgarized *mediatorship*, in which one afflicted with this faculty is supposed to become an agent of communication between a living man and a departed "spirit." There exist regular methods of training for the development of this undesirable acquirement.

Mercavah (*Heb.*). "A chariot. The Kabalists say that the Supreme, after he had established the ten Sephiroth—which, in their totality, are Adam Kadmon, the Archetypal Man—used them as a chariot or throne of glory in which to descend upon the souls of men."

Mesmerism. The term comes from Mesmer, who rediscovered this magnetic force and its practical application toward the year 1775, at Vienna. It is a vital current that one person may transfer to another, and through which he induces an abnormal state of the nervous system that permits him to have a direct influence upon the mind and will of the *subject* or mesmerized person.

Metaphysics. From the Greek *meta*, beyond, and *physica*, the things of the external material world. It is to forget the spirit and hold to the dead letter, to translate it "beyond nature" or *supernatural*, as it is rather beyond the natural, visible, or concrete. Metaphysics, in ontology and philosophy, is the term to designate that science which treats of the real and permanent being as contrasted with the unreal, illusionary, or phenomenal being.

Microcosm. The "little universe," meaning man, made in the image of his creator, the Macrocosm, or "great universe," and containing all that the latter contains. These terms are used in Occultism and Theosophy.

Mishnah (*Heb.*). Lit., a "repetition," from the word *shânâh*, "to repeat" something said orally. A summary of written explanations from the oral traditions of the Jews, and a digest of the Scriptures on which the later Talmud was based.

Moksha (*Sans.*). The same as *nirvâna;* a post-mortem state of rest and bliss of the "soul-pilgrim."

Monad. It is the "unity," the "one"; but in Occultism it often means the unified duad, Âtmâ-Buddhi, or that immortal part of man which, incarnating in the lower kingdoms and gradually progressing through them to man, finds thence way to the final goal, *nirvâna*.

Monas (*Gr.*). In the Pythagorean system the Duas emanates from the higher and solitary Monas, which is thus the First Cause.

Monogenes (*Gr.*). Lit., the "only begotten"; a name of Proserpina and other goddesses and gods, as also of Jesus.

Mundaka Upanishad (*Sans.*). Lit., the "Mundaka Esoteric Doctrine." A work of high antiquity.

Mysteries. The Sacred Mysteries were enacted in the ancient temples by the initiated Hierophants for the benefit and instruction of candidates. The most solemn and occult were certainly those which were performed in Egypt by "the band of secret-keepers," as Mr. Bonwick calls the Hierophants. Maurice describes their nature very graphically in a few lines. Speaking of the Mysteries performed in Philæ (the Nile-island), he says: "It was in these gloomy caverns that the grand mystic arcana of the goddess (Isis) were unfolded to the adoring aspirant, while the solemn hymn of initiation resounded through the long extent of these stony recesses." The word "mystery" is derived from the Greek *muô*, to close the mouth, and every symbol connected with them had a hidden meaning. As Plato and many of the other sages of antiquity affirm, these Mysteries were highly religious, moral, and beneficent as a school of ethics. The Grecian Mysteries—those of Ceres and Bacchus—were only imitations of the Egyptian; and the author of *Egyptian Belief and Modern Thought* informs us that our own word "*chapel* or *capella* is said to be the *caph-el* or college of *el*, the solar divinity." The well-known Kabiri are associated with the Mysteries.

In short, the Mysteries were in every country a series of dramatic performances, in which the mysteries of cosmogony and Nature in general were personified by the priests and neophytes, who enacted the parts of various gods and goddesses, repeating supposed scenes (allegories) from their respective lives. These were explained in their hidden meaning to the candidates for initiation, and incorporated into philosophical doctrines.

Mystery Language. The sacerdotal secret "jargon" used by the initiated priests, and employed only when discussing sacred things. Every nation had its own "mystery" tongue, unknown to all save those admitted to the Mysteries.

Mystic. From the Greek word *mysticos*. In antiquity, one belonging to those admitted to the ancient Mysteries; in our own times, one who practises Mysticism, holds mystic, transcendental views, etc.

Mysticism. Any doctrine involved in mystery and metaphysics, and dealing more with the ideal worlds than with our actual, matter-of-fact universe.

N.

Nazarene Codex. The Scriptures of the Nazarenes and of the Nabatheans also. According to sundry church fathers

—Jerome and Epiphanius especially—they were heretical teachings, but are in fact one of the numerous Gnostic readings of cosmogony and theogony, which produced a distinct sect.

Necromancy. The raising of the images of the dead, considered in antiquity and by modern Occultists as a practice of black magic. Iamblichus, Porphyry, and other theurgists deprecated the practice no less than Moses, who condemned the "witches" of his day to death, the said witches being often only mediums—e.g., the case of the witch of Endor and Samuel.

Neoplatonists. A school of philosophy which arose between the second and third centuries of our era, and was founded by Ammonius Saccas of Alexandria. The same as the Philaletheians and the Analogeticists; they were also called Theurgists and by various other names. They were the Theosophists of the early centuries. Neoplatonism is Platonic philosophy plus *ecstasy*, divine Râja Yoga.

Nephesh (*Heb.*). "Breath of life," *anima, mens vitæ*, appetites. The term is used very loosely in the Bible. It generally means Prâna, "life"; in the Kabalah it is the animal passions and the animal soul. Therefore, as maintained in Theosophical teachings, *nephesh* is the prâna-kâmic principle, or the vital animal soul in man.

Nirmânakâya (*Sans.*). Something entirely different in Esoteric Philosophy from the popular meaning attached to it, and from the fancies of the Orientalists. Some call the *nirmânakâya*, or body, "*nirvâna* with remains" (Schlagintweit), on the supposition, probably, that it is a kind of nirvânic condition during which consciousness and *form* are retained. Others say that it is one of the *trikâya* (three bodies), with "the power of assuming any form of appearance in order to propagate Buddhism" (Eitel's idea); again, that "it is the incarnate *avâtara* of a deity" (*ibid.*). Occultism, on the other hand, says (*Voice of the Silence*) that *nir-*

mânakâya, although meaning literally a transformed "body," is a state. The form is that of the Adept or *yogî* who enters, or chooses, that post-mortem condition in preference to the *dharmakâya* or *absolute* nirvânic state. He does this because the latter *kâya* separates him forever from the world of form, conferring upon him a state of *selfish* bliss, in which no other living being can participate, the Adept being thus precluded from the possibility of helping humanity, or even *devas*. As a *nirmânakâya*, however, the Adept leaves behind him only his physical body, and retains every other "principle," save the kâmic, for he has crushed this out forever from his nature during life, and it can never resurrect in his post-mortem state. Thus, instead of going into selfish bliss, he chooses a life of self-sacrifice, an existence which ends only with the life-cycle, in order to be enabled to help mankind in an invisible, yet most effective, manner. (See *Voice of the Silence*, Third Treatise, "The Seven Portals.") Thus a *nirmânakâya* is not, as popularly believed, the body "in which a Buddha or a Bodhisattva appears on earth," but verily one who, whether a *chutuktu* or a *khubilkhan*, an Adept or a *yogî*, during life, has since become a member of that invisible Host which ever protects and watches over humanity within karmic limits. Mistaken often for a "spirit," a deva, God himself, etc., a *nirmânakâya* is ever a protecting, compassionate, verily a guardian angel to him who is worthy of his help. Whatever objection may be brought forward against this doctrine, however much it is denied—because, forsooth, it has never hitherto been made public in Europe, and therefore, since it is unknown to Orientalists, it must needs be a "myth of modern invention"—no one will be bold enough to say that this idea of helping suffering mankind at the price of one's own almost interminable self-sacrifice is not one of the grandest and noblest that was ever evolved from the human brain.

Nirvâna (*Sans.*). According to the Orientalists, the entire "blowing out," like the flame of a candle; the utter extinction of existence. But in the esoteric explanations it is the state of absolute existence and absolute consciousness, into which the Ego of a man who had reached the highest degree of perfection and holiness during life goes after the body dies, and occasionally, as in the case of Gautama Buddha and others, during life.

Nirvâni (*Sans.*). One who has attained *nirvâna*—an emancipated Soul. That *nirvâna* means something quite different from the puerile assertions of Orientalists, every scholar who has visited India, China, or Japan is well aware. It is "escape from misery," but only from that of matter; freedom from *kleshâ* or *kâma*, and the complete extinction of animal desires. If we are told that the *Abhidhamma* defines *nirvâna* as "a state of absolute annihilation," we concur, adding to the last word the qualification "of everything connected with matter or the physical world," and this simply because the latter (as also all in it) is illusion or *mâyâ*. Shâkyamuni Buddha said in the last moments of his life, "The spiritual body is immortal." As Mr. Eitel, the scholarly Sinologist, explains it: "The popular exoteric systems agree in defining *nirvâna negatively* as a state of absolute exemption from the circle of transmigration; as a state of entire freedom from all forms of existence—to begin with, freedom from all passion and exertion; a state of indifference to all sensibility;" and he might have added "death of all *compassion* for the world of suffering." And this is why the Bodhisattvas who prefer the *nirmânakâya* to the *dharmakâya* vesture stand higher in the popular estimation than the *nirvânis*. But the same scholar adds that "positively [and esoterically] they define *nirvâna* as the highest state of spiritual bliss, as absolute immortality through absorption of the soul [spirit, rather] into itself, but preserving *individuality*, so that, e.g., Buddhas, after entering *nirvâna*, may reappear on earth [i.e., in the future *manvantara*]."

Noumenon (*Gr.*). The true essential nature of Being as distinguished from the illusive objects of sense.

Nous (*Gr.*). A Platonic term for the higher mind or soul. It means spirit as distinct from animal soul, *psyche;* divine consciousness or mind in man. The name was adopted by the Gnostics for their first conscious *eon*, which, with the Occultists, is the third *logos*, cosmically, and the third "principle" (from above), or Manas, in man.

Nout (*Eg.*). In the Egyptian Pantheon it meant the "One-Only-One," because it does not proceed in the popular or exoteric religion higher than the *third* manifestation which radiates from the Unknowable and the Unknown in the Esoteric Philosophy of every nation. The *nous* of Anaxagoras was the *mahat* of the Hindûs—Brahmâ, the first *manifested* deity—"the mind or spirit self-potent." This creative principle is the *primum mobile* of everything to be found in the universe—its soul or ideation.

O.

Occultism. See "Occult Sciences."

Occultist. One who practises Occultism, an Adept in the secret sciences, but very often applied to a mere student.

Occult Sciences. The science of the secrets of Nature —physical and psychic, mental and spiritual; called Hermetic and esoteric sciences. In the West the Kabalah may be named; in the East, Mysticism, magic, and Yoga-philosophy. The latter is often referred to by the *chelâs* in India as the *seventh darshana* or school of philosophy, there being only six *darshanas* in India known to the world of the profane. These sciences are, and have been for ages, hidden from the vulgar, for the very good reason that they would never be appreciated by the selfish educated classes, who would misuse them for their own profit, and thus turn the divine science into black magic ; nor by the uneducated, who would not understand them.   It is often brought forward as an accusation against the Esoteric Philosophy of the Kabalah that its literature is full of " a barbarous and meaningless jargon," unintelligible to the ordinary mind. But do not *exact* sciences—medicine, physiology, chemistry, and the rest—plead guilty to the same impeachment ?   Do not official scientists veil their facts and discoveries with a newly coined and most barbarous Greco-Latin terminology ?   As justly remarked by our late brother, Kenneth Mackenzie, " to juggle thus with words, when the facts are so simple, is the art of the scientists of the present time, in striking contrast to those of the seventeenth century, who called spades spades, and not ' agricultural implements.'" Moreover, while their "facts" would be as simple and as comprehensible if rendered in ordinary language, the facts of occult science are of so abstruse a nature that in most cases no words exist in European languages to express them. Finally, our "jargon" is a double necessity, (*a*) for describing clearly these *facts* to one who is versed in the occult terminology ; and (*b*) for concealing them from the profane.

Occult World.   The name of the first book treating of "Theosophy," its history, and certain of its tenets, written by A. P. Sinnett, then editor of the leading Indian paper, the *Pioneer*, of Allahabad.

Olympiodorus.   The last Neoplatonist of fame and celebrity in the school of Alexandria.   He lived in the sixth century under the Emperor Justinian.   There were several writers and philosophers of this name in pre-Christian as in post-Christian periods.   One of these was the teacher of Proclus, another a historian in the eighth century, and so on.

Origen.   A Christian churchman, born at the end of

the second century, probably in Africa, of whom little, if anything, is known, since his biographical fragments have passed to posterity on the authority of Eusebius, the most unmitigated falsifier that has ever existed in any age. The latter is credited with having collected upward of one hundred letters of Origen (Origenes Adamantius), which are now said to have been lost. To Theosophists the most interesting of all the works of Origen is his "Doctrine of the Preëxistence of Souls." He was a pupil of Ammonius Saccas, and for a long time attended the lectures of this great teacher of philosophy.

P.

Pantænus. A Platonic philosopher in the Alexandrian school of the Philaletheians.

Pandora. In Greek mythology, the first woman on earth, created by Vulcan out of clay to deceive Prometheus and counteract his gift to mortals. Each god having made her a present of some quality, she was made to carry them in a box to Prometheus, who, however, being endowed with foresight, sent her away, changing the gifts into evils. Thus, when his brother Epimetheus afterward married her, on opening the box all the evils now afflicting humanity issued from it, and have remained since then in the world.

Pantheist. One who identifies God with Nature and *vice versa*. If we have to regard deity as an infinite and omnipresent principle, this can hardly be otherwise, Nature being thus simply the physical aspect of deity, or its body.

Parabrahman (*Sans.*). A Vedântin term meaning "beyond Brahmâ." The supreme and the absolute principle, impersonal and nameless. In the Veda it is referred to as "That."

Paranirvâna. In the Buddhistic philosophy, the highest form of *nirvâna*—beyond the latter.

Parsis. The present Persian followers of Zoroaster, now settled in India, especially in Bombay and Gujerat; sun and fire worshipers. One of the most intelligent and esteemed communities in the country, generally occupied with commercial pursuits. There are between fifty and sixty thousand now left in India, where they settled some one thousand years ago.

Personality. The teachings of Occultism divide man into three aspects—the *divine*, the *thinking* or rational, and the *irrational* or animal man. For metaphysical purposes, also, he is considered under a septenary division, or, as it is agreed to express it in Theosophy, he is composed of seven " principles," three of which constitute the higher *triad*, and the remaining four the lower *quaternary*. It is in the latter that dwells the *personality*, which embraces all the characteristics, including memory and consciousness, of each physical life in turn. The *individuality* is the higher Ego (Manas) of the triad considered as a unity. In other words, the *individuality* is our imperishable Ego which reincarnates and clothes itself in *a new personality* at every new birth.

Phallic Worship. Sex-worship; reverence and adoration shown to those gods and goddesses which, like Shiva and Durgâ in India, symbolize respectively the two sexes.

Philadelphians. Lit., "those who love their brothermen." A sect in the seventeenth century, founded by one Jane Lead. They objected to all rites, forms, or ceremonies of the church, and even to the church itself, but professed to be guided in soul and spirit by an internal deity, their own Ego, or God within them.

Philaletheians. See " Neoplatonists."

Philo Judæus. A Hellenized Jew of Alexandria, a famous historian and philosopher of the first century; born about the year 30 B.C., and died between the years 45 and 50 A.D. Philo's symbolism of the Bible is very remarkable.

The animals, birds, reptiles, trees, and places mentioned in it are all, it is said, "allegories of conditions of the soul, of faculties, dispositions, or passions; the useful plants were allegories of virtues, the noxious of the affections of the unwise, and so on through the mineral kingdom; through heaven, earth, and stars; through fountains and rivers, fields and dwellings; through metals, substances, arms, clothes, ornaments, furniture, the body and its parts, the sexes, and our outward condition." (*Dict. Christ. Biog.*) All of which would strongly corroborate the idea that Philo was acquainted with the ancient Kabalah.

Philosopher's Stone. A term in Alchemy; called also the *powder of projection*, a mysterious "principle" having the power of transmuting the base metals into pure gold. In Theosophy it symbolizes the transmutation of the lower animal nature of man into the highest divine.

Phren. A Pythagorean term denoting what we call the Kâma-Manas, still overshadowed by Buddhi-Manas.

Plane. From the Latin *planus*, level, flat. An extension of space, whether in the physical or metaphysical sense. In Occultism, the range or extent of some state of consciousness, or the state of matter corresponding to the perceptive powers of a particular set of senses or the action of a particular force.

Planetary Spirits. Rulers and governors of the planets. Planetary gods.

Plastic. Used in Occultism in reference to the nature and essence of the astral body, or the "protean soul."

Plerôma. "Fullness"; a Gnostic term used also by St. Paul. Divine world or the abode of gods. Universal space divided into metaphysical *eons*.

Plotinus. A distinguished Neoplatonic philosopher of the third century, a great practical mystic, renowned for his virtues and learning. He taught a doctrine identical with that of the Vedântins, namely, that the spirit-soul emanated from the one deific principle, and after its pilgrimage on earth was reunited to it.

Porphyry (Porphyrius). His real name was Melech, which led to his being regarded as a Jew. He came from Tyre, and having first studied under Longinus, the eminent philosopher-critic, became the disciple of Plotinus at Rome. He was a Neoplatonist and a distinguished writer, specially famous for his controversy with Iamblichus regarding the evils attending the practice of Theurgy, but was, however, finally converted to the views of his opponent. A natural-born mystic, he followed, like his master Plotinus, the pure Indian Râja Yoga system, which, by training, leads to the union of the soul with the over-soul of the universe, and of the human with its *divine* soul, Buddhi-Manas. He complains, however, that in spite of all his efforts he reached the highest state of ecstasy only once, and that when he was sixty-eight years of age, while his teacher Plotinus had experienced the supreme bliss six times during his life.

Pot Amun. A Coptic term meaning "one consecrated to the god Amun," the Wisdom-god. The name of an Egyptian priest and Occultist under the Ptolemies.

Prajñâ (*Sans.*). A term used to designate the "universal mind." A synonym of *mahat.*

Pralaya (*Sans.*). Dissolution, the opposite of *manvantara*, one being the period of rest and the other of full activity (death and life) of a planet, or of the whole universe.

Prâna (*Sans.*). Life-principle, the breath of life, *nephesh.*

Protean Soul. A name for the *mâyâvi rûpa* or thought-body, the higher astral form which assumes all forms and every form at the will of an Adept's thought.

Psychism. The word is used now to denote every kind of mental phenomena, e.g., mediumship as well as the higher form of sensitiveness. A newly coined word.

Purânas (*Sans.*). Lit., "the ancient," referring to Hindû mythological writings or scriptures, of which there is a considerable number.

Pythagoras. The most famous Greek mystic philosopher, born at Samos about 586 B.C., who taught the heliocentric system and reincarnation, the highest mathematics and the highest metaphysics, and who had a school famous throughout the world.

Q.

Quaternary. The four lower "principles" in man, those which constitute his *personality* (i.e., body, astral double, Prâna or life, organs of desire, and lower Manas or brain-mind), as distinguished from the higher ternary or triad, composed of the higher spiritual soul, mind, and Âtman (Higher Self).

R.

Recollection, Remembrance, Reminiscence. Occultists make a difference between these three functions. As, however, a glossary cannot contain the full explanation of every term in all its metaphysical and subtle differences, we can only state here that these terms vary in their applications, according to whether they relate to the past or the present birth, and whether one or the other of these phases of memory emanates from the spiritual or the material brain, or, again, from the "individuality" or the "personality."

Reincarnation, or Rebirth. The once universal doctrine which taught that the Ego is born on this earth an innumerable number of times. Nowadays it is denied by Christians, who seem to misunderstand the teachings of their own Gospels. Nevertheless the putting on of flesh periodically and throughout long cycles by the higher human soul (Buddhi-Manas) or Ego is taught in the Bible, as it is in all other ancient scriptures, and "resurrection" means only the rebirth of the Ego in another form.

Reuchlin, John. A great German philosopher and philologist, Kabalist and scholar. He was born at Pforzheim, in Germany, in 1455, and early in youth was a diplomat. At one period of his life he held the high office of judge of the tribunal at Tübingen, where he remained for eleven years. He was also the preceptor of Melanchthon, and was greatly persecuted by the clergy for his glorification of the Hebrew Kabalah, though at the same time called the "Father of the Reformation." He died in 1522, in great poverty, the common fate of all who in those days went against the dead letter of the church.

S.

Sacred Science. The epithet given to the occult sciences in general, and by the Rosicrucians to the Kabalah, and especially to the Hermetic philosophy.

Samâdhi (*Sans.*). The name in India for spiritual ecstasy. It is a state of complete trance, induced by means of mystic concentration.

Samkhâra (*Pâli*). One of the five Buddhist *skandhas* or attributes. "Tendencies of mind."

Samma Sambuddha (*Pâli*). The sudden remembrance of all one's past incarnations, a phenomenon of memory obtained through Yoga. A Buddhist mystic term.

Samothrace. An island in the Grecian Archipelago, famous in days of old for the Mysteries celebrated in its temples. These Mysteries were world-renowned.

Samyuttaka Nikaya (*Pâli*). One of the Buddhist *sûtras.*

Saññâ (*Pâli*). One of the five *skandhas* or attributes, meaning "abstract ideas."

Séance. A term now used to denote a sitting with a medium for sundry phenomena. Used chiefly among the Spiritualists.

Self. There are two *Selves* in men—the higher and the lower, the impersonal and the personal Self. One is divine, the other semi-animal. A great distinction should be made between the two.

Sephiroth. A Hebrew Kabalistic word for the ten divine emanations from Ain Suph, the impersonal, universal principle, or deity.

Skandhas. The *attributes* of every personality, which after death form the basis, so to say, for a new karmic re-incarnation. They are five in the popular or exoteric system of the Buddhists: i.e., *rûpa*, form or body, which leaves behind it its magnetic atoms and occult affinities; *vedanâ*, sensations, which do likewise; *saññâ*, or abstract ideas, which are the creative powers at work from one incarnation to another; *samkhâra*, tendencies of mind; and *viññâna*, mental powers.

Somnambulism. "Sleep-walking." A psychophysiological state, too well known to need explanation.

Spiritism. The same as the following, with the difference that the Spiritualists almost unanimously reject the doctrine of reincarnation, while the Spiritists make of it the fundamental principle in their belief. There is, however, a vast difference between the views of the latter and the philosophical teachings of Eastern Occultists. Spiritists belong to the French school founded by Allan Kardec, and the Spiritualists of America and England to that of the "Fox girls," who inaugurated their theories at Rochester, N. Y. Theosophists, while believing in the mediumistic phenomena of both Spiritualists and Spiritists, reject the idea of "spirits."

Spiritualism. The modern belief that the spirits of the dead return on earth to commune with the living.

St. Germain, Count. A mysterious personage, who appeared in the last century and early in the present one in France, England, and elsewhere.

Sthûla Sharira (*Sans.*). The human physical body in Occultism and Vedântic philosophy.

Sthûlopâdhi (*Sans.*). The physical body in its waking, conscious state (*jagrat*).

Sûkshmopâdhi (*Sans.*). The physical body in the dreaming state (*svapna*), and *kâranopâdhi*, the "causal body." These terms belong to the teachings of the Târaka Râja Yoga school.

Summer-land. The fancy name given by the Spiritualists to the abode of their disembodied "spirits," which they locate somewhere in the Milky Way. It is described, on the authority of *returning* "spirits," as a lovely land, having beautiful cities and buildings, a congress hall, museums, etc., etc. (See the works of Andrew Jackson Davis.)

Swedenborg, Emanuel. A famous scholar and clairvoyant of the past century, a man of great learning, who had vastly contributed to science, but whose Mysticism and transcendental philosophy placed him in the ranks of hallucinated visionaries. He is now universally known as the founder of the Swedenborgian sect, or the New Jerusalem Church. He was born at Stockholm (Sweden) in 1688, from Lutheran parents, his father being the Bishop of West Gothland. His original name was Swedberg, but on his being ennobled and knighted in 1719 it was changed to Swedenborg. He became a mystic in 1743, and four years later (in 1747) resigned his office (of Assessor Extraordinary to the College of Mines) and gave himself up entirely to Mysticism. He died in 1772.

T.

Taijasa (*Sans.*). From *tejas*, fire; meaning the "radiant," the "luminous"; referring to the *mânasa-rûpa*, "the body of *manas*," also to the stars and the *starlike* shining envelopes. A term in Vedântic philosophy, having other meanings besides the occult signification just given.

Târaka Râja Yoga (*Sans.*). One of the Brâhmanical Yoga systems, the most philosophical, and, in fact, the most secret of all, as its real tenets are never given out publicly. It is a purely intellectual and spiritual school of training.

Tetragrammaton (*Gr.*). The deity-name in four letters, which are in their English form IHVH. It is a Kabalistical term, and corresponds on a more material plane to the sacred Pythagorean *tetraktys*.

Theodidaktos (*Gr.*). The "God-taught," a title applied to Ammonius Saccas.

Theogony. From the Greek *theogonia*, lit., the "genesis of the gods."

Theosophia (*Gr.*). Lit., "divine wisdom or the wisdom of the gods."

Therapeutæ, or Therapeuts (*Gr.*). A school of Jewish mystic healers, or esotericists, wrongly referred to by some as a sect. They resided in and near Alexandria, and their doings and beliefs are to this day a mystery to the critics, as their philosophy seems a combination of Orphic, Pythagorean, Essenian, and purely Kabalistic practices.

Theurgy. From the Greek *theiourgia*. Rites for bringing down to earth planetary and other spirits or gods. To arrive at the realization of such an object the Theurgist had to be absolutely pure and unselfish in his motives. The practice of Theurgy is very undesirable and even dangerous in the present day. The world has become too corrupt and wicked for the practice of that which such holy and learned men as Ammonius, Plotinus, Porphyry, and Iamblichus (the most learned Theurgist of all) could alone attempt with impunity. In our day Theurgy, or divine, beneficent magic, is but too apt to become goetic, or, in other words, sorcery. Theurgy is the first of the three subdivisions of magic, which are theurgic, goetic, and natural magic.

Thread Soul. The same as *sûtrâtmâ*, which see under "Manas-sûtrâtmâ."

Thumos (*Gr.*). A Pythagorean and Platonic term; applied to an aspect of the human soul, to denote its passionate kâma-rûpic condition; almost equivalent to the Sanskrit word *tamas*, the quality of darkness, and probably derived from the latter.

Timæus of Locris. A Pythagorean philosopher, born at Locris. He differed somewhat from his teacher in the doctrine of metempsychosis. He wrote a treatise on the soul of the world and its nature and essence, which is in the Doric dialect and still extant.

Triad, or Trinity. In every religion and philosophy, the three in one.

U.

Universal Brotherhood. The subtitle of the Theosophical Society, and the first of the three objects professed by it.

Upâdhi (*Sans.*). Basis of something, substructure; as in Occultism substance is the *upâdhi* of spirit.

Upanishad (*Sans.*). Lit., "esoteric doctrine." The third division of the Vedas, and classed with revelation (*shruti* or "revealed word"). Some one hundred and fifty or even two hundred of the Upanishads still remain extant, though no more than about twelve can be fully relied upon as free from falsification. These twelve are all earlier than the sixth century B.C. Like the Kabalah, which interprets the esoteric sense of the Bible, so the Upanishads explain the mystic sense of the Vedas. Professor Cowell has two statements regarding the Upanishads, as interesting as they are correct. Thus he says: (1) These works have "one remarkable peculiarity, the total absence of any Brâhmanical exclusiveness in their doctrine. . . . They breathe an entirely different spirit, a freedom of thought unknown in any earlier work except the *Rig Veda* hymns themselves"; and (2) "the great teachers of the higher knowledge [*gupta-vidyâ*], and Brâhmans, are continually represented as going to Kshatriya kings to become their pupils [*chelâs*]." This shows conclusively that (*a*) the Upanishads were written before the *enforcement* of caste and Brâhmanical power, and are thus only second in antiquity to the Vedas; and (*b*) that the occult sciences, or the "higher knowledge," as Cowell puts it, are far older than the Brâhmans in India, or, at any rate, than the caste system. The Upanishads are, however, far later than *gupta-vidyâ*, or the "secret science," which is as old as human philosophical thought itself.

V.

Vâhan (*Sans.*). "Vehicle." A synonym of *upâdhi.*

Vallabâchâryas (*Sans.*). The "sect of the Mahârâjas"; a licentious phallic-worshiping community, whose main branch is at Bombay. The object of the worship is the infant Krishna. The Anglo-Indian government has been compelled several times to interfere in order to put a stop to its rites and vile practices, and its governing Mahârâja, a kind of high priest, was more than once imprisoned, and very justly so. It is one of the blackest spots of India.

Vedânta (*Sans.*). Meaning, literally, the "end of [all] knowledge." Among the six *darshanas* or schools of philosophy it is also called Uttaramîmânsâ, or the "later" Mîmânsâ. There are those who, unable to understand its esotericism, consider it atheistical; but this is not so, as Shankarâchârya, the great apostle of this school, and its popularizer, was one of the greatest mystics and Adepts of India.

Vidyâ (*Sans.*). Knowledge, or rather "wisdom-knowledge."

Viññâna (*Pâli*). One of the five *skandhas;* meaning, exoterically, "mental powers."

W.

Wisdom-Religion. The same as Theosophy. The name given to the secret doctrine which underlies every exoteric scripture and religion.

Y.

Yoga (*Sans.*). A school of philosophy founded by Patanjali, but which existed as a distinct teaching and system of life long before that sage. It is Yâjnavalkya, a famous and very ancient sage, to whom the *White Yajur Veda*, the *Shatapatha Brâhmana*, and the *Brihad Âranyaka* are attributed, and who lived in pre-Mahâbhâratean times, who is credited with inculcating the necessity and positive duty of religious meditation and retirement into the forests, and who, therefore, is believed to have originated the Yoga doctrine. Professor Max Müller states that it is Yâjnavalkya who prepared the world for the preaching of Buddha. Patanjali's Yoga, however, is more definite and precise as a philosophy, and embodies more of the occult sciences than any of the works attributed to Yâjnavalkya.

Yogî, or Yogin (*Sans.*). A devotee, one who practises the Yoga system. There are various grades and kinds of Yogîs, and the term has now become in India a generic name to designate every kind of ascetic.

Yuga (*Sans.*). An age of the world, of which there are four, which follow each other in a series, namely, *krita* (or *satya*) *yuga,* the golden age; *tretâ yuga, dvâpara yuga,* and finally *kali yuga,* the black age—in which we now are.

Z.

Zenobia. The queen of Palmyra, defeated by the Emperor Aurelianus. She had for her instructor Longinus, the famous critic and logician in the third century A.D.

Zivo, Kabar or Jukabar. The name of one of the creative deities in the Nazarene Codex.

Zohar (*Heb.*). The Book of "Splendor," a Kabalistic work attributed to Simeon ben-Iochai, in the first century of our era.

Zoroastrian. One who follows the religion of the Parsîs, sun or fire worshipers.

[Readers requiring fuller information about any particular term should consult *The Theosophical Glossary.*]

INDEX.